A

B O O K

The Philip E. Lilienthal imprint
honors special books in commem-
oration of a man whose work at the
University of California Press from
1954 to 1979 was marked by dedi-
cation to young authors and to high
standards in the field of Asian Studies. Friends, family, authors, and
foundations have together endowed
the Lilienthal Fund, which enables
the Press to publish under this imprint selected books in a way that
reflects the taste and judgment of a
great and beloved editor.

NATIVE SOURCES OF JAPANESE INDUSTRIALIZATION, 1750–1920

THOMAS C. SMITH

UNIVERSITY
OF
CALIFORNIA
PRESS

BERKELEY
LOS ANGELES
LONDON

University of California Press
Berkeley and Los Angeles, California

University of California Press, Ltd.
London, England

© 1988 by
The Regents of the University of
California

First Paperback Printing 1989

Library of Congress Cataloging-in-Publication Data

Smith, Thomas C. (Thomas Carlyle), 1916–
    Native sources of Japanese industrialization, 1750–1920 / Thomas
C. Smith
        p.   cm.
    "A Philip E. Lilienthal book"—Series t.p.
    Includes index.
    Contents: Premodern economic growth: Japan and the West—The
land tax in the Tokugawa period—Farm family by-employments in
preindustrial Japan—Peasant families and population control in
eighteenth-century Japan—Japan's aristocratic revolution—The
discontented—"Merit" as ideology in the Tokugawa period—Ōkura
Nagatsune and the technologists—Peasant time and factory time in
Japan—The right to benevolence: dignity and Japanese workers,
1890–1920.
    ISBN 0-520-05837-2 (alk. paper).   ISBN 0-520-06293-0 (pbk.)
    1. Japan—Economic conditions.   2. Japan—Social conditions.
3. Japan—Industries—History.   I. Title.
HC462.S617   1988
330.952—dc19   87-27470
                                                            CIP

Printed in the United States of America
    3   4   5   6   7   8   9

TO J.M.S.

CONTENTS

ACKNOWLEDGMENTS

In the course of writing these articles, I have had more help and encouragement from friends and strangers than I can properly acknowledge in a short space. I hope I have expressed my gratitude for these kindnesses in print and less public ways sufficiently that I may be excused from listing names. It would be a very long list and lists are poor acknowledgment. Instead, I would like to use the occasion to express my special gratitude to two friends for things that have no ostensible connection to these essays but much to do with them. I am deeply indebted to my undergraduate teacher Harry Girvetz, who first excited me with the possibilities of history by abolishing the hard-and-fast distinction in my mind between what has been and what is; and to my colleague Irwin Scheiner, whose gift for friendship and intellectual discourse has made a difference in life for me as for many others.

It is an honor to have this book become the first in a series to be published by the University of California Press in memory of Phil Lilienthal, whom I liked and admired from our first meeting in Palo Alto in 1948. In this and other ways, friends at the press have made the production of this book a pleasure; I owe special thanks to Betsey Scheiner, who in editing the manuscript rarely put pencil to a sentence without improving it.

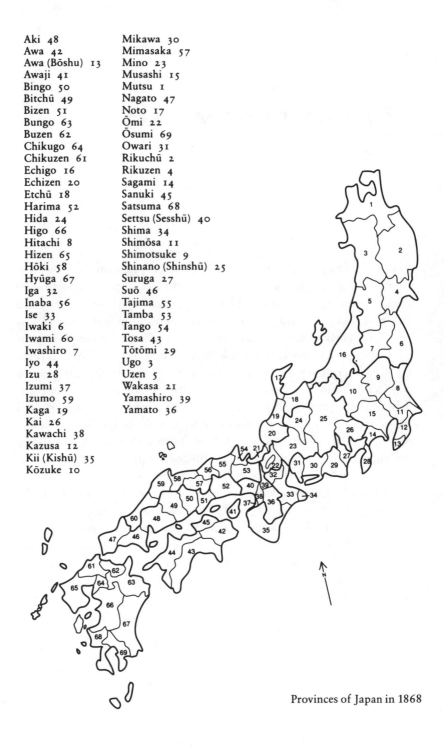

Aki 48	Mikawa 30
Awa 42	Mimasaka 57
Awa (Bōshu) 13	Mino 23
Awaji 41	Musashi 15
Bingo 50	Mutsu 1
Bitchū 49	Nagato 47
Bizen 51	Noto 17
Bungo 63	Ōmi 22
Buzen 62	Ōsumi 69
Chikugo 64	Owari 31
Chikuzen 61	Rikuchū 2
Echigo 16	Rikuzen 4
Echizen 20	Sagami 14
Etchū 18	Sanuki 45
Harima 52	Satsuma 68
Hida 24	Settsu (Sesshū) 40
Higo 66	Shima 34
Hitachi 8	Shimōsa 11
Hizen 65	Shimotsuke 9
Hōki 58	Shinano (Shinshū) 25
Hyūga 67	Suruga 27
Iga 32	Suō 46
Inaba 56	Tajima 55
Ise 33	Tamba 53
Iwaki 6	Tango 54
Iwami 60	Tosa 43
Iwashiro 7	Tōtōmi 29
Iyo 44	Ugo 3
Izu 28	Uzen 5
Izumi 37	Wakasa 21
Izumo 59	Yamashiro 39
Kaga 19	Yamato 36
Kai 26	
Kawachi 38	
Kazusa 12	
Kii (Kishū) 35	
Kōzuke 10	

Provinces of Japan in 1868

INTRODUCTION

Any fair-minded reader will discover two or three consistent biases running through this book. In one way or another all the essays concern how Japan became a modern society and were written with a generalized notion drawn from Western history of how such transformations occur. This perspective is often held to be the source of bias because historians who apply it—whatever their persuasion and nationality—tend to look for the confirmation of Western models and to see departures from them as backwardness and weakness. In my case the model gave rise to a rather different bias: I tend to pass over Japanese similarities with the West as possibly important but uninteresting and concentrate on the positive aspects of differences. These essays are therefore a bit like a trip abroad undertaken in the hope of extending rather than repeating experience and in the hope that the experience will be edifying, not merely new. Put differently, I have paid particular attention to factors that contributed to making modern Japanese society similar to but profoundly different from Western counterparts.

One essay tries to explain how a modern revolution was made by elements of an aristocracy; another how and with what consequences workers' criticism of the early factory called for status justice rather than the fulfillment of rights; yet another how time discipline in modern industry came to be based on a principle rather different from "time is money." Thus the cumulative sense of these essays, as well as other things I have written, goes against the widely accepted notion that the constraints of a common technology make industrial societies ever more alike (which usually means others are becoming more like us). I can see little in what I have studied to justify that belief, but admittedly my subjects of study have not been random choices.

If the emphasis on divergences from the model may be called intellectual—and I doubt that is the right word—a less obtrusive bias is aesthetic. I have been drawn, as many others have, to what is old in Japan rather than to what is new, preferring, as Tanizaki Jun'ichirō put it, the writing brush to the fountain pen (although I cannot operate either competently). I mean the vital "old," not its widely ritualized or commercialized reproductions. What gives particular pleasure is finding the past animating and informing the present and itself changing and being renewed in the process. I was delighted to discover an agriculture in the Tokugawa and Meiji periods where progress was not associated with economies of scale; to follow the transformation of loyalty to the lord into a bureaucratic ideal of performance in office; and to observe in the factory the concept of the benevolence owed by a superior to a dependent becoming a "right to benevolence." Whether this kind of pleasure has led to or results from a propensity for discovering elements in the past that turn out to be modern strengths, the two clearly go together.

The third bias is perhaps a corollary of the other two. In slighting much about the Japanese past that did not prove useful to the present, I have no doubt also slighted the cost of what occurred. There is little in what I have written about such subjects as the Temmei famine; or the condition of tenant farmers; or the vastly increased number of wanderers, scavengers, peddlers, and street entertainers that early industrialization produced. Nor have I paid much attention to the daughter and only child in Nakahara who served her aged and widowed father until his death, probably doing most of the work on their tiny farm; only then, at the age of forty-three, did she marry for the first of three times to young men.

I have not thought such subjects less legitimate or inherently less interesting than those I wrote about. But when I began studying Japanese history immediately after World War II, the dark side of the Japanese past needed no elaboration and had many distinguished analysts. What seemed to me to need study was how, in such darkness, so much that was admirable about Japanese life, even under the most trying postwar conditions, had flourished. No question in that connection intrigued me more than whether modern Japanese industry had strong indigenous roots or was merely a cunning transplant made possible by the combination of a talent for imitation and an absolutist government able to mobilize popular energies on behalf of national expansion. In the one case there was great hope for revival; in the other, decidedly less, since at least one of the conditions of earlier success was not likely to be repeated.

After writing a doctoral thesis in the late 1940s on early factory industry in Japan, I turned to the study of Tokugawa agrarian history, looking for economic and social change among the people who farmed that might help explain subsequent industrialization. The search was in part prompted by reading in Western economic history, but the major stimulus was the role rural people played in the development of the silk industry in the Meiji period. Behind that impressive display of enterprise, I thought, must lie some recent cultural preparation worth understanding.

I soon discovered profoundly contradictory evidence. On the one hand, countrywide indices of the economy were decidedly negative. About 1700, after a century of extraordinary economic expansion in which arable had greatly increased, castle-towns in all parts of the country grown rapidly, and national population more than doubled, the economy seemingly settled into long-term stagnation. From the first Tokugawa census in 1721 to the last in 1846, national population hovered around 26 million commoners. Castle-towns and other major urban centers, with some notable exceptions, suffered severe losses of population. Famine occurred on an unprecedented scale, the land tax relative to assessed yields reached startling levels, and peasant uprisings grew in frequency and scale.

On the other hand, I discovered that the evidence accumulating from local studies by Japanese scholars, often of single villages, occasionally of the records of individual farmers or merchants, gave a distinctly more optimistic impression. These studies suggested that agricultural technology was advancing, trade and industry growing in the countryside, village schools being founded, literacy spreading, and peasant families in some number moving up as well as down the economic and social scale by the purchase and mortgage of rights to land.

There seemed no way to reconcile the conflicting sets of impressions. On the whole the gloomier view prevailed, partly because immediately after the war Japanese scholars found little that was helpful in their past and partly because the optimistic evidence seemed scarcely more than scattered local instances.

One major Tokugawa transformation affecting agriculture and most people who farmed was difficult to classify. Although it began earlier and proceeded more rapidly in some regions than others, it appeared to be under way in all but the most remote and economically backward places. This was a transition on large holdings from holder to tenant cultivation (from *tezukuri* to *kosaku*). At the beginning of the process, most villages contained one or several large holdings that were worked with the labor services of dependents who either lived as long-term (sometimes hereditary) servants in the holder's family or on small allotments of land from him. There were usually also a considerable number of small and middling holdings that were not integrated into these groupings of large holder and dependents even though the groupings (or, rather, their heads) dominated the communities in which they were located. With the development of trade and industry these groupings gradually broke up. Step by step, large holders withdrew from farming, entrusting at first some and then more and more land to tenants in return for rent in kind, while they themselves turned increasingly to commodity trading, putting-out, and money lending.

Many historians took a negative view of this transformation and to underline the point described the landlords emerging from it as "parasitic." On the narrowest construction the term meant taking much from agriculture and giving little in return. But it also meant in some lexicons a system of exploitation that kept tenants poor, blocked the way to capitalist farming, and in important degree cut Japan off from the possibility of a liberal state and society. In this view, the tragic agricultural role of landlords was not significantly altered by landlord activity in trade and industry. The two roles were inextricably associated. Profits flowed from each to support and extend the other, and the power over tenants that gave reputation and influence in a village and district was the ultimate source of security for property of all kinds.

The business activity of landlords, therefore, seemed less to modify than to fortify an oppressive agrarian regime.

I had become skeptical of this view by the time I began work on *The Agrarian Origins of Modern Japan* (published in 1959). Clearly, commercial and industrial activities associated with the exploitation of land through tenants was radically different from the same activities free of such association. But the positive aspects of these activities could not be discounted, and I was also convinced that the agricultural transformation in itself was liberating—widening rather than restricting the possibilities of economic, social, and individual development. Its effect was to transfer the power of decision over the use of land, labor, and time from the head of a hierarchical group of kin and fictive kin to nuclear and stem families.

These small domestic units had three significant advantages over the larger and more heterogeneous groups. (1) Families, being more coherent and their members more directly motivated, were better able than the larger group to exploit improvements in farm technology that generally called for more care, knowledge, and initiative from each member of the labor force. (2) Because of the family's small size and internal discipline, it was better able than the large group to integrate farming with commercial and industrial by-employments. (3) Small holders and tenants had greater control over their lives and economic fortunes than their counterparts in the large group who lived by labor services, which were less parts of an economic exchange than expressions of personal dependence.

I do not know to what degree, if any, these views were my own, since *Agrarian Origins* was in large part based on Japanese research and I had discussed crucial points at length with Japanese colleagues. In any case, the argument of the book raised problems that kept me busy for some years. I had been able to work the argument out in my own mind only by concentrating on the transition from large-holder to tenant cultivation and its effects, avoiding any attempt to square those developments with long-term trends in population, taxation, and peasant uprisings. It would have been fatal to the completion of the manuscript to have introduced the monumental problems of evidence and interpretation these subjects raised. Just these problems, nevertheless, left doubts in my mind about the tenability of the unstated but clear implication of the book that the output of the economy during the last century or so of the Tokugawa period was probably growing in per capita terms. I was therefore intent on testing that proposition insofar as I could.

The first four chapters of the present book were efforts at such tests. Each sought to analyze quantitative data collected for the promise they held of throwing useful light on a key aspect of the question of growth. In all cases the data were local—from scattered villages, counties, castle-towns—and so raised obvious problems of representativeness. But my hope was not to prove that per capita growth had indeed taken place, something that can perhaps never be satisfactorily done, but only to give a certain credence to that possibility. I will discuss these chapters here in the order written to suggest the direction that my thinking took; they appear in slightly different order in the book itself to provide a more coherent account of premodern economic growth. None of these essays or any of the others has been changed in the book except to improve readability and correct errors of fact, although some express opinions I would now phrase differently or substantially revise.

The first of the four that I wrote, "The Land Tax in the Tokugawa Period," was based on tax records from eleven villages in seven daimyo territories; it cast doubt on the notion that the land tax was everywhere high and probably rising after 1700. This common view weighed heavily against the probability of rising yields in agriculture. Taxes were indeed high (often more than 50 percent) relative to assessments of the productivity of fields (kokudaka). But in none of the eleven villages did either the land tax or the assessments on which it was based change significantly from the early eighteenth century to the mid-nineteenth. This evident stagnation of taxation was almost certainly the result of the financial inability of daimyo governments to carry out new surveys, along with their fear of peasant resistance to raising tax rates, especially in the absence of new assessments. If this condition was common, as seemed possible from the wide geographic scattering of the villages, any rise in agricultural yields (of which there was some evidence in records kept by farmers) would result in a long-term decline in real tax burden. This would have given peasant families a powerful incentive to improve their farming; their success was accompanied by the appearance of a large number of farm manuals in the last century of the Tokugawa period.

The second of the essays concerned farm family by-employments in preindustrial Japan. By-employments were potentially an immense source of income growth in peasant families, and although widely mentioned in secondary literature and published village documents, to the best of my knowledge no systematic effort had been made as of 1969 to estimate the significance of by-employments for the rural economy. My attempt at such an estimate was based on a remarkable economic survey of the two provinces of Chōshū Domain in 1843, which I worked on for longer than I like to remember. For each district in the domain, the survey listed the number of households by occupation and all important items of input and output in physical quantities or money or both. The sheer mass of the data necessitated limiting the study to the returns from a single county (Kaminoseki), which contained 6,510 households and comprised an economically highly developed coastal area and relatively backward districts in the hilly interior. Analysis revealed that 55 percent of net income (outputs minus inputs) in the county came from nonagricultural sources—mainly trade, industry, and transport—and that most of this was produced by farm families. Still more surprising was the fact that, in the county's fifteen districts, the proportion of farm family income earned from nonagricultural production varied from a low of 16 percent to a high of 74, with a median of 43.

These data certainly suggested that commercial and industrial skills were widely disseminated among the farm population and that by-employments were an important cultural preparation for subsequent industrialization. They also confirmed the immense potential of by-employments for the growth of per capita income. They said nothing, however, about the degree to which that potential may have been realized, since there was the possibility that increased income from by-employments had been wholly offset, or more than offset, by the growth of population because of more frequent and younger marriages induced by the widened possibilities of employment. On the other hand this offsetting would not have occurred if, despite everything, farm families had chosen and been able to restrict marriage to a single son in each generation in order to avoid further fragmenting holdings. Unfortunately, the Chōshū data gave no clue as to which of these possibilities was more likely.

One of the major reasons for doubting that the economy was growing in the last century of the Tokugawa period was the decline of castle-towns. The third of the essays, "Premodern Economic Growth," attempted to discover how widespread and severe that decline was and to account for it. Thirty-five castle towns on which I was able to collect data, with rare exceptions the largest urban centers in their districts, lost 18 percent of their combined population between the early eighteenth and mid-nineteenth centuries; moreover, except in economically backward regions nearly all castle-towns suffered severe population loss. It was clear, however, from the comment of contemporary observers and the measures taken by governments to arrest urban losses, that the decline reflected a shift of trade and industry from cities to the countryside. This was owing partly to the greater freedom of the country from taxes and governmental controls and partly to advantages in the country of nearness to raw materials, fuel, and cheap labor in farm families. The decline of castle-towns therefore did not necessarily mean overall economic decline and may even have been associated with overall growth.

But if overall growth was to be regarded as a serious possibility, some explanation consistent with it was needed for the secular stagnation of national population from the early eighteenth century on. And such an explanation would have to center on the reproductive behavior of farm families, which made up the greater part of the population and whose output in trade and industry was evidently growing. I had suggested that farm families may have been restricting marriage—and therefore indirectly fertility—in order to protect the integrity of their already small holdings. But I had no explanation of why the growth of rural trade and industry would not in Japan, as it had in Europe, allow noninheriting sons to find independent livings mainly or wholly *outside* agriculture.[1]

1. Osamu Saito's remarkable book *Puroto-kōgyōka no jidai: The Age of Proto-Industrialization—Western Europe and Japan in Historical and Comparative Perspective* (Tokyo, 1985) is addressed to the differences in proto-industry between Japan and

Meanwhile I had begun to wonder whether farm families were not practicing some form of family limitation, a line of speculation suggested by French and English studies in demographic history and by Hayami Akira's study of the village of Yokouchi. In the fourth article, "Peasant Families and Population Control in Eighteenth-Century Japan," Robert Eng and I sought to confirm Hayami's findings by an analysis of the population registers from the village of Nakahara for the years from 1717 to 1830. We confirmed what he (and by that time a few others) had found: low registered fertility and mortality, wide spacing of births, early stopping of childbearing by married women, and small completed families. Much to our astonishment, we also found evidence that married couples tended at each birth order to balance the sexes of their children by means of infanticide. Although large holders had somewhat larger families than small, this balancing tendency was present in both groups, so infanticide seemed not to be wholly a function of poverty. I should mention that there was nothing in these findings necessarily at odds with subsequent work by others emphasizing the gender division of labor in connection with by-employments; indeed, sex balancing may well have reflected and would surely reinforce that tendency. Of course, Nakahara was a single case and warranted no general conclusion about demographic behavior in the Tokugawa period. Happily, a large-scale project is now under way for the study of population registers from upward of forty villages on the Nobi Plain, where Nakahara is situated, which will add immensely to our knowledge of the dynamics of premodern Japanese population growth.

Earlier I mentioned writing a doctoral thesis on Japanese industry in the Meiji period. The thesis stressed the importance to early indus-

---

Europe. Saito's explanation turns in large measure on the absence or weakness in Japan of the tendency for proto-industrialization to lead to regional specialization between agriculture and rural industry. It was this tendency, which was marked in Europe, that in proto-industrial districts led to earlier marriages and larger families. Saito attributes the absence or weakness of such specialization in Japan mainly to the gender division of labor in the farm family—with women chiefly responsible for industry and men for farming—in conjunction with the continuing ability of small farms to achieve increases in agricultural productivity.

trialization of the revolutionary political and administrative changes of the Restoration, the character of which I attributed in part to the influence of wealthy farmers (gōnō) on samurai in the Restoration movement. I did not pursue the subject but continued to be intrigued as to how samurai, the chief beneficiaries of the Tokugawa government, came to overthrow that regime and lead the nation on a course eliminating samurai privileges.

A part of the answer that should have been obvious all along dawned on me while working on the Tokugawa land tax. The stagnation of tax rates and assessments brought home how radically the removal of samurai from the land in the seventeenth century changed the character of that class, transforming it from landholders with assured incomes and a dominating local presence in the countryside into city-dwellers living on stipends from the lord's treasury and subject to his repeated and arbitrary exaction of contributions (kariage). In conjunction with rising standards of consumption among rich townsmen, such exactions exposed lower and middling samurai, who were financially unable to live up to costly status requirements, to daily humiliation (or the fear of it) at the hands of commoners. Some of the resulting complications in class relations are discussed briefly in "The Discontented."

Removal from the land fatefully changed the samurai's relation to political as well as to economic power. For samurai, power had previously meant personal control over land and people and had been exercised as an inherited right. Now it became impersonal and bureaucratic, deriving from an appointed office from which the incumbent could be and often was removed. Relations with the lord changed accordingly. Once intensely personal and emotional, relations became distant and formal, hedged about with ceremonies and taboos, and vassals increasingly looked on the lord less as a leader in war than as a symbol of administration. Loyalty came to mean disinterested advice and personal conduct that was a credit to the lord's administration: qualities of the ideal bureaucrat had come to be viewed as the essence of the warrior. "Japan's Aristocratic Revolution" tries to show how these changes prepared samurai for centralized bureaucratic government, without shogun or daimyo, and for a meritocratic society in which rank was determined by education rather than birth.

Another chapter, "'Merit' as Ideology," elaborates on the conflict between the feudal ideal of personal service defined by rank and passed down from father to son and the Confucian and bureaucratic ideal of meritocratic appointment to office. At first the merit ideal became a weapon of discontented samurai in criticizing the policies of governments staffed by samurai who were, in practice, selected according to inherited rank; then it was seen as a practice calculated to destroy character and make men unfit for government; and finally it was used to call into question the legitimacy of "present-day rulers," who it was alleged had been corrupted by inherited rank beyond the possibility of personal redemption. Because these ideas were commonplace by late Tokugawa among samurai of all condition and especially those of low and middling rank, they prepared the samurai for the abolition of the privileges of birth in the early Meiji period, a measure that owed less to Western inspiration than meets the eye.

The last two chapters in the book, on early factory workers, may seem at first glance to have no particular relation to the others. At least I thought not when I wrote them as articles; I was pleased to turn to the study of Meiji labor with a sense of taking up a new subject. I had become so committed to certain views of Tokugawa social and economic history I was fearful that I would go on rather too long repeating them without adding anything. But two things soon changed my mind about how new the new subject of labor really was.

One was seeing a striking similarity between early factory strikes and Tokugawa peasant uprisings: the ritual petition for redress of grievances; the moral language of protest; the taking from participants of loyalty oaths signed in a circle to avoid identifying leaders; the use of shrines and temples as meeting places; the parallel leadership and organizational roles of village headmen and foremen on the one hand and villages and workshops on the other. Second was discovering that, unlike Western counterparts, Japanese industrial workers rarely mentioned rights before 1918—even though intellectuals did, insistently— and that they appealed instead to the idea of status justice. That is, they appealed for the sympathy, consideration, respect, and protection that superiors in a hierarchical society were thought to owe dependents and denounced the absence of these sentiments among employers as unrighteous, selfish, inhumane, cruel, and violent. Since this ideal was all but universal in Meiji society, the appeal to it in labor disputes could not be attributed particularly to fundamentalist workers from the countryside; finding it as the prime source of workers' ideology was a concrete reminder, though, that the culture many workers brought to the factory was rooted in a recent agrarian past.

The chapter on labor that I wrote first, "The Right to Benevolence," traces the concept of status justice among workers from 1890 to 1920. This concept was neither a false consciousness nor a mere prelude to rights consciousness (as it is sometimes seen), but an original, effective, and evolving criticism of the factory that tapped the deepest Japanese feelings about social justice. At first the criticism was highly personal, directed against the employer or factory head or *oyakata* (work boss). Increasingly it was turned against the company, although the language of criticism remained much the same: "benevolence" remained the key term describing a sentiment that ought to inform all actions of superordinates toward subordinates. But the emphasis in usage gradually moved away from designating acts of personal kindness, generosity, and recognition to describing institutional entitlements covering pay, benefits, and welfare measures. In the name of status justice workers won some of the key entitlements they demanded from management (although at low levels of payment) before unions played a significant role in labor relations. When unions came into prominence after 1917, they took over the earlier demands, rephrasing them in the language of rights and class struggle—with an uncertain effect on worker consciousness.

The other essay, "Peasant Time and Factory Time," traces time discipline in contemporary Japanese factories to premodern attitudes toward time. I had been led by E. P. Thompson's powerful essay "Time, Work Discipline, and Industrial Capitalism" to expect an intense conflict in Japanese industry between managers and workers over time. But in fact I found little such conflict, and upon consulting Tokugawa farm manuals for an impression of the time sense of preindustrial Japanese, I began to see why. The lax task-oriented sense of time Thompson described in preindustrial England was not much in evidence in these sources. Prominent, instead, was an insistence on the value of time and hence on planning, saving, stretching, and profiting from time. This advice neatly fitted the nature of late Tokugawa farming: family-size farms worked with little aid from hired labor or animals and where each member of the labor force had a direct interest in results; farms typically composed of scattered small plots planted to different crops requiring the intricate coordination of planting, harvesting, fertilizing, weeding, and irrigating and where farming was widely integrated with industrial and commercial occupations in the family.

A critical dimension of time sense unremarked by Thompson was prominent in Japanese farm manuals and ethnographic descriptions: time did not belong to individuals but to the farm family and, through it, to kin, friends, neighbors, and the village. There was no immediate close mesh between these premodern attitudes toward time and factory discipline, but the result was less a conflict over time between management and worker than a certain give-and-take in adjusting to the new situation. Workers worked extraordinarily long hours with little complaint but paced themselves accordingly. Managers arbitrarily lengthened the workday and canceled holidays as orders required, tolerating in turn considerable absenteeism, lateness, and even soldiering. But as the employment relationship evolved away from the employers' paradigm of contract and toward the worker ideal of a community of shared benefits, shared obligations, and select membership, time discipline steadily tightened. Today it rests less on the principle that time is money and hence that a fair day's pay deserves a fair day's work than on the clear priority of the firm's claim over conflicting private claims to time. Hence the widespread practice in Japanese business of employees' working during part of their legally mandated and paid vacations and their determination of the length of the workday more by the amount of work to be done than by stipulated starting and quitting times.

Writing an introduction to a book of this kind, containing essays composed over many years, presents a special hazard. The point of such an introduction is to show unity among the essays, demonstrating that they belong together and this is indeed a book. It requires downplaying some themes in favor of others and in the end gives a rather misleading impression of how the essays took form. False starts, vigorous forward movements into dead ends, random trying of first one idea and then another to make sense of things—these and other kinds of mucking about get left out. I began the Chōshū study with the idea of finding among the fifteen districts of the region a correlation between nonagricultural income and per capita income; encountering technical difficulties that in time proved insuperable, I turned the hand-processed data into a study of by-employments. But only the subject of by-employments figures in the account of the research given here. Such suppression of part of the story in the interests of coherence and regard for the reader's patience gives a process that might be compared to groping over unfamiliar terrain the air of a brisk and knowing movement from one objective to another. For me, it has never been like that.

1

PREMODERN
ECONOMIC GROWTH:
JAPAN AND THE WEST

I begin with a definition of the term "premodern growth," which is used here in a very restricted sense to mean economic growth only during the century or so immediately before industrialization. There was such growth in England and France and some other Western countries, and it was apparently an important factor in their subsequent industrialization.[1] According to Simon Kuznets's estimates, presently ad-

Reprinted from *Past and Present*, no. 60 (August 1973).

1. François Crouzet, "England and France in the Eighteenth Century: A Comparative Analysis of Two Economic Growths," in *The Causes of the Industrial Revolution in England*, ed. Ronald M. Hartwell (London, 1967), 139–74; Frederick J. Fisher, "The Sixteenth and Seventeenth Centuries: The Dark Ages of Economic History?" *Economica*, n.s. 24, no. 93 (February 1957): 2–19; Jean Marczewski, "The Take-off Hypothesis and French Experience," in *The Economics of Take-off into Sustained Growth*, ed. Walt W. Rostow (New York, 1965), 119–38.

vanced countries, which are nearly all European or derive from Europe, enjoyed per capita incomes on the eve of industrialization several times those of underdeveloped countries today.[2] Surely this astonishing advantage was crucial to their early industrialization, and "premodern growth" important in achieving the advantage.

This inference is strengthened by the case of Japan, the earliest non-Western industrializer, which also experienced "premodern growth."[3] From the early eighteenth century until the middle of the nineteenth, approximately the last half of the Tokugawa period, the output of the country grew slowly but steadily, while the population remained nearly unchanged. The growth of output is indicated by a variety of indirect evidence: rising crop yields, increased by-employments among farmers, a very large number of minor technical innovations, the spectacular growth of manufacturers catering to mass consumption (especially textiles), and a spate of books stressing the efficient use of land and labor. About population we have more precise, if not essentially better, evidence. Between the first and last countrywide "censuses" of the period, in 1721 and 1846, which Japanese historians regard as approximately accurate, the total number of commoners increased barely 3 percent.[4] The combination of factors that held the population in check for this long in the face of expanding output—especially after the previous rapid growth—is one of the more important mysteries of Japanese social history. Whatever it was, it gave every percentage gain in output for over a century an equivalent percentage gain in per capita income. It is perhaps unnecessary to insist that the benefits were not very evenly distributed and that large numbers of Japanese were not better off as a result.

It seems unlikely that by 1860 Japan had attained anything approaching the preindustrial level of per capita income of nations like

2. Simon Kuznets, "Underdeveloped Countries and the Pre-Industrial Phase in the Advanced Countries," in *The Economics of Underdevelopment,* ed. A. N. Agarwala and S. P. Singh (New York, 1963), 143–44; also David Landes, *The Unbound Prometheus* (Cambridge, 1969), 13.

3. For a summary of statistical evidence, see Nakamura Satoru, "Hōkenteki tochi shoyū kaitai no chiikiteki tokushitsu," *Jinbun gakuhō,* 1964, pp. 130–52.

4. Sekiyama Naotarō, *Kinsei Nihon no jinkō kōzō,* 2d printing (Tokyo, 1957), 95–96, 123.

England, the Netherlands, or Sweden. But there can be no doubt that the country was far better prepared for industrialization than it had been a century before. Commercial institutions were larger and more specialized, businessmen more numerous and more widespread geographically and socially; labor was more mobile, literacy much more common, agriculture more productive, and capital more plentiful. This is not to mention a changed political climate, perhaps the most important new element of all. If we imagine away these changes, the transformation of the economy following the overthrow of the Tokugawa in the late 1860s becomes unthinkable.

So there is a seeming parallel between widely separated countries: "premodern growth" followed by industrialization; and to the best of my knowledge, the second term of the sequence did not occur anywhere in the world without the first during the nineteenth century. But the first itself was strikingly different in Japan and the West. "Premodern growth" in the West was accompanied by marked urban growth: towns and cities grew in size and number, and probably their inhabitants also grew as a percentage of total population.[5] But in Japan during the eighteenth century and the first half of the nineteenth, towns generally stagnated or lost population. The heaviest losses were suffered by the largest towns or towns located in regions with growing

5. In the century 1650–1750, London grew from 7 to 11 percent of the English population: E. Anthony Wrigley, "A Simple Model of London's Importance in Changing English Society and Economy, 1650–1750," *Past and Present*, no. 37 (July 1967): 44–45. Phyllis Deane and W. A. Cole, *British Economic Growth, 1688–1959* (Cambridge, 1962), 7, estimate that the proportion of the British population living in towns of over five thousand rose from about 13 to 25 percent in the course of the eighteenth century. See also Roger Mols, *Introduction à la démographie historique des villes d'Europe du XIVe au XVIIe siècle* (Louvain, 1955), 3 : 526; and Thomas S. Ashton, *An Economic History of England: The Eighteenth Century* (London, 1955), 8, 95–96.

Mols lists the population of thirty-four large French towns at five dates between 1726 and 1801. These figures give a picture of vigorous growth: only seven of the thirty-four towns lost population and many of the others grew dramatically; overall growth of the thirty-four between 1726 and 1801 was 40 percent. According to census figures, the twenty-five largest French cities grew from an aggregate 1,949,574 in 1801 to 2,725,452 in 1846, again a 40 percent increase. Paris at these dates was 547,736 and 1,053,897. French towns of fifty thousand or more grew at an annual rate of 1.18 percent between 1801 and 1851. Mols, *Introduction* 2 : 513–16; Charles H. Pouthas, *La population française pendant la première moitié du XIXe siècle* (Paris, 1956), 98; Marczewski, "Take-off," 130.

economies; on the other hand, rare instances of town growth occurred only in backward and economically stagnant parts of the country.[6]

By towns I mean places of five thousand inhabitants or more, or places legally designated "towns" regardless of size. The more important such places were castle-towns, most of which had grown from small beginnings during the century and a half before 1700. There were about two hundred[7] of them scattered over the country roughly as population was distributed, ranging in size from dusty little places of several thousand up to Edo (Tokyo) with about a million inhabitants in the 1720s.

In view of the subsequent loss of urban population, it is pertinent to suggest in passing what may account for the dramatic growth of castle-towns before 1700,[8] although this is much too complex a question to answer in a few words. (1) Most important was the forced removal of almost the entire samurai class, including families, retainers, and servants, from the land to compact residential quarters laid out around the daimyo's castle. This measure aimed at firmer control by the great lords over their vassals and the vassals' domains. (2) Samurai

6. This paragraph overstates the contrast between Japan and Europe. It is now clear from Jan de Vries's path-breaking study of European urbanization that the growth of Europe's urban population in the seventeenth and eighteenth centuries was owing to a relatively small number of large cities—mostly capitals and ports—and that the bulk of cities barely kept pace with, or lost some slight ground relative to, overall population growth. The reason for this stagnation was similar to the decline of Japan's castle-towns: namely, "a transfer of industrial production to the countryside, and the rise of numerous villages and local market towns as the nuclei of the putting-out system." Although the parallel is striking, significant differences remain between Japan and Europe in respect to urban trends and proto-industrialization. Whereas cities of forty thousand and over in Europe grew in aggregate, cities of this size (taking their samurai population into account) declined sharply in Japan; and whereas in Europe proto-industry was sufficiently divorced from agriculture for de Vries to speak of "migration" from agriculture to rural industry, the two activities were typically integrated within the peasant family in Japan. This difference may have made the demographic effects of the growth of proto-industry very different in the two cases. Such differences notwithstanding, a number of comparative statements in the text exaggerate the contrast, and I have tried here to alert the reader to them. Jan de Vries, *European Urbanization, 1500–1800* (Cambridge, Mass., 1984), 66–69, 71–76, 101, 239–46.

7. Toyoda lists 141 castle-towns of daimyo with domains of fifty thousand *koku* or more, whereas many daimyo, perhaps another 50, with lesser domains also had castles. Toyoda Takeshi, *Nihon no hōken toshi* (Tokyo, 1952), 302.

8. For an account of castle-towns in English, see John Hall, "The Castle Town and Japan's Modern Urbanization," in *Studies in the Institutional History of Early Modern Japan,* ed. John Hall and Marius Jansen (Princeton, 1968), 169–89.

removal in turn resulted in the gathering of merchants and artisans in the growing castle-towns to provide goods and services. (3) This tendency was reinforced by legislation drastically restricting the practice of crafts and trade outside legally designated towns, including castle-towns. (4) Rapid population increase during apparently the whole of the seventeenth century, perhaps at a rate approaching 1 percent a year, permitted the growth of towns and, simultaneously, a sufficient expansion of arable land and agricultural population to feed the enlarging urban population. (5) After a long period of civil war, the achievement of peace and order and a substantial degree of political centralization through the Tokugawa hegemony made all the other developments possible.

The decline of town population during the latter half of the Tokugawa period was offset to an unknown extent by the growth of a multitude of places in the country that, although small and not legally designated as "towns," contained a considerable number of artisans and merchants. By any conceivable standard, however—size, residential density, occupational diversity, culture—these places were far less urban than the declining towns. It must be kept in mind, too, that Japan remained a conspicuously urban country for its time, with towns everywhere and several cities of great size. We are remarking a trend, not an absolute level. Nothing perhaps bespeaks the trend so dramatically as the sad decline of urban culture, which reached a peak of creativity at the end of the seventeenth century and gradually lost life and originality thereafter.

The decline of towns in the course of "premodern growth" calls for an explanation. I will argue that the decline was neither a statistical illusion (as I first thought) nor an inexplicable aberration, but a function of growth itself. Without a considerable degree of de-urbanization, no growth could have taken place. This mode of "premodern growth," so different from the Western type, will be seen to have had ramifications throughout the society and to have influenced powerfully the character of Japan's subsequent industrialization.[9] But let us try now to get some notion of the magnitude of town decline.

9. See n. 6.

I have assembled all the figures available at scattered dates in the Tokugawa period for thirty-seven castle-towns, about 18 percent of the total number (see the appendix to this chapter). The figures come indirectly from the annual registers of population kept in nearly all towns and villages after the late seventeenth century, which listed—or were supposed to list—every commoner man, woman, and child (usually over Japanese age two, or our age one on average) resident in the jurisdiction. Village registers survive in substantial number, but town registers rarely do. Nevertheless town population figures have been preserved, although haphazardly and usually only as global figures, in administrative documents and local histories and gazetteers. Hence in most cases no way exists to check the original registers for mistakes of transcription and addition, and the originals were themselves probably never free of considerable error. Still, with few exceptions the town figures may be regarded as approximately accurate;[10] in any case we are interested less in absolute figures than in trends, and there is no reason to suggest that errors in the figures would impart a consistent upward or downward bias over many towns.[11] Also, the down-

10. As anyone who has worked with them knows, Japanese population registers from the Tokugawa period contain many errors. Persons who moved from one jurisdiction to another, especially if they left families behind, sometimes continued to be listed for years afterward in the original place. New residents in a place were not always registered immediately upon arrival; and even old residents were occasionally omitted through oversight and possibly a conviction that some categories of people (children, maiden aunts, servants) were less important than others. It is possible that such misregistrations and omissions increased over time. But Japanese demographic historians have done enough detailed work with population registers extending in nearly unbroken series over long periods, which permit individuals to be followed year by year from birth to death and tabulation to be made of persons unaccountably appearing or disappearing, to give some confidence in the general accuracy of registration. Certainly registration aimed at universality for commoners, and the passport system made an approach to this goal possible.

11. In comparing population figures from the same town at different dates, there is always a problem of comparability: do the figures refer to the same age and status groups and geographical areas? A substantial change in any of these respects would of course give a wholly erroneous impression of population change. Fortunately definitions of social and geographical boundaries at various registrations have been preserved in a fair number of cases. From these cases it seems that changes in the scope of registration were infrequent and more likely to result in an upward than a downward bias, because of a tendency to bring places on the outskirts of a town under the same commercial regulations as the town itself and a bureaucratic desire to make registration ever more comprehensive within a given jurisdiction. Population figures survive for a few town wards near the center of castle-towns, where there is little possibility of a change of ei-

ward trend shown by the figures is confirmed everywhere by the complaints of town officials of population loss and merchants of declining prosperity.

The appendix to this chapter presents in tabular form the changes that took place in the commoner population from 1700 to 1850 (Table 1.1) and a description of the method used to construct the table. It will be seen that twenty-four towns declined by 10 percent or more: nine of these declined severely (DD), or by more than 30 percent; fifteen declined at a more moderate rate (D). Seven others, with a population change of less than 10 percent, may be regarded as stable (S), and four with gains of 10 percent or more as growing (G). The groups of towns with the same observation dates declined, in the order used in the table, by 21, 13, 18, 13, 34, and 32 percent. When the six groups are aggregated, the overall loss of population is 18 percent.

Edo and Osaka were omitted from the table in order to avoid overweighting with two places far larger than the others, since each had a commoner population approaching half a million in the early eighteenth century. But their inclusion would not have changed the results significantly. Edo was nearly static from the early eighteenth century to the mid-nineteenth. Osaka continued to grow until 1763, somewhat later than most castle-towns; then it lost population steadily until 1868, when the number of inhabitants stood at 67 percent of the figure of a century before.[12]

I have not attempted a systematic sampling of other towns. The number of towns is great and population data for them scarce and difficult to come by. The figures that are at hand give an impression of a decline similar to the castle-towns;[13] but the sample is small and geo-

---

ther geographical or status boundaries. These show the same tendency to population decline as the towns as a whole, and in some places a sharper decline, suggesting that for some reason the center of the town lost population more heavily than outlying wards.

12. Nishiyama Matsunosuke, "Ōsaka, Hyōgo, Nishinomiya, Shiakujima jinkō tōkeihyō," Rekishigaku kenkyū, no. 157 (May 1952): 26–29; Kōda Shigetomo, "Edo no chōnin no jinkō," Shakai keizai shigaku 8 (April 1938): 1–24.

13. Kaizuka declined from 6,807 in 1721 to 3,956 in 1869; Nishinomiya from 9,778 in 1769 to 7,669 in 1850; Ōmi Hachiman from 7,568 in 1721 to 5,629 in 1869; Sakai from 62,860 in 1688 to 37,153 in 1859. Other sizable declining towns in the general Kinki–Inland Sea region were Gifu, which declined from 6,203 in 1726 to 4,808 in 1840, and Tomo (Fukuyama's port), which fell from 7,204 in 1711 to 4,794 in 1816.

graphically skewed, coming mainly from the central, Kinki district, and no conclusion is warranted. The most one can say is that complaints of urban decline came from all over the country and made no distinction between castle and other towns. On the other hand, as noted before, there were a large number of growing places that, although usually designated legally as "country" (zaikata), were socially partly urban, some even approaching town size. I will refer to these settlements, for lack of a better term, as "country places."

The distribution over the landscape of castle-towns in different stages of growth and decline (Map 1.1) is suggestive, with three features especially standing out. First, severely declining castle-towns were concentrated in the Kinki and the Inland Sea regions, economically the most advanced parts of the country, but growing towns were located without exception in remote and economically backward districts. Second, severely declining castle-towns tended to be ports[14] and hence to have access to relatively cheap, fast, and long-ranging transport. But stable and growing towns were located inland, where transport was mainly overland and so relatively expensive, slow, and short-range. This situation is, of course, the opposite of what one would expect; taken in conjunction with the first, it suggests that town decline was somehow associated with economic development and superior communications, and stability or growth with their opposites.

Third, castle-town and regional population change often ran strongly counter to one another, as is shown in the appendix to this chapter. Of twenty-four declining and severely declining castle-towns, fifteen were located in provinces with some population increase, and in many cases the divergence was striking. Hiroshima, for example, a castle-town and port with a magnificent location on the Inland Sea, sustained a population loss of 33 percent while the population of its province, Aki, increased by 69 percent—a divergence of 102 percent.

The one place legally classified as a town that grew substantially in this region, so far as I know, was Yokkaichi, a station on the Tokaidō, which grew from 5,868 in 1724 to 7,461 in 1839. *Fukuyama shishi* (Fukuyama, 1968), 2:261–62; *Yokkaichi shishi* (Osaka, 1961), 224–25; *Kaizuka shishi* (Osaka, 1955), 1:487–89; *Nishinomiya shishi* (Kyoto, 1960), 2:79; *Aichi kenshi* (Tokyo, 1938), 2:229–31; *Sakai shishi* (Sakai, 1930), 3:161–63; *Shiga Hachiman chōshi*, 2d ed. (Osaka, 1969), 1:352–55.

14. Six of ten were ports; another two were located near the coast.

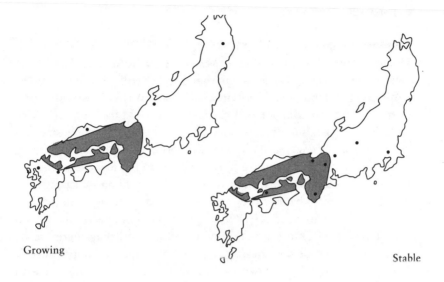

Growing

Stable

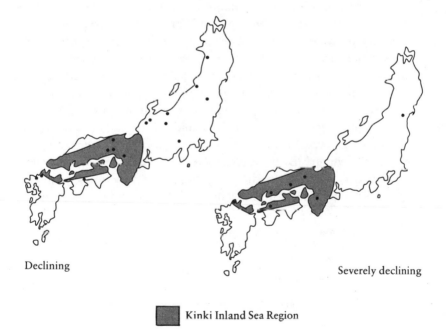

Declining

Severely declining

Kinki Inland Sea Region

Map 1.1   Types of Castle-Town Population Change

This was an unusual case; but Kokura, Ueda, Kōchi, Takada, Karatsu, Hakata, Tottori, Himeji, Akita, Matsuyama, Kōfu, and Fukuyama were other declining castle-towns that were sharply at odds with the demographic trend of their provinces. Cases of this kind would, more-over, probably be commoner if castle-towns could be compared with counties rather than with provinces, which because of their size and geographical diversity usually included both growing and declining districts. Such comparison is rarely possible. In the few cases where it is, however—in Okayama, Fukuyama, and Hiroshima—fast-growing counties tended to be near the castle-town and declining counties at a distance. These are all cases from neighboring domains on the Inland Sea, a region of extreme castle-town decline, and may therefore be unrepresentative of the country as a whole. Yet our impression is strengthened that castle-town decline was somehow associated with surrounding economic growth.

Each declining castle-town lost population for a somewhat differ-ent set of reasons, but the commonest cause cited by contemporaries was the development of trade and industry in the surrounding coun-tryside. Government attempted to block this development, which it re-garded as likely to divert labor from farming and make the peasants lazy, quarrelsome, and greedy. It also sought to confine trade and in-dustry to the towns in order to assure their provisioning and to facili-tate price control and the taxation of nonagricultural income.[15]

Complex legislation designed to achieve these ends was largely in-effectual, however, for the putting-out system spread to nearly every part of the country. By the early nineteenth century as large a number of different, nonagricultural occupations could be found within a radius of a few miles in many rural areas as in fair-sized cities.[16]

15. Ishii Ryōsuke and Takayanagi Shinzō, *Ofuregakisho tenmei shūsei* (Tokyo, 1958), 867–77; and Ishii Ryōsuke, ed., *Hanpōshū* (Tokyo, 1959–61), vol. 1, pt. 1, pp. 451–93, pt. 2, pp. 221–29; vol. 2, pp. 153–337.
16. Seventy-seven occupations appear on a list of 2,954 families making contribu-tions to a temple in the castle-town of Hikone in 1695. Compare this figure with the fifty-one by-employments represented in a group of fourteen villages in Sasayama that had a combined population of 538 families; also compare the seventy-four occupations represented among 494 commercial households in Ichinomiya in 1842 with the fifty oc-cupations in Iwakura Village with 420 households in 1835—both in Owari Province. Kawaura Yasuji, *Kisei jinushiron* (Tokyo, 1960), 70–74; *Hikone shishi* (Kyoto, 1962), 2:4–5; Oka Mitsui, *Hōken sonraku no kenkyū* (Tokyo, 1962), 196.

Whole districts came to earn a major part of their living from by-employments[17] and commodities shipped directly from country places to remote towns and to other country places without passing, as the law stipulated, through nearby towns. The determination of the government to stop these circumventions gradually weakened, so that by the end of the Tokugawa period much of the restrictive legislation on behalf of towns had become a dead letter.

The growth of rural trade and industry might have redounded to the benefit of castle-towns by expanding their markets in the countryside, but in fact it was apparently achieved at some net cost to their prosperity. From the early eighteenth century the towns complained loudly that their merchants and artisans were being ruined by country competition.[18] In 1789 a city magistrate in Okayama, a severely declining castle-town with a commoner population of over twenty thousand, alleged that ships were putting in, in growing numbers, at country ports in order to avoid selling their cargoes at less favorable prices in the town. Ships entering the town had consequently fallen to one-third of the number for the period 1736–50.[19] A statute of about the same time describes what this loss meant to the inhabitants.

> Commerce in this city has steadily declined and many small merchants find themselves in great difficulty. On the other hand, ships from other provinces stopping at places such as Shimoshii Village and Saidaiji Village have steadily increased, bringing trade in the country [*zaikata*] into a flourishing condition. People used to come into the castle-town from the surrounding area to shop or to take goods on consignment in order to sell them in the country. But now people from the castle-town go to the country to shop, and town shopkeepers send agents to the country to arrange to receive goods on consignment. Thus the distinction between front and

17. Thomas C. Smith, *The Agrarian Origins of Modern Japan* (Stanford, 1959), chaps. 6–12; "Farm Family By-Employments in Preindustrial Japan," *Journal of Economic History* 29, no. 4 (December 1969): 687–715; Oka, *Hōken sonraku*, 192–97.

18. For some examples in addition to those cited below, see Ono Hitoshi, *Kinsei jōkamachi no kenkyū* (Tokyo, 1928), 286; Yasuoka Shigeaki, *Nihon hōken keizai seisaku shiron* (Tokyo, 1958), 171–73; Chihōshi Kenkyū Kyōgikai, ed., *Nihon sangyōshi taikei* (Tokyo, 1962), 6:36–39; Kitajima Masamoto, "Kōshinchi ni okeru nōminteki shukōgyō no seikaku," *Nihonshi kenkyū*, no. 12 (February 1946): 15–16; Itō Yoshiichi, *Edo jimawari keizai no tenkai* (Tokyo, 1966), 214–17; Takemoto Ryūhei, "Kannōsaku," in *Nihon keizai sōsho*, ed. Takimoto Seiichi (Tokyo, 1917), 20:599–600; Andō Seiichi, *Kinsei zaikata shōgyō no kenkyū* (Tokyo, 1958), 270–72, 286–96, and 320–29.

19. *Okayama ken no rekishi* (Okayama, 1962), 417.

back, town and country, has been lost; farmers and tradesmen have exchanged positions. Naturally this has resulted in the impoverishment of many people in the town.[20]

Nor was it only merchants who suffered from country competition; the brewers of the town alleged in 1802 that their number had been reduced from sixty-seven to forty-four by business failures in the past thirty years. This, they said, was because country rivals enjoyed the advantage of lower production costs and freedom from guild and municipal restriction and hence were able to make and sell "just as they please." [21] Characteristically, the town brewers asked not for equal freedom for themselves but for the suppression of country brewers.

Complaints of this kind came from nearly all castle-towns; only the details are different, as one illustration must suffice to suggest. A petition of 1819 from the rice merchants of Mito, a backward district, charged that the rice brought by peasants into the town for sale was only about half the amount of former times, since country merchants were buying up rice and other products for shipment and sale elsewhere—where presumably they received a higher return. The village of Aoyagi, located near the castle-town, had become a prosperous port because of this illegal trade, it was said. The petition also charged that the brewing industry, once concentrated in the castle-town, had spread through the rice-growing region in the southern part of the fief, adversely affecting the castle-town brewers and the town rice merchants who supplied them. Remedies were suggested but proved difficult to enforce.[22] Two years after this petition, for example, the headmen of the wards of Mito town complained about retail shops in the country. Except for a few items of daily use, the sale of manufactured goods within a prescribed radius of the town had been strictly prohibited in 1636 and the prohibition repeated many times since; yet

> year after year the retail trade in country districts increases. Sake, dyes, dry goods, toilet articles, hardware, lacquerware—everything you can think of—are sold in villages. Moreover, recently [village shops] have begun to buy directly from Edo [rather than from the castle-town]. And as

20. Ono, *Kinsei jōkamachi*, 417.
21. Ibid., 288–89.
22. Kidota Shirō, *Meiji Ishin no nōgyō kōzō* (Tokyo, 1960), 45.

for rice, wheat, and other cereals, it is well known that they are bought up in the country and that the amount coming into the castle-town has been greatly reduced. The result of all this is that the castle-town declines more and more, and every year the number of vacant stores and houses increases.[23]

One finds fragmentary and scattered evidence indirectly supporting such complaints. A list of 197 "men of wealth" in the Mito *han* drawn up in 1804 showed that less than one-quarter were residents of the castle-town.[24] When the lord of Miyazu, a rich textile region opposite Kyoto on the Japan Sea, called on the wealthy merchants and manufacturers of his domain for financial contributions in 1860, more large contributions and more contributors came from outside than inside the castle-town.[25] In the textile district around Hachiōji, more middlemen buyers (*nakagai*) of cocoons, silk yarn, and cloth lived in villages than in the fifteen towns of the district.[26]

But the most impressive evidence of the country's hurting the towns is the growth of scores—perhaps hundreds—of country places because of the expansion of industry, trade, and transport. Contemporaries often alluded to such places.[27] I have made no systematic effort to collect population figures on growing country places but there were undoubtedly a great many. A list of twenty-one compiled haphazardly, excluding those thought to be growing because of the expansion of arable land and hence of the agricultural population, presents several features worth noting.[28]

First, most of the places were small compared to the average castle-town; all but eight had under three thousand inhabitants and most had under one thousand. Second, the majority, as far as can be determined, were legally villages rather than towns. Third, all grew fairly rapidly during the century and a half after 1700, several doubling or

23. Ibid., 57.
24. Ibid., 59.
25. *Nihon sangyōshi taikei* 6:85.
26. Shōda Ken'ichirō, *Hachiōji orimonoshi* (Tokyo, 1965), 302–3.
27. *Ashikaga orimonoshi* (Tokyo, 1960), 13.
28. The twenty-one (with their provinces in parentheses) were Takasaki (Kōzuke), Zenkōji (Shinano), Narita (Shimōsa), Toraiwa (Shinano), Mitarai (Aki), Hachiōji (Musashi), Sannohe (Mutsu), Fukiage (Bizen), Kofurue (Aki), Atsuta (Owari), Urato (Tosa), Kōbe (Settsu), Shimotsutsuga (Aki), Utsui (Nagato), Tsuichi (Nagato), Takehara (Aki), Kawado (Iwami), Tsunozu (Iwami), Kushiro (Iwami), Hieshima (Settsu), Kiryū (Kōzuke).

tripling in that time. Although the irregular and wide spacing of observations makes generalization difficult, there seems to have been more
growth in the group after 1750 than before, and a number of places
show a distinct acceleration of growth after 1800. Fourth, in nearly all
cases growth was accompanied by the local expansion of trade or industry, and it is not surprising therefore that eighteen of the twenty-
one were ports. They included a number on the Inland Sea, a location
that in castle-towns almost guaranteed decline. In fact, some of these
Inland Sea ports were located near severely declining castle towns; for
example, Mitarai and Kofurue were near Hiroshima, and Fukiage near
Okayama.

Little is known about the demographic mechanisms of castle-town
decline and country-place growth, but migration was clearly among
them. Castle-towns were probably like contemporary European towns
in normally recording an excess of deaths over births, hence in depending on immigration for the maintenance or increase of population. In
the latter half of the Tokugawa period, when Edo's population was
static, a quarter of the commoners in the city were found to have been
born elsewhere,[29] and a high ratio of immigrants also appears in other
towns.

Many immigrants were live-in "servants" (genin) who came into
town from the country on yearly or seasonal employment contracts.
As employment opportunities expanded in the country, the flow of
rural labor to the towns evidently slowed. For example, live-in servants in two wards of Tennōji, a town on the outskirts of Osaka, declined from eighty-four in 1806 to a mere five in 1858, at the same
time that the ward population fell from 755 to 451, or 40 percent.
There was also a decline of 24 percent in the number of households
in these wards, which was especially severe among families renting
houses in contrast to house-owning families. Some of the regular residents of the town were obviously leaving in hope of bettering their
luck elsewhere.[30]

29. Hayami Akira, "Nihon keizaishi ni okeru chūsei kara kinsei e no tenkan,"
Shakai keizai shigaku 37, no. 1 (1971): 98–99; Kōda, "Edo no chōnin," 1–24.
30. Robert J. Smith, "Town and City in 'Pre-Modern' Japan: Small Families, Small
Households,and Residential Instability," mimeograph (Cornell University), 22–23.

It would be surprising if migrants went in large number directly from declining castle-towns to growing country places. Patterns of migration were more complex and diffuse. Every town and village annually registered people moving to and from many other places for marriage, adoption, and employment or as a result of the termination of such arrangements. When towns or villages gained or lost population over the long term because of migration, it would seem to have been the outcome of small changes in net flows between many points on a grid rather than of large transfers between a few.

In any case, growing places were augmented by migration as declining towns were diminished. Kiryū, a textile town or village—significantly, documents use both designations—in Kōzuke Province, tripled in size between 1757 and 1855. A document of 1835 tells how: "Weavers who came to make a living hired women operatives to spin and weave, and people came crowding into the town from other provinces, renting houses there and even in surrounding hamlets."[31] Nor was Kiryū unique in this respect, for in 1846 we find the village (or town) complaining of a local labor shortage and blaming it on the neighboring village of Ashikaga, which was said to be tempting Kiryū workers away at "exorbitant" wages. Some Ashikaga weavers were allegedly employing as many as "thirty, forty, fifty, or a hundred or more" operatives each. The figures ought not to be taken literally, but the competitive hiring was real enough.[32]

Servants, who appear in the population registers of growing country places in large numbers, often came from surprising distances, suggesting a shortage of labor not only locally but also in the surrounding district. Of 23 workers employed by a silkworm egg producer in a Fukushima village in 1815, 20 came from outside the province.[33] The large servant population in the rapidly growing commercial and salt-making town of Takehara-Shimoichi came mainly from Iyo Province across the Inland Sea.[34] A record of the servants in a Settsu village near Osaka showed a total of 221 servants employed from outside the vil-

31. *Kiryū shishi* (Kiryū, 1958), 1:819.
32. Ibid., 857.
33. *Nihon sangyōshi taikei* 3:86.
34. Watanabe Norifumi, "Zaigōmachi to shūben nōson to no kankei," in *Nihon machi*, ed. Chihōshi Kenkyū Kyōgikai (Tokyo, 1958), 297; *Nihon sangyōshi taikei* 7:45.

lage between 1707 and 1810—180 of these from other provinces.[35]
The records of a master weaver in Kiryū show him employing 132
operatives between 1788 and 1817, nearly half of whom came from
outside the province.[36]

The ability of country places to attract and hold labor in competition with castle-towns bespeaks comparative economic advantages, five
of which were mentioned by contemporaries or can be read between
the lines: (1) nearness to raw materials and water power; (2) closeness
to the growing rural market for goods and services; (3) tighter and
more reliable networks of face-to-face relations at a time when, in the
absence of a developed commercial law, such relations, rather than
contracts, were the principal basis of security in commercial transactions; (4) the ability of workers in the country to shift back and forth
between farming and other employments; and (5) greater freedom
from taxation and guild restrictions. These advantages require no special comment since, with the possible exception of the third, all were
widespread in Europe before the nineteenth century. But another advantage that contemporaries did not see clearly, and the ineffectiveness
of economic legislation on behalf of the towns—which they did see—
need some explanation.

After the mid-eighteenth century, governments increasingly attempted to confine the sale of certain staples in each region to licensed
wholesalers in towns who paid for their monopolies handsomely in financial "contributions," "thank-money" (reikin), and taxes.[37] The
government's need of revenue, already pressing in the eighteenth century, became more acute with time, and these monopolies were its
chief device for taxing trade and industry, the most vigorously growing
sectors of the economy. Producers and buyers invariably tried to cir-
cumvent them in order to avoid rigged prices, taxes, and the high

35. Imai Rintarō and Yagi Akihiro, Hōken shakai no nōson kōzō (Tokyo, 1955),
157.
36. Kiryū shishi 1:977–98. For other cases, see Furushima Toshio, Nihon hōken
nōgyōshi (Tokyo, 1941), 308.
37. Oka, Hōken sonraku, 122–48; Yasuoka, Nihon hōken keizai seisaku, 129,
168–69, 173, 178; Ono Masao, "Okayama ni okeru Kokura orimono no ryūtsū kei-
tai," in Nihon shakai keizaishi kenkyū: Kinsei, ed. Hōgetsu Sensei Kanreki Kinenkai
(Tokyo, 1967), 439–56.

transport charges consequent upon circuitous shipping. Nevertheless, monopolies were relatively well enforced in towns, where guild organization could be utilized and the surveillance area was limited in extent and swarming with samurai officials and police. Enforcement was far more difficult in the country, where few guilds existed and the obstacles to surveillance presented by space and terrain were great. Moreover, enforcement there was largely in the hands of village authorities, except for a sprinkling of district magistrates who were rarely in a locality long enough to know its people intimately. Samurai had for a century or more been removed from most of the countryside and concentrated in castle-towns to give the daimyo security against his vassals. No serious thought was ever given to reversing this practice. But the result of the concentration of the samurai in towns was the need to delegate the day-to-day enforcement of the law in the countryside to solidary communities whose members, in this and other matters, had a strong interest in noncompliance. This interest was often especially marked on the part of village officials, who were likely to be merchants as well as landholders.[38]

There were, of course, offsetting advantages on the side of the castle-towns; the most important was the degree of occupational specialization they permitted.[39] Nevertheless the overall advantage in many expanding branches of industry probably lay with the country, as scattered wage data suggest. Real daily wages (money wages converted to rice at local prices) were higher in villages around Osaka, a

38. Evasion of the monopolies, which castle-town merchants continually complained of, could not have occurred on the scale it did without the connivance of whole villages and their officials; village resistance to monopolies is dramatically shown in the leagues of Kinai villages that banded together to petition against them. Yagi Akihiro, *Kinsei no shōhin ryūtsū* (Tokyo, 1968), 166–73. The connivance of Tokugawa village headmen in evading the law has parallels elsewhere. Michael Moerman, "A Thai Village Headman as a Synaptic Leader," *Journal of Asian Studies* 29, no. 3 (May 1969): 535–49. For an eighteenth-century English example of justices of the peace failing to enforce industrial regulations enacted on behalf of a town, see Herbert Heaton, *The Yorkshire Woolen and Worsted Industries* (Oxford, 1965), 228–29.

39. This advantage may not have been as great as one would suppose. The rare and marvelous specialities of Edo and Osaka were not to be found in the country. (For a contemporary literary description, see Howard Hibbett, *The Floating World in Japanese Fiction* [New York, 1959], 45.) But many of them had little to do with the output of significant industries. The operative division of labor was often not greatly different in country districts from that in fair-sized towns; see n. 15.

region of exceptional rural economic development, than in Kyoto, a
city of about four hundred thousand, thirty miles away. Carpenters'
wages were approximately the same in the two places in 1810 but distinctly higher in the country by 1846; plasterers' wages were higher in
the country at the three dates (1814, 1835, and 1846) at which comparisons can be made; and most significant perhaps, day laborers'
wages were over 50 percent higher in the country at the only two observation dates we have (1810 and 1814). Nor was this a unique situation, although it is impossible to say how common it was; as early as
1762, the Sasayama regional government set identical money wages
for male and female servants in the castle-town and country, which
almost certainly meant higher real wages in the latter.[40]

Yet, when one looks at Europe, it is clear that the comparative advantages of country places alone cannot account for the decline of
castle-towns. These same advantages were present in Europe with different results. Much of the history of European industry before the factory is the story of its spread in the countryside, which leads David
Landes to term the characteristic locational pattern of preindustrial
manufacturing "rural settlement."[41] As a consequence of rural compe-

40. Nakamura Satoru, "Nihon ni okeru hongenteki chikuseki no ichi tokushitsu,"
Nihonshi kenkyū, no. 92 (July 1967): 77; Oka, *Hōken sonraku*, 153. This is not inconsistent with the earlier statement that low wages were normally one of the advantages of
the country over the town. Higher real wages in the country were confined to districts
where agriculture, trade, and industry had created an intense local demand for labor;
industry could always find cheaper labor by moving deeper into the countryside, although at some cost in higher transport charges.
41. Landes, *Unbound Prometheus*, 188, 554; Michael M. Postan and Edwin E.
Rich, eds., *The Cambridge Economic History: Trade and Industry in the Middle Ages*
(Cambridge, 1952), 409–26; Eleanora M. Carus-Wilson, "Evidence of Industrial
Growth on Some Fifteenth-Century Manors," *Economic History Review*, 2d ser. 12
(1959–60): 190–206; Joan Thirsk, "Industries in the Countryside," in *Essays in the
Economic and Social History of Tudor and Stuart England*, ed. Frederick J. Fisher
(Cambridge, 1961), 70–88; Jan Dhondt, "The Cotton Industry at Ghent During the
French Regime," in *Essays in European Economic History*, ed. François Crouzet (Lon-
don, 1969), 15; Rudolf Braun, "The Impact of Cottage Industry on an Agricultural
Population," in *The Rise of Capitalism*, ed. David Landes (New York, 1969), 53–65.
Even after steam power came into use in the textile industry, the shift toward the towns
was slow. Many water-powered spinning mills installed steam engines but remained at
their old sites. Wilfred Smith, *An Economic Geography of Great Britain* (New York,
1948), 76–93, 101.

tition, it is true, towns declined in parts of Europe for long periods,[42] but this was never the overall pattern. Roger Mols states that, except perhaps for the period 1350–1450, the major cities of Europe grew in number and size in every century from 1300 to 1800.[43] In any case, however, our comparison is with the period of "premodern growth," when, despite rural settlement, the growth of urban population in Western Europe is not in doubt.[44]

Contemporary explanations of the decline of castle-towns suffice only within the system of which they were a part; similar factors in England and on the Continent led to rather different results. We need therefore to look to the larger environment, where differences in foreign trade and overall population growth attract particular attention. Limitations of knowledge and space rule out a detailed treatment of the interplay of these factors with urban growth and decline, and I have consequently had recourse to two crude models—one for Europe and one for Japan.

In both models foreign trade, urban growth, and population increase are interdependent.[45] In the European model, the increase of foreign trade—which has already reached an intercontinental scale and in Europe alone embraces a dozen countries with a combined population of over a hundred million—encourages population growth.[46] It

42. Henri Sée, "Remarques sur la caractère de l'industrie rurale en France et les causes de son extension au XVIIIᵉ siècle," *Revue historique* 142 (1923): 47–53; Alfred P. Wadworth and Julia de Lacy Mann, *The Cotton Trade and Industrial Lancashire, 1600–1780* (Manchester, 1931), 54–71; Heaton, *Yorkshire Woolen and Worsted Industries*, 217–47; Henri Pirenne, *Histoire de Belgique* (Brussels, 1922–23), 2:422–44, 3:220–61; Eleanora M. Carus-Wilson, "An Industrial Revolution of the Thirteenth Century," in *Essays in Economic History*, ed. Eleanora M. Carus-Wilson (London, 1954), 1:41–60.

43. Mols, *Introduction* 2:47, 528.

44. See n. 6.

45. Crouzet, "England and France," 145–46; for the foreign trade of England earlier, see Fisher, "Sixteenth and Seventeenth Centuries," 9.

46. The population of England and Wales probably increased slowly in the century 1650–1750 and then more rapidly in the next half century: Deane and Cole, *British Economic Growth*, 5–6. Wrigley ("A Simple Model," 48) stresses the slowness of population growth in the century 1650–1750. French population is estimated to have increased from 21 or 22 million in 1700 to 29.5 million in 1806: Louis Henry, "The Population of France in the Eighteenth Century," in *Population in History*, ed. David V. Glass and David E. C. Eversley (London, 1965), 440. For other European countries, see

makes possible food imports in bad years, especially in towns, and it widens employment.[47] The resulting demand for labor encourages migration, earlier marriage, and a higher marriage rate. Towns—and above all, port towns—are the chief places of settlement of the new population.[48] Excellent harbors are scarce, and the docks and warehouses, bankers and lawyers, shipwrights and drayers concentrated in them provide the facilities, capital, and specialized skills necessary for overseas trade, with its long voyages and precious cargoes. The demand for labor cannot be continuously met, short of significant labor-saving innovations, unless population grows. Should this growth fail, foreign trade must cease to grow or—what comes to much the same thing—labor must be withdrawn from farming, bringing on food and raw material shortages with consequent price rises that wipe out comparative advantages in foreign trade.[49]

The difference between the two models is that foreign trade and population are both growing in the European model, whereas foreign trade is nonexistent and population static in the Japanese. The absence of foreign trade in the latter is the result of a political decision made

H. Gille, "The Demographic History of the Northern Countries in the Eighteenth Century," *Population Studies* 3, no. 1 (June 1949): 19; Michael Drake, *Population and Society in Norway, 1735–1865* (Cambridge, 1969), 42, 43; Carlo Cipolla, "Four Centuries of Italian Demographic Development," in *Population in History,* ed. Glass and Eversley, 573.

47. The growth of overseas trade enabled a national deficiency to be overcome by drawing grain from overseas. And better facilities for storage led to the holding of large reserves. "Such a run of wet seasons [a commentator wrote in 1773] as we have had in the last ten or twelve years would have produced a famine a century or more ago": cited in Ashton, *Economic History,* 8. For the seventeenth century, see Barry E. Supple, *Commercial Crisis and Change in England, 1600–1642* (Cambridge, 1959), 14–19.

48. London, Bristol, Liverpool, King's Lynn, Yarmouth, Exeter, and Hull in England; Marseilles, Bordeaux, Dunkerque, Le Havre, Brest, Cherbourg, and Rochefort in the eighteenth century in France. Patterns of urban growth shifted in the early nineteenth century in France, but ports continued to be well represented among fast-growing places. Mols, *Introduction* 2: 513–16, 526; Pouthas, *Population française,* 99–102; Deane and Cole, *British Economic Growth,* 7–8; Smith, *Economic Geography,* 76–77; Charles Wilson, *England's Apprenticeship, 1603–1763* (Oxford, 1965), 42.

49. Two articles by Jonathan D. Chambers, "Enclosure and the Small Landowner," *Economic History Review* 10 (1939–40): 118–28, and "Enclosure and Labour Supply," ibid., 2d ser. 5 (1952–53): 319–44, show that the new agricultural practices associated with enclosure created a new demand for labor and that the population of agricultural villages grew about as rapidly as the population of industrial areas. The decline in agricultural population in England did not begin until the mid-nineteenth century.

possible by hemispheric location amid countries not making up an international state system and not each avidly seeking trade. Coastal shipping is growing but this is hardly equivalent to foreign trade; its overall dimensions in a single country of about thirty million people are of puny order by comparison. Already short shipping distances are made still shorter by frequent stops along the way at night and in bad weather. Ships and cargoes, although numerous, are individually insignificant in size and value. Shipping may be dispersed through a multitude of small ports rather than being forced to gather in a few great ones; it therefore stimulates the growth of "country places," where other occupations are typically combined with farming, instead of the towns, where such combination is rare.

A new factor must now be introduced to account for the decline of towns in the Japanese model: despite everything, the economy is slowly expanding, by virtue of a host of mousetrap innovations, a positive investment rate, and the progressive relaxation of government control over the economy. The expansion of the economy in the absence of foreign trade and population growth induces the decline of towns. For as per capita income rises, so inevitably does the demand for the products of secondary industry and services, which therefore require more labor. For obvious reasons, including the danger of widespread starvation, labor cannot be withdrawn from farming. It can nonetheless be supplied amply and well and in a stable social environment by peasant family members, who can rarely be kept busy full-time in farming. As industry and trade spread in the country, therefore, by-employments on the farms begin to reduce the annual flow of migrants to the towns, and the towns, unable to sustain themselves by natural increase, lose population. The loss is most marked in the economically more advanced parts of the country, where rural trade and industry are growing, and is less noticeable or nonexistent in the backward districts, where such development is slight.

It will now be convenient to relax the assumption that population is static overall and ask why, with increased employment in the country, population does not begin to grow. I believe the reason is that nonagricultural occupations continue to be carried on mainly in conjunction with family farming. They do not create many independent new livings, many new slots for new families. Parents still cannot provide for "surplus" children (in excess of replacements for themselves) without parceling already small holdings and so endangering family continuity. Instead, they continue, as they have for generations whenever arable land is not expanding sufficiently to allow for additional families, to use abortion and infanticide and perhaps other means to limit the number of children to be raised.[50] This practice increases the chance of dying or reaching old age without a natural male heir, a prospect that anthropologists tell us peasants abhor; but in this case the culture offers a happy evasion. It has always been possible in Japan to adopt a male heir, even of adult age, as a husband for a daughter or outright, so long as there is property to inherit. If only property is not dispersed, the heir will not be a problem. Moreover, he is in every sense but sentimentally, and perhaps not always with that exception—legally, socially, religiously, even genealogically—the exact equal of a natural heir; and he has the bonus advantage that if he works out badly, he can be disinherited and replaced.

Family priorities, which keep population in check, would presumably change if the country were opened to foreign trade, thus accelerating economic expansion and making a limited number of ports the focal points of growth. Then better prospects for children off the farm would reduce the incentive to limit families. And in fact when foreign trade commenced in the 1850s, both national and town populations began to grow rapidly, after more than a century of stagnation.

It is not to be hoped that these models will constitute a satisfactory explanation of the difference in "premodern growth" between Japan and the West, but only that they may be suggestive. In any case, we are not dealing with chance differences but rather different modes of growth, one urban-centered and the other (if such a phrase may be used) rural-centered, which color a great many other aspects of society.[51] Let me cite a single illustration. Consider certain changes in the relations of social classes accompanying "premodern growth" in Japan

---

50. For evidence of family limitation among the farming population, see Hayami Akira, "Shinshū Yokouchi mura no chōki jinkō tōkei," *Keizaigaku nenpō* 10 (1968): 59–105.

51. See n. 6.

that would have struck a contemporary European of almost any nationality as extremely odd.

For one thing, although "premodern growth" brought gains to the Western bourgeoisie, it unquestionably imposed losses on the urban class in Japan, which was smaller and less prosperous in 1850 than in 1700 and also less spirited. Castle-towns, of course, continued to perform vital economic functions. But by 1850 their merchants had been suffering for several generations from country competition on the one hand and oppressive taxation and regulation on the other. One might expect urban merchants to help themselves in such circumstances by political means, at least in time, but they seem to have been quite unable to do so. Living in the shadow of the lord's castle and in the midst of his soldiers, without corporate freedoms and representative assemblies, townsmen could not conceive of a change in government brought about by themselves. Indeed, the more difficult their economic plight became, the more they clung to government. All over the country as towns declined, townsmen asked for more laws, more strictly enforced, against country trade and industry,[52] and their pleas were anything but assertive. The authors asked government to give them relief not as a matter of right or justice but out of sympathy for their sufferings and in consideration of past loyalty, obedience, and payment of taxes.

Second, the decline of castle-town merchants was more than matched by the rise of rural entrepreneurs, who were consequently not only more important to their society than their counterparts in England and France but, I believe, a rather different breed. The history of this class, unfortunately for us, has yet to be written. It sprang from diverse origins: at one extreme from large holders who had once worked land with unfree labor and who descended remotely from warriors left on the land; and at the other extreme from new men, coming from no one knew where, who made their way up through petty trade and money lending. The origins of capital were similarly mixed. Some capital came from commercial farming, some from the exploitation of unfree labor, some from the profits of money lending,

52. Hayashi Reiko, *Edo ton'ya nakama no kenkyū* (Tokyo, 1967), 175–81.

and some from loans by city capitalists. Contemporaries who wrote of this class, who were generally Confucian and nearly always disapproving, may have exaggerated its wealth and power in order to alarm readers. Yet there was undoubtedly truth in their accounts. Surviving business records show cases of country merchants trading across greater distances, with larger amounts of capital at risk, than many town merchants. Local documents show them amassing land, entertaining famous scholars, building fine houses, sending sons off to town to school, writing poetry, collecting ceramics, wearing swords, and celebrating masses to the dead in samurai style.[53] Such men were far from peasants with an abacus.

It is impossible to go beyond impressions, and we know little about variations in the class from one line of business and locality to others. Sometimes country merchants faintly resemble a business class as it is supposed to behave in feudal societies. At these times they are at odds with government over taxation and commercial legislation, opposing openly, sabotaging, and evading.[54] We also find them in conflict with government over its intervention in local affairs, in matters concerning village common land, irrigation rights, and the selection of headmen,[55] since such intervention was sometimes against the powerful of the village on behalf of the weak. Country merchants were also inclined to be restive, hankering after honors reserved to the samurai and access to office and influence in the higher levels of government. Judging from opinions expressed in the books on agriculture and rural industries they wrote—and read—some, dissenting from the orthodox ideal of a hierarchical society of stable ranks, thought that men with enough intelligence, education, and enterprise to alter their social position by their own efforts ought to be able to; and if there were enough such men, society would be changed for the better.[56]

53. *Seji kenmonroku*, in *Kinsei shakai keizai sōsho*, ed. Honjo Eijirō (Tokyo, 1927), 1:48–50.
54. For evidence regarding the land tax, see Chapter 2; on opposition to commercial regulations, see Yagi, *Kinsei no shōhin ryūtsū*, 266–75.
55. Aso Naohiro, "Bakumatsu ni okeru ryōshu to nōmin," *Nihonshi kenkyū*, no. 29 (September 1956), 54–76; Furushima Toshio and Nagahara Keiji, *Shōhin seisan to kisei jinushisei* (Tokyo, 1954), 129–32; Tsuda Hideo, "Hōken shakai hōkaiki ni okeru nōmin tōsō no ichi ruikei ni tsuite," *Rekishigaku kenkyū*, no. 168 (February 1954): 6–9.
56. See Chapter 8, pp. 188–92.

But if some members of this class favored a more open system above, nearly all opposed any such thing below. There was a certain logic in this position. Almost without exception these people were large landowners by local standards, exploiting their holdings with tenants and hired labor. Partly for this reason but also by virtue of their commercial activities and often the claims of old family, they were powerful men. The man who spoke for his village, with its autonomous administration and solidarity toward the outside, was inevitably an important man in the district. This circumstance had obvious commercial and social uses and also gave rise to large political ambitions.[57] Hence their desire for openness above. But the whole structure of influence that made this desire understandable depended on the continued solidarity of the village, which was increasingly in doubt. As trade and industry spread to the countryside, there was an increase in rural disorder and threats of violence, even occasional acts of violence, against the rural rich, and chilling millenarian slogans about "remaking the world" (yonaoshi).[58] This was the first challenge for many centuries to the existing order of rural society. As often happens when things long taken for granted are threatened, the chief beneficiaries of that order became its passionate defenders and so transformed the wonted solidarity and structure of rural villages into an ideology of community.[59]

Third, the samurai class, which might be compared to the European aristocracies, fell on the hardest of times for reasons linked to the decline of towns. Government revenues, which were nearly the sole source of samurai income and came in large part from the land tax, remained approximately the same in real terms after 1700,[60] while

57. An extraordinary example was Kikuchi Yasusada, a member of the rural elite, who memorialized his lord in 1858 suggesting, in effect, that samurai be done away with and replaced in their functions by members of the rural gentry who would be attached to the lord by direct bonds of loyalty. He argued that samurai were hated, feared, and incompetent, whereas rural leaders had powerful, local followings and were greatly respected by the people of their districts.

58. Sasaki Junnosuke, Bakumatsu shakairon: "Yonaoshi" jōkyō kenkyū joron (Tokyo, 1969), 53–68; Shōji Kichinosuke, Meiji Ishin no keizai kōzō (Tokyo, 1958), 211–70.

59. See the marvelously rich and suggestive study by Shibata Hajime, Kinsei gōnō no gakumon to shisō (Tokyo, 1966), 309–53.

60. Furushima Toshio, "Shōhin ryūtsū no hatten to ryōshu keizai," in Iwanami kōza

government expenditure rose. Thus, government became poorer as the country grew richer. The chief reason was not the incompetence or extravagance of government, as often alleged, but the removal of the samurai from the land in the seventeenth century and the consequent investiture of the village with the functions of local government—especially the collection of taxes and the reporting of new arable land and changes in the productivity of old arable.

Unable in these circumstances to increase income from the land tax, the government sought to reduce expenditure, and the readiest way was to cut the payments to the samurai, which in most *han* amounted to half or more of all government expenditure. It applied methods too numerous and too diverse to list. The most straightforward was to withhold a portion of samurai pensions as a "contribution" to the lord's treasury. In many domains this withholding tax took 30 or 40 percent of nominal samurai income.[61] Contributions

---

Nihon rekishi (Tokyo, 1963), 12:53–92, shows that Bakufu land tax in kind and in money converted to kind (presumably at the rate actually used, although this is not clear) did not increase between 1716 and 1841. Whether taxes other than the land tax increased in real terms is doubtful. Yamazaki Ryūzō, "Edo kōki ni okeru nōmin keizai no hatten to nōminsō bunkai," in *Iwanami kōza Nihon rekishi* 12:342–43, gives data on the rice income from the land tax in six major daimyo territories (*han*) by ten-year averages from the late seventeenth through the early eighteenth century. Without exception they show a peak of income before 1760, usually in the early eighteenth century, and a decline thereafter. Since, however, the figures do not include money income from either the land tax or other taxes, although suggestive they are not conclusive. In yet another *han* (Matsushiro) for which we have continuous data, revenues from the land tax declined sharply in the 1730s to a level at which they stayed until the end of the Tokugawa period. Yoshinaga Akira, "Han senbai seido no kiban to kōzō," in *Nihon keizaishi taikei: Kinsei* (Tokyo, 1965), 4:253–55. The revenue of the Hiroshima *han* from all sources (money taxes being converted to rice, presumably at market price), exclusive of "borrowings" from samurai, was approximately 14 percent lower in 1848 than in 1719. Note that in this case we are comparing isolated years for which there happen to be records and may therefore be misled as to the general trend. Note also that there was no change in the boundaries of the Hiroshima *han* after 1719, when a considerable territory was added; and that 1848 was not a bad harvest year. *Hiroshima shishi* (Hiroshima, 1959), 2:443–44; "Hiroshima karō kyūchi no bunpu," *Geibi chihōshi kenkyū* 12 (June 1962): 58–61.

61. Dazai Shundai in 1744 claimed that all daimyo large and small had become impoverished and "borrowed" from their vassals' stipends. He went on to say that the "borrowings" often took up to 50 or 60 percent of stipends; hence the term *hanchi*, or halving, stipends came into use. The Matsuyama *han* "borrowed" from stipends every year but one in the 160 years 1709–1869; the lowest rate of "borrowing" (as a percentage of individual stipends) was 10 percent and the highest 60 percent. In 87 percent of the years of record, the rate was 30 percent or more. Tanaka Toshio, "Matsuyama han

and other exploitive measures impoverished large numbers of samurai, especially in the middle and lower pay grades, demoralizing and embittering them and driving them to degrading expedients such as domestic industry, taking in lodgers, housebreaking, cheating retainers, selling rank, pimping, and pawning armor. It also turned loyalty to the lord into anger,[62] which became among the most powerful internal causes of the overthrow of the Tokugawa.

The reduction of samurai stipends would seem to have contributed to the decline of castle-towns since it reduced consumer demand there. But what was taken from the samurai by the government was then spent by it on other goods and services in the town, so the net effect was about nil. A more important income factor would seem to have been a secular decline in the price of rice relative to other commodity prices. A large part of government and samurai income was received in rice, while a large and growing share of other commodities, manufactured as well as agricultural, came from the countryside. Yet the government might have compensated for this shift in real income toward the countryside and away from itself, the samurai, and the towns by increased taxes on the country people. It tried desperately to do just this, and failed. Once the samurai were removed from the land, even though the government could keep the peace and suppress uprisings readily enough, it could no longer enforce its will in the countryside in the details of daily life except by the cooperation of self-governing villages run by the people it would tax. One might almost argue that although in the West towns often enjoyed "liberties" not normally found in the country, the situation was just the reverse in late Tokugawa Japan—except, of course, that the liberty enjoyed by Japanese villages had no legal basis. It was instead the practical result of institutional weakness on the part of the government, of a kind not to be overcome without revolutionary political and administrative change.

Perhaps the preceding sketch of class change will be enough to suggest how widespread the effects of "premodern growth" in Japan

---

no kariage ni tsuite," *Aichi Daigaku kiyō,* December 1955, pp. 233–46; *Tsuruoka shishi* (Tsuruoka, 1962), 1:321–25.

62. See Chapter 7, pp. 170–71.

were, and how different from those in Europe.[63] The likelihood that these differences account in part for the distinctive features of Japanese industrialization may be brought out by comparison with the Gerschenkron model of European industrialization before 1914.[64] According to Alexander Gerschenkron, the major differences in the speed, methods, and other characteristics of industrialization among European countries before that date arose mainly from the different levels of economic backwardness at which industrialization began. The more backward the country, the greater the gap between the possibilities offered by the most advanced technology and the country's actual condition, and the greater the obstacles to be overcome. In bridging the gap between present and promise, backward countries typically borrowed technology most aggressively from the most advanced industries of advanced countries for two reasons: these industries were where the greatest benefits from borrowing could be realized; because they were capital-intensive, their technologies would compensate to an extent for one of the severest barriers to development, the scarcity of a disciplined and stable labor force cut off definitively from the land. From this choice came the main characteristics of European industrialization outside England, a country that was never backward in Gerschenkron's sense. These characteristics—varying "in direct relation to the *degree* [my italics] of backwardness"—included a dependence on technological borrowing, rapid industrial growth, stress on the bigness of plant and enterprise, and a utilization of banks and government in capital formation and the coordination of effort.[65]

If Gerschenkron's model may be taken as a fair approximation of what happened,[66] Japanese industrialization differed from the European on several counts. These have been pointed out at some length by Henry Rosovsky in his excellent book on capital formation in Japan.[67]

63. See n. 6.
64. Alexander Gerschenkron, *Economic Backwardness in Historical Perspective* (Cambridge, Mass., 1962), 1–52.
65. Alexander Gerschenkron, *Europe in the Russian Mirror* (Cambridge, 1970), 99.
66. An interesting attempt to test the Gerschenkron hypothesis against quantitative evidence is Steven L. Barby, "Economic Backwardness and the Characteristics of Development," *Journal of Economic History* 29, no. 3 (September 1969): 449–73.
67. Henry Rosovsky, *Capital Formation in Japan, 1868–1940* (Glencoe, 1961), 55–104.

The most important is the only one we need note here, however, since it goes to the heart of the model. Until the 1930s, the leading sector of modern industry in Japan was not heavy industry but textiles, where labor was a relatively important factor, units of production often rather small, private capital predominant, and the role of government and banks modest and mostly indirect. Rosovsky accounts for this radical divergence from Gerschenkron's model by emphasizing the surprising ability of the Japanese, despite backwardness, to create a disciplined and reliable labor force.[68] This ability made highly profitable industries based on relatively labor-intensive technologies that would otherwise have been unprofitable.

Rosovsky seems to say that this ability turned on the astuteness of Japanese entrepreneurs in building a factory system around preindustrial values, which eased the problem of recruiting and training an industrial labor force.[69] It avoided the costly resistances and inefficiencies this task typically met in backward countries. Here Rosovsky's analysis stops; but it leaves open the further question, How did it happen that preindustrial values[70] were adaptable to modern industry in Japan and that Japanese entrepreneurs were sensitive to them?

My answer to this question brings us back to rural-centered "premodern growth," although I can do no more here than list some of its connections with industrialization. (1) At the end of this growth, a very large proportion of Japanese farm families, approaching 100 percent in some places, had behind them a generation or more of experience in working part-time at nonagricultural occupations, often off the farm and for an employer. (2) Handicraft, artisan, and commercial skills of all kinds were accordingly widespread among them. So was the habit of moving for work, and the custom of depending on an employer in some degree for housing and social credentials in a strange community. (3) No industry gave so much nonfarm employment to peasant families as textiles; but other industries such as paper, ceramics, metals, mining, brewing, wood products, transport, and food pro-

68. Ibid., 102–3.
69. Ibid., 103–4.
70. By this term, which he uses only in a quotation, Rosovsky means "paternalism" as described by James Abegglen in *The Japanese Factory* (Glencoe, 1958).

cessing were equally important in some localities. (4) Networks of commercial institutions covered the countryside linking rural districts to towns and to one another. Given the technical limitations on transport and communication, these institutions were effective in integrating different processes of manufacture, disseminating price information, mediating transactions at a distance, signaling investment opportunities, and distributing labor where it seemed most needed.

My argument is that the growth of the modern textile industry was made possible by the specific skills, attitudes, roles, capital accumulations, and commercial practices brought into being mainly during the period of "premodern growth." Without these preconditions, the stimulus of foreign technology and foreign markets would not have resulted in the rapid expansion of the textile industry under private auspices after 1880. This contention is impossible to prove. But it is strongly supported by the following considerations: the modern textile industry grew mainly in districts of traditional manufacture; much of the growth occurred in villages and former "country places"; entrepreneurs, plant managers, buyers, shippers, and labor contractors came from the same districts; and the labor came overwhelmingly from farm families.

The preindustrial values incorporated in the emergent factory system were not immemorial. Insofar as they included willingness to work for long periods off the farm for wages and were associated with industrially useful skills, they were mainly the product of the Tokugawa period, and of its last century especially. Modern Japanese industry took over these *new* preindustrial values, changing them in the process, although—as many observers have noticed—less than one would think. In fact, in the early decades the changes may have consisted largely of a self-conscious codification.

This was a natural and efficient development. Workers, foremen, and entrepreneurs, many of whom were "carryovers" from traditional industry, were all sensitive to those values. It is probable, indeed, that many personal relationships in traditional industry were transferred intact to the new era. No one thought that any radical change in the modes, customs, and spirit of relations between persons in authority and those under them was necessary or desirable; no such proposal for change was made except by union organizers. The carryover of skills and values was easiest in light industry. It was more difficult in heavy industry, where technology created a gap between past experience and new requirements. But even here traditional skills and attitudes, conditioned by "premodern growth," were immensely useful. In 1880, for example, only eight years after British engineers had built the first railroad in the country between Yokohama and Tokyo, Japanese engineers and workers laid a more difficult line over about the same distance through the broken country between Kyoto and Ōtsu, entirely without foreign engineers. They had learned from the British, of course. But to have learned so quickly, they must have brought useful experience and relevant motives as well as raw aptitude to their study.

To summarize, Japanese industrialization differed radically from Gerschenkron's model of European in that textiles were the leading sector (and traditional light industry generally important) during the first four or five decades. This peculiarity, which gave the whole process a distinctive look, was a consequence of rural-centered "premodern growth." Such growth spread the skills, attitudes, and roles adaptable to modern industry more widely among the rural population than the country's relative degree of economic backwardness would suggest.

In this (and some other respects) the crucial influence seems to have been not the degree, but a particular cultural variant, of backwardness. This variant, as we have seen, was deeply rooted in the historical circumstances of Japan's "premodern growth," closed economy, a nearly unchanging population, and isolation from war—surely a rare combination for long. Although clearly associated with backwardness in a very general way, it would be difficult to argue that this variant (de-urbanization) was associated with a particular degree of backwardness, especially as it became more rather than less marked with the growth of the economy in the last century of the Tokugawa period. These remarks are not intended as a criticism of Gerschenkron's model, which concerns the *degree* of backwardness and is explicitly limited to Europe before 1914. But they do raise questions about Gerschenkron's argument for the model from the experience of European history, in which he relies heavily on cultural and institutional factors to explain national differences in industrialization.[71] Are such factors uniquely associated (at least conceptually) with particular degrees of backwardness? If not, then insofar as the argument relies on them rather than on degrees of backwardness, it seems to reduce to a statement that backward countries are different in many ways and hence the modes of industrialization are also many.

APPENDIX

The following method was used in constructing Table 1.1:

1. Five periods were established, centering on the years 1680, 1714, 1740, 1794, and 1834. The periods are not uniform in length; they vary from twenty to thirty-one years, long enough to smooth out short-term changes but perhaps not so long as to obscure major ones. The five periods, 1664–95, 1700–27, 1730–50, 1781–1807, and 1821–46, average 25.8 years.
2. Observations within periods tended to cluster. In order to obtain population figures, each of the five periods was divided into three subperiods of as equal length as possible. Observations in each subperiod were averaged, and the averages of all three were taken as the figure for the period.
3. For each castle-town, the highest population figure for any of the first three of the five periods was compared with the figure for the last period that had

71. For example, Gerschenkron states, "The role of the state distinguishes the type of Russian industrialization from its German or Austrian counterpart." In Germany the banks played the role taken by the state in Russia; and he goes on to explain as follows: "The basic elements of a backward economy were, on the whole, the same in Russia of the nineties and in Germany of the fifties. But quantitatively the differences were formidable. The scarcity of capital in Russia was such that no banking system could conceivably succeed in attracting sufficient funds to finance a large-scale industrialization; the standards of honesty in business were so disastrously low, the general distrust of the public so great, that no bank could have hoped to attract even such small capital funds as were available, and no bank could have successfully engaged in long-term credit policies in an economy where fraudulent bankruptcy had been almost elevated to the rank of a general business practice. Supply of capital for the needs of industrialization required the compulsory machinery of the government" (*Economic Backwardness*, 19). Gerschenkron elsewhere traces low standards of honesty in business in Russia to the absence of a long tradition of craft guilds; the moral consequences of this absence "remained as a long-term obstacle to economic growth, to be painfully overcome in the very course of industrialization" (*Europe in the Russian Mirror*, 60). I agree that low standards of honesty in business are an obstacle to economic development, under state or private auspices, but I fail to see how standards of honesty can be thought to vary with the degree of economic backwardness.

data available. The population trend between these observation periods, representing roughly the middle and late Tokugawa periods, was expressed as the percentage change between them. According to the magnitude and direction of this change, as explained in the text, towns were classified as growing (G), stable (S), declining (D), or severely declining (DD). In order to express trends yet more broadly, towns with the same observation periods were aggregated and the percentage change calculated for the group.

4. In cases where castle-town populations were large and underwent significant change between comparison dates, they were subtracted from the populations of their home provinces in order to obtain the population of the surrounding province.

TABLE I.I   Changes in Commoner Population, ca. 1700–1850

| | Population of Castle-Town | | | | Population of Province (Excludes Castle-Town) | | Divergence |
Name	First Year	Last Year	(1) % Change	Type of Change	Name	(2) % Change	Between (1) and (2)
	1714–1834					1721–1834	
Morioka	14,797	19,505	+32	G	Morioka	−6[b]	38
Tsuruoka	9,526	8,406	−12	D	Dewa	+7	19
Hiroshima[a]	37,155	24,776	−33	DD	Aki	+69	102
Imabari	4,871	5,110	+5	S	Iyo	+18	13
Kokura	18,065	8,917	−51	DD	Buzen	+4	55
Tatsuno	4,020	3,466	−14	D	Harima	−4	10
TOTAL	88,434	70,180	−21	D		+15	36
	1714–1794					1721–1798	
Ueda	2,746	2,180	−21	D	Shinano	+7	28
Fukui	21,103	18,364	−13	D	Echizen	−5	8
Ōgaki	5,757	5,343	−7	S	Mino	+3	10
Kanazawa	64,987	56,355	−13	D	Kaga	−4	9
Takaoka	11,732	15,465	+32	G	Etchū	+6	26
Kōriyama	12,869	7,430	−42	DD	Yamato	−17	25
Fukushima	4,261	3,360	−21	D	Iwashiro	no data	
Ueno	11,195	8,459	−24	D	Iga	−15	9
TOTAL	134,650	116,956	−13	D		1	12
	1680–1834					1721–1834	
Tanabe	3,999	3,786	−5	S	Kii	0	5
Kōchi	17,054	14,867	−13	D	Tosa	+32	45
Takada	19,397	18,276	−6	S	Echigo	+31	37
Karatsu	3,972	2,999	−24	D	Hizen	+15	39
Kuwana	12,520	8,527	−32	DD	Ise	−9	23
Ōtsu	17,822	14,893	−16	D	Ōmi	−15	1

TABLE I.I *continued*

	Population of Castle-Town				Population of Province (Excludes Castle-Town)		Divergence
Name	First Year	Last Year	(1) % Change	Type of Change	Name	(2) % Change	Between (1) and (2)
Okayama	30,112	20,173	−33	DD	Bizen	−3	30
Kuruma	8,764	11,208	+28	G	Chikugo	+12	16
Hakata	19,468	14,619	−25	D	Chikuzen	+14	39
TOTAL	133,108	109,348	−18	D		+14	32
	1740–1834				1750–1834		
Tottori	13,125	11,440	−13	D	Inaba	+11	24
Himeji	18,769	13,872	−26	D	Harima	+10	36
Matsumoto	9,578	9,700	+1	S	Shinano	+18	17
Sendai	21,736	13,749	−37	DD	Sendai[c]	−21	16
Matsue	13,545	20,506	+51	G	Izumo	+33	18
Akita	21,313	16,387	−23	D	Dewa	+12	35
TOTAL	98,066	85,654	−13	D		+9	22
	1680–1794				1721–1797		
Hikone	7,814	7,892	+1	S	Ōmi	−11	12
Matsuyama	16,604	11,528	−31	DD	Iyo	+7	38
Kōfu	13,552	9,566	−29	D	Kai	+6	35
Tsuyama	16,284	7,086	−56	DD	Mimasaka	−16	40
TOTAL	54,254	36,072	−34	DD		−3	31
	1740–1794				1750–1797		
Fukuyama	12,678	7,900	−38	DD	Bingo	+5	43
Sasayama	2,678	2,529	−6	S	Tanba	+2	8
TOTAL	15,356	10,429	−32	DD		+3	35
TOTAL[d]	523,868	428,639	−18	D		+8	26

SOURCES (castle-towns).

Morioka: Takahashi Bonsen, *Nihon jinkōshi no kenkyū* (Tokyo , 1963), 3:251–54.
Tsuruoka: *Tsuruoka shishi* (Tsuruoka, 1962), 1:555.
Hiroshima: *Shinshū Hiroshima shishi* (Hiroshima, 1960), 3:115.
Imabari: *Imabari shishi* (Imabari, 1938), 36.
Kokura: *Kokura shishi* (Kokura, 1921), 1:169–71.
Tatsuno: Yazaki Takeo, *Nihon toshi no hatten katei* (Tokyo, 1962), 240.
Ueda: *Ueda shishi* (Ueda, 1940), 2:232–39.
Fukui: *Fukui shishi* (Fukui, 1941), 1:19–32.
Ōgaki: *Ōgaki shishi* (Ōgaki, 1968), 1:429, 520.
Kanazawa: *Kanazawa shishi* (Kanazawa, 1917), 3:791–98.
Takaoka: *Takaoka shishi* (Takaoka, 1963), 3:418–31.
Kōriyama: *Kōriyama chōshi* (Hyōgo, 1953), 285–86.
Fukushima: *Fukushima kenshi* (Fukushima, 1970), 3:973–1013.

TABLE I.I *continued*

Ueno: *Ueno shishi* (Ueno, 1961), 47–48.
Tanabe: *Tanabe shishi* (Tanabe, 1938), 325–26.
Kōchi: *Kōchi shishi* (Kōchi, 1958), 1:367–69.
Takada: *Takada shishi* (Takada, 1958), 1:242–44.
Karatsu: *Karatsu shishi* (Fukuoka, 1962), 631–33.
Kuwana: *Kuwana shishi* (Kuwana, 1959), 1:326–30.
Ōtsu: *Ōtsu shishi* (Ōtsu, 1937), 1:444–67, 524.
Okayama: *Okayama shishi* (Okayama, 1964), 6:212.
Kuruma: Yazaki, *Nihon toshi no hatten katei,* 240.
Hakata: *Fukuoka kenshi* (Fukuoka, 1963), vol. 2, pt. 2, p. 457.
Tottori: Yazaki, *Nihon toshi no hatten katei,* 239–40.
Himeji: *Himeji shishi* (Himeji, 1962), 2:4–5.
Matsumoto: *Matsumoto shishi* (Tokyo, 1933), 1:769–72.
Sendai: Takahashi, *Nihon jinkōshi no kenkyū* (Tokyo, 1955), 2:36–39.
Matsue: *Shinshū Shimane kenshi* (Matsue, 1968), 1:578.
Akita: *Akita kenshi* (Tokyo, 1965), 3:233.
Hikone: *Hikone shishi* (Kyoto, 1962), 1:641–45.
Matsuyama: *Matsuyama shishi* (Matsuyama, 1962), 94.
Kōfu: *Kōfu ryakushi* (Kōfu, 1935), 214–18.
Tsuyama: Andō Seiichi, "Kinsei machikata shōgyō tōsei: Tsuyama han no baai," *Keizai riron,* no. 34 (November 1956):63–64.
Fukuyama: *Fukuyama shishi* (Fukuyama, 1968), 2:761–62.
Sasayama: Oka Mitsuo, *Hōken sonraku no kenkyū* (Tokyo, 1962), 179.
SOURCES (provinces).
Sendai: Takahashi, *Nihon jinkōshi* 2:137–39.
All others: Sekiyama Naotarō, *Kinsei Nihon no kinkō kōzō* (Tokyo, 1957), 137–39.

[a]Figures do not include the *shinkai,* an area of reclaimed land settled with agricultural villages although under the administration of the town. *Shinshū Hiroshima shishi* 6:311–12.

[b]1720–1838.

[c]1747–1808.

[d]Excludes Nagoya, whose figures included a large agricultural population settled on land reclaimed in the course of the eighteenth century. *Nagoya shishi* (Nagoya, 1915) 2:359–62.

2

THE LAND TAX
IN THE TOKUGAWA PERIOD

Few notions are so widely held among students of Japanese economic history as that the land tax during the Tokugawa period was cruelly oppressive. It is thought to have left the peasantry no significant surplus after production costs and to have become heavier as time passed.[1] I propose to examine certain evidence bearing on this view, which strongly influences the interpretation of modern Japanese history.

It is commonly held that the increasing weight of the land tax impoverished the peasantry and drove it to rebellion, thus weakening the economic and political foundations of the Tokugawa regime and has-

Reprinted from the *Journal of Asian Studies* 18, no. 1 (November 1958).
1. Representative statements of this view may be found in Toya Toshiyuki, *Kinsei nōgyō keiei shiron* (Tokyo, 1949), 13–73; and Kajinishi Mitsuhaya et al., *Nihon ni okeru shihonshugi no hattatsu* (Tokyo, 1951), 1:13–23.

tening its end. The tax burden also is thought to have deeply colored the society that emerged from the downfall of the Tokugawa. Because capitalist development was blocked in the countryside, which consequently remained "feudal" in a social sense long after the Restoration, modernization in general and industrial development in particular were primarily achievements of the state. In its ultimate extension, this argument is held to account in considerable measure for the abortiveness of political democracy in Japan before World War II.

Of course no one attempts to explain any of the developments—or absence of them—wholly by reference to the land tax. Disproof of the assumptions made about the tax, therefore, would not necessarily make untenable any particular view of Japanese history. It would suggest, though, that the views outlined above bear reexamination.

Historians have generally been content to support their views about the severity of taxation by citing the proportion of the assessed yield of holdings that was normally taken by the land tax, but they have been nearly silent on the relation of assessed to actual yield. The figures cited mean very little and may even be misleading, since it is probable that agricultural productivity increased substantially in the two and a half centuries after 1600. During the first half of the period, agricultural technology improved[2] and the urban population increased notably.[3] During the second half there was a striking rise in crop yields in some regions: on individual fields for which we have production data, it ran as high as 112 percent in fifty years.[4] These may well have been exceptional cases, but even a much smaller increase would imply

2. Chiefly by the development of new plant varieties and more intensive fertilization; see Furushima Toshio, *Gaisetsu Nihon nōgyō gijitsushi* (Tokyo, 1951).

3. Sekiyama Naotarō, *Kinsei Nihon no jinkō kōzō* (Tokyo, 1948), 231–32; Furushima Toshio, *Kinsei Nihon nōgyō no kōzō* (Tokyo, 1943), 611.

4. This is not implausibly high: "To illustrate, a project just now getting underway in India indicates that, for a set of 6 representative case study farms in 2 districts in Uttar Pradesh . . . an addition of Rs. 321 cash expenditures per farm, mostly spent on fertilizer and seeds, would add Rs. 1,219 or 77 per cent to the gross value of output per farm." John D. Black, review in the *American Economic Review* 47, no. 6 (December 1957): 1033–34.

For increments in productivity during the Tokugawa period, see the figures on rice yields between 1787 and 1856 in Aki Province in Gotō Yōichi, "Jūku-seiki Sanyōsuji nōson ni okeru tōnō keiei no seikaku," *Shigaku zasshi* 63, no. 7 (July 1954): 12; and the estimates for a holding in Settsu Province in Imai Rintarō, *Hōken shakai no nōgyō kōzō* (Tokyo, 1955), 47.

that cultivators had both powerful incentives to increase yields and the ability to invest in commercial fertilizers to bring it about—a condition not suggestive of confiscatory taxation.

This is not to deny that the tax burden was uncomfortably heavy; but it was perhaps not as oppressive as is sometimes made out, and it became lighter with time—at least in some places for some people—as surviving tax records leave little doubt. Before considering the evidence of these documents, however, a word needs to be said about the Tokugawa tax system.

The main tax levied on the peasants was the land tax, called *nengu,* based on the estimated productivity of land. With certain local exceptions (noted later), all other taxes were negligible by comparison. Like other taxes imposed by the lord, this one was levied on village communities as a whole rather than on individual proprietors or families. In order to levy the land tax, it was obviously necessary for the lord to know the extent and productivity of the arable land in every village under his control. For that purpose each field in each village was surveyed and assigned a grade that expressed its per-acre yield in normal years—yield being measured in units of unhulled rice, or rice equivalents in the case of other crops. Multiplying the size times the grade therefore produced the normal yield of the field—a datum called *kokudaka,* which might be translated as taxable or assessed yield. From the data on individual fields, it was simple to compute the *kokudaka* of holdings and villages.

The village *kokudaka* was the lord's basic referent in setting the land tax, which he announced annually to the village in a document called a *menjō.* The *menjō* recorded both the assessed yield of the village and the percentage demanded as land tax. Upon receipt of this document, the village, by consultative processes unknown in detail, allocated the tax bill among its individual holders. The register that recorded the resultant allocation (*waritsukechō*), along with the register of payments (*kaisai mokuroku*) and of course the *menjō* itself, were for obvious reasons exceedingly important records for village administration. They were consequently preserved with special care and survive in considerable number. Sometimes it is possible to find a series of such documents recording the assessed yield and annual tax payments of a village for a period of well over a century.

Figures 2.1–2.11 record the tax data for a total of eleven villages, in each case beginning sometime before 1700 and terminating after 1850. The top line shows assessed yield and the bottom line what percentage of that figure was taken by the land tax. Note that the two lines refer to different scales and therefore might have been plotted on separate graphs; here they are plotted on one in order to make a comparison of their gross contours possible, but the distance between them has no significance whatever.

The first feature of these graphs that strikes our attention is the surprising stability of the top lines. Remember that these lines represent village *kokudaka,* the official assessment of productivity on which taxes were based. One therefore confidently expects them to move upward to reflect the increasing productivity of land—or at least to show frequent movements of *some* kind, reflecting successive assessments of productivity. But in fact there is no movement at all for long periods. It is evident that in these villages from about 1700 on, land ceased to be periodically surveyed; by the middle of the nineteenth century, therefore, taxes were based on assessments a century to a century and a half old.

This is puzzling. Why should the samurai class, always in need of additional revenue, have failed to revise the tax base at a time when yields were rising? One deterrent to revision was the massive administrative effort that was required to survey an entire domain. But the surveying could have been done village by village rather than all at once; besides, great though administrative inertia may have been, it can hardly have blocked a measure so clearly advantageous. Is it possible that, since the peasants would as patently lose as the samurai would gain by reassessment, the decisive deterrent was a fear of resistance?

Whatever the reasons, reassessment was neglected. The graphs for nine villages show either no change in assessed yield, or negligible change only, from about 1700 to the middle of the nineteenth century; and several show no change whatsoever from sometime in the seventeenth century. In the sole case (Fig. 2.6) of a considerable increase after 1700—from 719 *koku* in 1699 to 752 in 1732, after which there was absolutely no change—the entire increment was the result of an addition of new arable to the tax rolls, not of a reassessment of yields.[5]

5. This explanation is obvious since in this, as in most *menjō,* old fields (*honden*) and new fields (*shinden*) were listed separately.

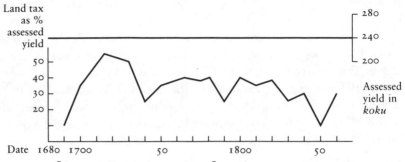

Fig. 2.1   Ōhama Village, Asai County, Ōmi Province

SOURCE: Documents on Ōhama Village, Shiga University, Hikone.

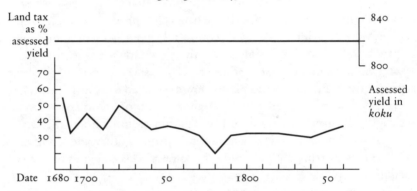

Fig. 2.2   Yamabe Village, Murayama County, Dewa Province

SOURCE: Documents on Yamabe Village, Kokuritsu Shiryōkan, Tokyo.

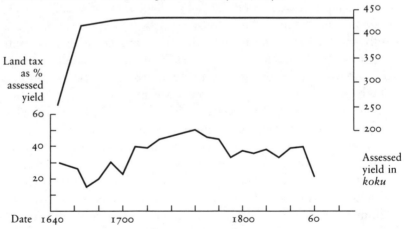

Fig. 2.3   Shima Village, Haibara County, Tōtōmi Province

SOURCE: Yamada family documents, Kokuritsu Shiryōkan, Tokyo.

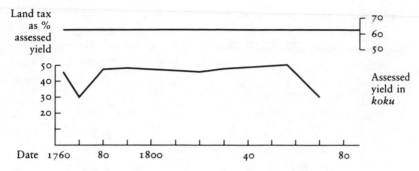

Fig. 2.4   Hoshikubo Village, Haibara County, Tōtōmi Province

SOURCE: Documents on Hoshikubo Village, Meiji Daigaku Keiji Hakubutsukan, Tokyo.

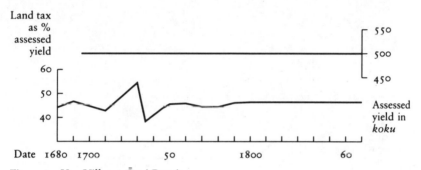

Fig. 2.5   Ura Village, Ōmi Province

SOURCE: Documents on Ura Village, Shiga Daigaku Shiryōkan, Hikone.

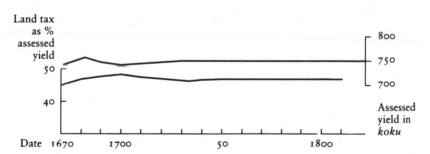

Fig. 2.6   Shimonishijō Village, Kako County, Harima Province

SOURCE: Ōnishi family documents, Kokuritsu Shiryōkan, Tokyo.

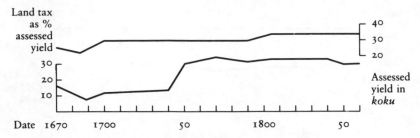

Fig. 2.7   Fukamachi Village, Kanbara County, Echigo Province

SOURCE: Yamaguchi family documents, Kokuritsu Shiryōkan, Tokyo.

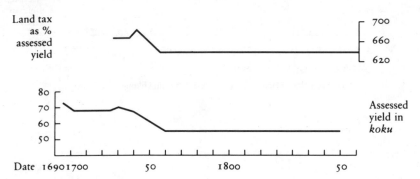

Fig. 2.8   Haruki Village, Senboku County, Izumi Province

SOURCE: Hara family documents, Haruki, Osaka.

NOTE: In 1800 the assessed yield of Haruki dropped from 646 to 377 *koku* because of the administrative separation of a part of the village in that year. Since there was no change thereafter, indicating that no reassessment took place, I have projected the line after 1800 at 646, which was undoubtedly the assessed yield of the whole village.

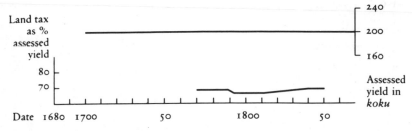

Fig. 2.9 Yamazaki Village, Naka County, Kii Province

SOURCE: Documents on Yamazaki Village, Wakayama Daigaku Kishū Keizaishi Bunkashi Kenkyūjo, Wakayama.

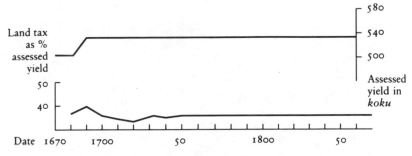

Fig. 2.10 Samegai Village, Sakada County, Ōmi Province

SOURCE: Documents on Samegai Village, Shiga Daigaku Shiryōkan, Hikone.

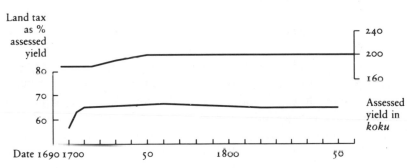

Fig. 2.11 Ichiba Village, Sennan County, Izumi Province

SOURCE: Documents on Ichiba, Wakayama Daigaku Kishū Keizaishi Bunkashi Kenkyūjo, Wakayama.

Map 2.1   Location of Eleven Villages and Kaga *Han*

Despite appearances, then, this village conforms to the same pattern as the others.

Almost certainly there were villages that would present a very different picture if we had the relevant documents. But even if numerous counterexamples should subsequently come to light, the pattern shown by the villages for which we now have data must be judged a common one. The villages were widely scattered geographically (Map 2.1), all but two were located in different domains, and all were chosen for no other reason than the availability of material.

Since the tax base was not significantly revised in any of these villages, we would expect to find the *rate* of taxation rising sharply in compensation. The trend was supposedly upward generally, and it should have been especially steep in these communities to make up for assessments that fell increasingly behind actual yields. But we find no such thing. Nine of the eleven villages show no significant long-term increase from 1700 or shortly thereafter until the end of the period; some show no change at all; a few register a long-term decline. Two villages only show a sizable increase; but in one of these (Fig. 2.1) the rate of taxation was uncommonly low to begin with and the increase short-lived. In the other (Fig. 2.3) the tax rate increased notably between 1700 and 1710, held firm from 1710 to 1780, but after that sank slowly to the original level. But the graphs speak for themselves.

We must not generalize too broadly from a few cases, but the similarities among the cases are impressive. It is difficult to understand fully why, with actual productivity rising and assessments static, the tax rate in these villages was usually not raised. Probably one very powerful reason was the technical difficulty of raising the tax rate without reassessment, for any considerable increase would then put an unbearable burden on peasants whose crop yields had not increased. This difficulty, incidentally, is one of the most cogent reasons for doubting that the trend in the rate of taxation could have been significantly upward generally—assuming that the reassessment of land after 1700 was actually as rare as it seems to have been, which itself needs additional proof and explanation.

Evidence from Kaga *han,* located on the Japan Sea, confirms the impression the graphs give that the tax burden did not necessarily increase with time. To understand the evidence, it is necessary to speak briefly of the tax system of the Kaga domain for it was different from the one typical of the rest of the country.

Instead of sending a tax bill down to the villages annually, the lord of Kaga left permanently in effect in each village the basic tax rate set for it in 1651. The effective rate might be altered from time to time, but only by adding to or subtracting from the initial rate—so that, for example, if a 10 percent increase in a tax of 50 percent were decreed, it would be expressed as 50 percent plus 10 percent, not 60 percent. This system made it clumsy to compute a village's effective tax rate in places where the rate had undergone numerous alterations, but the system had the advantage for the historian of keeping in the expression of the current rate a permanent record of prior changes.

Table 2.1 shows the net change in taxation after 1651 in each of

TABLE 2.1   Changes in Land Tax in Kaga *Han* Villages After 1651
(*N* = 424)

Percentage Change	Number of Villages		
	Decrease	No Change	Increase
Under 1	7		151
1–5	10		72
6–10	25		11
11–20	23		4
21–30	15		3
31–40	17		2
Over 40	20		0
TOTAL	117	64	243

SOURCE: Compiled from *Fugeshi gun muramura takamenki* and *Haka ryōgun takamenki* (undated manuscripts), nos. 164–99, Kanazawa City Library.

424 villages in three counties of Kaga *han*. The table is based on a tax register for these villages that was copied in the early Meiji period from a late Tokugawa document. Since the register is a copy, and a copy moreover of a document that may itself have been compiled from other documents, it is probable that individual entries were miswritten or dropped somewhere along the line. We cannot be certain, therefore, that the computations for all villages are precisely accurate; nevertheless, it is unlikely that they are generally erroneous or that they err consistently in one direction so as to exaggerate either increases or decreases.

It will be seen that more villages experienced a net increase than a net decrease—243 to 117. But with very few exceptions the net increases were negligible: 151 were under 1 percent and 223 under 5 percent. On the other hand the great majority of the net decreases were over 5 percent, and more than half were over 10 percent. Since Kaga was a large, compact domain and one of the more backward in the country, we should expect to find here, if anywhere, that the tax burden was increasing through time.[6] What we discover in fact is that, from the middle of the seventeenth century to the end of the Tokugawa period,

6. The land tax is thought to have been generally more oppressive in such domains than in the small, fragmented domains of the Kinai. The samurai class in the former was in a stronger political and military position against the peasantry.

the land tax in most villages remained unchanged for all practical purposes, and in the remainder it was more often reduced than not.

Are we to conclude, then, that as time passed taxation left a larger and larger surplus[7] in the hands of the peasants in many if not most villages? This seems to have been the case as concerns the land tax; but there are three other categories of taxes or dues to be considered: the corvée, irregular exactions by officials, and a multitude of supplementary taxes generally called *komononari*. Let us consider each of these categories briefly in turn.

Corvée labor was used in three types of work: castle construction and other work that was exclusively for the benefit of the samurai class; more generally beneficial work such as the construction of roads and irrigation projects; and overland transport. It is very important to remember that there was almost no direct use of peasant labor by the samurai class in agriculture,[8] even though this accounted for the bulk of peasant labor services in medieval Europe and possibly earlier in Japan.

Labor employed in the construction and maintenance of roads and irrigation works had a distinct benefit for the peasant; far from being an economic loss, such labor may properly be considered a form of involuntary investment that yielded long-run returns to him. But even labor on castle walls and moats, although distasteful, was an economic loss only insofar as the peasant was compelled to forego a profitable alternative use for his labor, which was by no means always the case. Castle construction work could be done in periods when work was otherwise slack, and common sense would caution against commanding it during the busiest seasons of the agricultural year.

There was, however, one important type of corvée that did often reduce the peasant's surplus. Labor was taken regularly from villages along the main routes of travel to move official parties and their equipage from one posting station to another, over mountain passes and

7. "Surplus" does not mean, of course, what was left after all necessary expenses—that is, savings—but the difference between what had been left after taxes earlier and what was left now, whether applied to savings or not.

8. The only exception was the relatively few samurai known as *gōshi*, who lived on the land instead of in castle-towns. *Gōshi* typically held land that they worked in part with the labor of neighboring peasants; a survival from an earlier period, they were found chiefly in Satsuma, Tosa, and Chōshū.

rivers and moors.[9] Since high-ranking warriors traveling with large retinues were constantly moving to and from the capital, the demands for
transport placed upon the wayside villages were often exceedingly
heavy; some communities were forced to maintain a larger animal
population than would otherwise have been required. This burden reduced the income left by the land tax; but even though the communities subject to it were numerous in absolute terms, they accounted
for no more than a small proportion of the several hundred thousand
villages in late Tokugawa.[10]

Irregular exactions in the form of bribes and gifts to tax officials
probably did not bulk large in the total economic burden of the village.
They may actually have reduced rather than added to it, for bribes of
all forms were offered in the hope of securing special consideration for
the village in the matter of taxes. Significantly, complaints against the
practice came not so much from peasants protesting an additional
burden as from officials lamenting the loss of revenue to the lord and
partiality in administration.[11]

Komononari, or supplementary taxes, consisted chiefly of dues imposed on forests, moors, rivers, and ponds; taxes on handicrafts and
other nonfarming occupations; and a great number of miscellaneous
taxes with little uniformity from one place to another. Frequently all
these taxes were listed in the same document that announced the land
tax (*menjō*). This was true of five of the eleven villages represented in
the graphs (Figs. 2.1–2.5); in these cases *komononari* has been added
to the land tax in plotting the bottom line.[12]

If these villages may be taken as representative, no conclusion justified by a study of the land tax would be materially altered by including *komononari*. It was negligible in all cases, and it showed the
same tendency to stability after 1700 as the land tax. This is reflected
in Figures 2.1–2.5; despite the addition of *komononari,* they show

9. Villages too far away to provide labor and animals were taxed in money or kind
for the support of posting stations; such taxes were included in *komononari.*

10. Yanagida Kunio, *Nihon nōminshi* (Tokyo, 1931), 21.

11. Tanaka Kyūgū (1662–1729) expressed the standard reaction to official corruption when he described it as stealing from one's lord. *Minkan seiyō,* in *Nihon keizai
sōsho,* ed. Takimoto Seiichi (Tokyo, 1914), 1:394.

12. Items of *komononari* expressed in money have been dropped, since in all cases
they were infinitesimal and remained so during the entire period covered by the data.

neither an unusually high rate of taxation nor a tendency for taxation to increase with time. It is always possible, of course, that our documentation is incomplete—that *komononari* in these villages was announced partly in the *menjō* and partly in other documents of which we have no record.

Two other factors deserve mention since either could have eliminated any "surplus" left the peasants. One was the commutation of taxes in kind; the other was population increase.

Although nearly always levied in kind, the land tax was sometimes actually paid partly in money, especially on land planted to cash crops. Insofar as it is possible to tell from the documents,[13] this was not the practice in any of our eleven villages. But wherever it was the practice, clearly the rate of commutation could have the effect of increasing the peasants' tax burden. But it could also have the opposite effect. If the commutation rate was not frequently altered, payment in cash could have the effect of lightening taxes since money steadily lost value throughout the Tokugawa period. What the actual effects of commutation were, however, is a question that requires special study and cannot be confidently answered here. The most that can be said is that there seem to have been few complaints from the peasants about commutation and in most regions no more than a small fraction of the land tax was commuted.

The other factor to be taken into account is population increase. Although the "surplus" after the land tax may have been steadily expanding, as our graphs suggest, if the farming population per acre of arable land was expanding at the same rate, the whole "surplus" would have been required to maintain living standards at their former level.[14] It seems unlikely, however, that the farm population increased significantly overall in the latter half of the Tokugawa period, when improvements in farm technology were spreading most notably. National population was approximately unchanged from the first national cen-

13. The documents announcing the land tax did not stipulate that any part of it was to be paid in money. This omission seems significant since in comparable documents from at least one other village, payments in money were stipulated. See documents on Nagatake Village, Meiji University Library, Tokyo.

14. This does not mean of course that the "surplus" would actually have been used for that purpose, especially if it was unevenly distributed.

sus in 1721 to the last in 1846; meanwhile rural employment in commercial and industrial occupations, usually but not always on a part-time basis, was increasing. The result was an acute shortage of farm labor that was felt nearly everywhere from about 1720 on and lasted into the Meiji period. A great many quotations from all parts of the country might be adduced as evidence of this trend.[15]

It would seem, then, that the size of the "surplus"—if one existed—was determined mainly by the land tax, except where the corvée was unusually heavy. The percentage of the *assessed* yield taken by the land tax was often fearfully high; 50 or 60 percent was not unusual, a fact frequently cited to illustrate the severity of taxation. But as we have seen, the tax was based on a quantity that had less and less relation to actual productivity as time passed. How greatly productivity increased between 1700 and 1868 is therefore a critical question, but it is an exceedingly complex one. Here we can only surmise that there was a geographically uneven but overall significant increase.

Although we must leave this question to one side and therefore that of the size of the "surplus," it is pertinent to ask who received such "surplus" as there was. Was it spread through the village more or less evenly, or did the greater part stick to the hands of some holders only? It would have had greater social and economic significance in the latter case than if its effects were widely dispersed.

This brings us to the question of how the village allocated the land tax and *komononari* among its holders. If allocated proportionately to the assessed yield of holdings, it is obvious that a cumulative inequity in taxation would result. Holders A and B would then be nominally subject to the same tax rate; but A, whose fields had gone unimproved for three generations, would be paying at twice the *actual* rate of B, whose crop-yields had doubled in the meantime. The point is that under such a system the "surplus" would have gone only to peasants

15. Typical is a village document from what is now Tottori Prefecture: "Since the opportunity for by-employments is abundant in the countryside, labor is scarce and there are many villages that suffer year after year because, owing to want of labor, they are late finishing the planting." Mihashi Tokio, "Edo jidai ni okeru nōgyō keiei no henkan," in *Nōson kōzō no shiteki bunseki*, ed. Miyamoto Mataji (Tokyo, 1955), 16. Also see Furushima Toshio, *Shōhin seisan to kisei jinushisei* (Tokyo, 1954), 88; Nomura Kanetarō, ed., *Mura meisaichō no kenkyū* (Tokyo, 1949), 26, 736; Oda Yoshinojō, *Kaga han nōsei shikō* (Tokyo, 1929), 578; Tanaka, *Minkan seiyō*, 260–61.

who improved their yields, and to each only in proportion as the productivity of his land had increased. This would have given such holders an important advantage in further improving their land and would presumably have led to even greater disparities in the incidence of taxation in the future.

But were taxes actually allocated in the village on the basis of assessments that went unrevised for generations on end? Perhaps the village made frequent assessments of its own to avoid the gross inequities of the lord's assessment, although I think it is fair to say no one knows for sure. Officials who wrote on such matters were interested in tax administration up to the boundaries of the village but no farther. We consequently find a great many detailed descriptions of how land was surveyed and graded, of the various factors to be taken into account in setting the tax rate, of the comparative advantages of setting it annually or for a period of years—but nothing to tell us how the villagers divided the annual tax bill among themselves.

There are reasons, nevertheless, for thinking the allocation was generally in proportion to the lord's assessments of yield. First is the sheer simplicity of this method. How easy it was to follow year after year the individual assessments of the land register, which bore the authority of the tax official and had once been more or less equitable; and how difficult for the villagers themselves to revise the assessments. Who, in the event of revision, would not claim that his fields yielded less than a neighbor's and less than they actually did? That some concession ought to be made for their clumsy location, poor drainage, and so on? The possibilities of disagreement were endless. Agreement would be the more difficult, moreover, because the improving farmers, who on the whole were bound to be the most influential members of the village, had the most to lose by any revision at all.

Second, many contemporary documents reported that good land and good farmers were taxed less heavily than poor. These statements are very perplexing unless we assume that assessments had gotten badly out of date and that consequently taxes were relatively low on improved land and high on unimproved. If this was the case, complaints like the following one in a memorial to the lord of Matsuyama become quite understandable: "Now one peasant whom we shall call Ichisuke is prosperous: since his fields are actually larger and their yield higher than registered, cultivation of his holding is profitable. But the holding of Nisuke is smaller and its yield less than registered, so however hard he works there is never profit but bitter suffering only. Within your lordship's domain *there are many cases like these two*" (italics added).[16]

There is, additionally, quite specific documentary evidence on this point, which consists of the case of Renkōji Village, located in Musashi Province in the domain of a Tokugawa retainer named Amano. There exists for this village, in the Shiryōkan in Tokyo, a very long series of *waritsukechō*, or registers of individual assessments. Each of these documents records for a different year how the land tax and *komononari*, taken together,[17] were allocated among the holders of the village. It lists every holder in the village, the amount of land he owned in each of the various grades, and the amount of tax rice he owed on land in each grade. It is a simple thing to determine that land within each grade was uniformly taxed.[18] The critical question then is whether assessments of fields were periodically revised. If not, they were bound to have fallen behind actual productivity on some fields, and inequities in taxation must have resulted.

We unfortunately cannot follow the assessments of particular fields through successive *waritsukechō*—if that were possible the question could be definitively answered for this village. Land was not listed in these documents by field but by grade only—"upper paddy," "middle paddy," "lower paddy," and so on. It is possible however to follow the composition of individual holdings by the total amount of land in each grade, as Table 2.2 illustrates. It shows the amount of land in each of several grades owned by a certain Shinpei (and his successive heirs) from 1753 to 1804. Note, first of all, that there were very few changes in the amount of land registered in the various grades; consider next that such changes as are recorded can mean two things only: either

16. Kan Kikutarō, "Matsuyama han ni okeru jōmensei no kenkyū," *Shakai keizai shigaku* 11, no. 8 (November 1941): 54.

17. Postscript to the *waritsukechō* for 1693, Tomizawa family documents, Shiryōkan, Tokyo.

18. For instance, in 1754 all holders paid a tax of .1920 *koku* of rice per *tan* on top-grade upland, .1610 on middle grade, .1320 on low grade, and .500 on residential land.

TABLE 2.2 Holding of Shinpei, Renkōji Village, Musashi Province
(Figures in *Tan* of Land)

Date	Paddy			Upland			Resi-dential
	upper	middle	lower	upper	middle	lower	
1753	.4726	.3920	1.1224	.7214	.5812	1.8726	.2015
1754		↓	↓		↓		
1755		.3012	.9729		.3401		
1756							
1757						1.8300	
1758						1.8512	
1759							
1760						↓	
1761						1.8315	
1762					↓	↓	
1763					.5327	2.1324	
1764							
1765							
1766						2.1525	
1767					↓	↓	
1768		↓	↓	↓	.4802	2.1607	
1782		.3118	.7829			2.0228	
1783		↓					
1784		.3020	.6418		.4902		
1785		.3012					
1786							
1787							
1789							
1790						2.040	
1791							
1792							
1793	↓						
1794	.4606						
1795							
1796							
1797							
1800				↓		↓	
1801				.7908		1.9720	
1802							
1803	↓	↓	↓	↓	↓	↓	↓

SOURCE: *Waritsukechō*, Tomizawa family documents, Shiryōkan, Tokyo.

NOTE: Arrows represent continuous, unchanged entries.

that land was bought or sold (or ownership otherwise transferred), or that it was moved from one grade to another without a change of ownership. The first kind of change would not indicate a regrading or a reassessment of land; but the second, if it occurred, obviously would.

The problem is, of course, to determine whether changes occurred in the second way and if so how often. Fortunately the problem is susceptible to a solution with a rather high degree of reliability. Let me illustrate: in 1761 the amount of "lower upland" belonging to Shinpei decreased from 1.8512 *tan* to 1.8315—a decrease of 0.197. Since there was no increase in the other grades totaling that amount—in fact, in this particular year, no change in any of them whatsoever—it seems probable that the land in question was transferred to another holder; hence no reassessment of land is indicated. All changes throughout the table except two seem to be of this kind.[19]

The two exceptional changes—one in 1784 and another in 1794— clearly did result from reassessments, for in both cases there is a notation in the *waritsukechō* to that effect. In the one, .0100 *tan* of lower paddy was regraded as middle upland, and in the other .0120 of upper paddy was taken off the tax rolls because it had "gone to waste." Since these are the only reassessments noted, it seems probable that the other changes occurred by a transfer of ownership. Moreover, there are good grounds for believing that these two particular changes were made for exceptional reasons and not as part of periodic, general reassessments. One plot of land had presumably gone out of production entirely, a fact that could not simply be ignored in allocating taxes; the other had been transformed from paddy to upland—a circumstance that may have been occasioned by a community decision with respect to water and one that in any case would have been registered by a notable physical change in the appearance of the field.

With these two exceptions, it seems that land was not reassessed

19. We cannot be absolutely sure; it is possible that both a purchase (or sale) *and* a reassessment of land took place, in such a way as to obscure the latter. For example, it is conceivable that in 1761 the .0197 of lower upland referred to was not sold but regraded, let us say, as middle upland and that this does not show in our data because in the same year exactly the same amount of middle upland was sold. This of course is highly unlikely when only one figure has changed during the year, but it is less improbable when several have changed.

during this period in Renkōji. Judging from statements by contemporaries that good land was taxed relatively lightly, this was probably also true of many other villages.

Using the preceding data, we can piece together something of a picture of the effect that taxes had on the lives of peasants during the Tokugawa period. In many villages the land tax and *komononari* were static or even declined slightly, although the productivity of land was generally rising. Thus a larger and larger "surplus" was left by these two taxes in the hands of peasants. How rapidly the "surplus" was increasing and, consequently, what its absolute size was at any given time, are questions that cannot be answered. Whatever the rate of increase, however, benefits were probably not spread evenly through the peasant population but conferred exclusively on peasants who contrived to increase crop yields.

Other types of taxes may have reduced the "surplus," but the reduction was probably not drastic in most cases. The facts of this matter, of course, are obscure. But no one doubts that other taxes were quantitatively much less significant than the land tax, and there was necessarily a tendency to hold them within limits tolerable to the average peasant family. They were therefore unlikely to have offset entirely the increment that accrued to improving peasants from the combination of rising yields and a static land tax; in no case would they have canceled the comparative advantage of such peasants.

It seems likely that for many peasant families in the Tokugawa period farming paid—for some it may even have paid handsomely by the standard of the times. This fact would help explain certain features of Tokugawa economic and social history that are otherwise puzzling: why land ownership tended to concentrate, although generally on a small scale—because it could be profitably exploited; why tenant farming spread—because with rising yields rent could be added to taxes and still leave the cultivator enough to live; why rural trade and industry developed so powerfully from about 1700 on—because purchasing power in rural areas was expanding and there were profits from farming to finance new enterprises. Most important, perhaps, it goes far toward explaining the existence of the large class of relatively wealthy, educated, and ambitious peasant families we find nearly everywhere at the end of the Tokugawa period, which contributed strikingly to the making of modern Japan.

It is necessary to guard against one possible misunderstanding. I do not wish to suggest that the many contemporary descriptions of agrarian distress are entirely misleading, although considered alone they give a one-sided picture. Not all peasant families were able to increase yields or to increase them fast enough to offset tax increases. Taxes moreover were not the unique cause of peasant distress. Usury, floods, droughts, immoderate spending for weddings and funerals, adverse price movements, and deeper involvement in the money economy all contributed to poverty for many. But widespread poverty—a condition by no means characteristic of all areas—was quite compatible with numerous instances of impressive wealth and elegance. It is a serious mistake to think of the Tokugawa peasantry as even a fairly homogeneous class. The upper strata of peasants were in many respects, not least in respect to standard of life, much nearer to the middle ranks of the samurai than to the majority of peasants.

3

FARM FAMILY
BY-EMPLOYMENTS
IN PREINDUSTRIAL JAPAN

By-employments ready preindustrial people for modern economic roles since they represent an incipient shift from agriculture to other occupations, spread skills useful to industrialization among the most backward and numerous part of the population, and stimulate ambition and geographical mobility. Although widespread in Western preindustrial societies, by-employments have been mainly treated there from the standpoint of the history of industry to the neglect of their effect on the habits, aptitudes, and outlook of farmers and their wives and children. Because the forms of by-employments are scattered and widely varied and changing, it is all difficult to know what proportion

Reprinted from the *Journal of Economic History* 29, no. 4 (December 1969).

of farmers practiced them and what part of their income they earned by them.

This circumstance lends special interest to a wonderfully detailed economic survey of a county in southwestern Japan on the eve of modern economic growth that throws some light on these questions. The survey shows unmistakably that the population consisted overwhelmingly of farm families; yet income was over half nonagricultural in origin, suggesting that most farmers were heavily engaged in by-employments. It is clear, too, that by-employments were oriented toward the market rather than home consumption and that they were part of an intricate division of labor between different parts of the county and between the county and other parts of Japan. Nor was this highly unusual. Contemporary descriptions as well as early Meiji occupation and production statistics lead to the supposition that by-employments were widespread and commercialized over much of the country.

Kaminoseki County—as I will call what in reality was an administrative district rather smaller than a county—was located in Chōshū, a domain at the extreme south of the main island of Honshū (Map 3.1). The county was roughly coterminous with a hilly peninsula some twenty-five kilometers long that projects into the Inland Sea and lies across the main sea route linking the southwest to central Japan. This is a region of ancient settlement and one that, owing to its position, was in close commercial relations with other parts of the country from early times. At the end of the seventeenth century Engelbert Kaempfer marveled at the amount of shipping in these waters, writing that they were "very much frequented, not only by Princes and Lords of the Empire, with their retinues, travelling to and from Court, but likewise by Merchants of the country going from one province to another to traffick and to dispose of their goods, and by others, and so one may chance, on some days, to see upwards of a hundred ships under sail."[1] A century later the Swedish botanist Thunberg confirmed Kaempfer's impressions: "The harbors are covered with large and small craft, the highroads are crowded with travellers, and wares that are transporting

1. Engelbert Kaempfer, *The History of Japan* (Glasgow, 1906), 2:297.

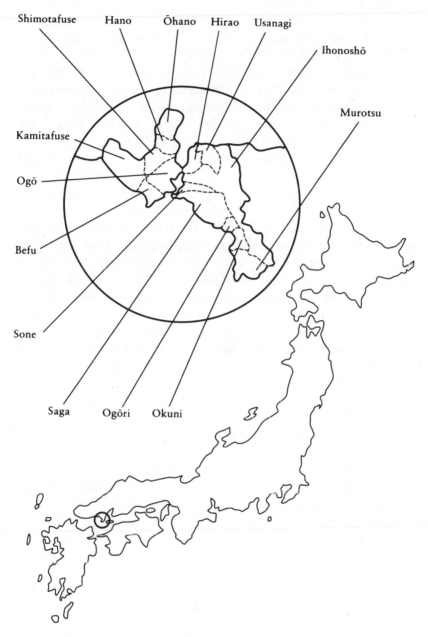

Map 3.1   Kaminoseki County, Chōshū

from one place to another, and the shops are everywhere filled with goods from every part of the Empire."[2]

Judging from fragmentary trade records of the port of Osaka at the eastern end of the Inland Sea, which show increases in imports of some articles of mass consumption ranging up to several hundred percent during the eighteenth century, trade along the Inland Sea may have doubled or trebled between Kaempfer's and Thunberg's visits.[3] The production of export goods in the southwest, which were shipped mainly to Osaka, must have undergone a large increase in the same period, and in Kaminoseki this meant mainly salt and cotton cloth.

Salt making was an ancient industry in the coastal villages of the county, but technique was primitive and output small until the late seventeenth century. Then production began to expand as new methods of carrying seawater to the evaporation "fields"—a system of ditches and dikes instead of hand labor and tides—were introduced. The new methods cut costs drastically, and both output and use increased while salt prices fell steadily against the upward trend of prices generally. By the end of the eighteenth century, Kaminoseki was a major salt exporter, with the greater part of its salt "fields" dating from after 1700.[4]

The growth of the textile industry in Chōshū roughly parallels in time the development of salt production. Cotton was grown hardly anywhere in Japan until the early Tokugawa period, when it began to replace hemp in the clothing of the commoners. Once begun, however, this revolution proceeded rapidly owing to cotton's greater warmth, softness, durability, and cheapness, and it was all but complete by the end of the seventeenth century. In Chōshū raw cotton was at first imported from other parts of the country and worked up into cloth in peasant households for home use; then cloth began to be exported, and by the 1730s Chōshū cottons were reaching the Osaka market in

2. C. P. Thunberg, *Travels* (London, 1795), 3:106.
3. Yamazaki Ryūzō, "Edo kōki ni okeru nōson keizai no hatten to nōminsō bunkai," in *Nihon rekishi: Kinsei* (Tokyo, Iwanami), 4:347.
4. Watanabe Norifumi, "Jūshū enden," in *Nihon sangyōshi taikei* (Tokyo, 1960), 7:26–32, 38, 55–58; Kodomo Yōichi, *Kinsei enden no seiritsu* (Tokyo, 1960), 562, for the development of the salt industry in a neighboring district, which throws light on Kaminoseki.

considerable quantity. As the volume of exports expanded thereafter, cotton cultivation and commercial ginning, spinning, and weaving spread from Ōshima and Kumage (Kaminoseki) counties, where they had first appeared, over the whole domain except for a district along the Japan Sea.[5]

Something should be said briefly about the origin and nature of the Kaminoseki survey materials before turning to the information in them. About 1840 the Chōshū *han* sent out a detailed questionnaire to the villages of the domain in order to gather material for administrative purposes and for the compilation of a gazetteer. Although the gazetteer was never completed, the questionnaire returns from nearly every village survived and have recently been published in twenty-two volumes, entitled *Bōchō fūdo chūshin'an* (Reports on the customs and economy of Suō and Nagato provinces).[6] Most of the returns, which vary somewhat in form from one county to another, are dated 1843, and all those from Kaminoseki bear this date. The Kaminoseki returns[7] are the most detailed of any county's, with the possible exception of the ones from neighboring Ōshima, which also exported large quantities of salt and cotton cloth and whose economy was generally similar. The Kaminoseki returns contain information on the following items for every district (a unit to be explained shortly) in the county: *Geography*—terrain, conditions of sunlight, soils, rainfall and water supply, sources and adequacy of natural fertilizers, climate, distances to other places, and rivers and bridges; *Agriculture*—crops, agricultural calendar, mountains and wasteland, and irrigation facilities with measurements; *Demography*—population by sex and household, households by occupation and status as *honbyakushō* and *mōdo* (a complex and changing distinction based essentially on size of holding and probably carrying differential rights in the village); *Income*—agricultural and industrial production, services with some obvious

5. Shinobu Seizaburō, *Kindai Nihon sangyōshi josetsu* (Tokyo, 1942), 47–49; Seki Jun'ya, *Hansei kaikaku to Meiji Ishin* (Tokyo, 1956), 25–34, 69.
6. Edited by the Yamaguchi Prefectural Archives; hereafter cited as *BFC* (Yamaguchi, 1960–66).
7. *BFC*, vols. 5, 6.

omissions (see the appendix to this chapter), *han* (domain) expenditures in the district, and remittances from persons working outside the district; *Expenditures*—land and other taxes in money and kind, fertilizer, replacement of farm tools and animals, raw materials and fuel for industry, services purchased outside the district, food consumption, and other consumer goods.

The production and expenditure figures given in the returns, as notations make clear, were either three-year averages or (for some items) estimates "taking good and bad years into account." These figures are not without perceptible omissions and bias, the most important of which have been corrected for in ways explained along with other technical matters in the appendix. From the corrected figures it is possible to calculate the output and income of each district and to break down output and income by sectors, although the results should be regarded as no more than approximations.

Much of the interest of the figures lies in differences among districts, of which there were fifteen in peninsular Kaminoseki.[8] Each was composed of from four or five to ten or more villages and contained a sizable population; one had nearly five thousand inhabitants; only one had less than a thousand. The districts were typically spread over a considerable territory; consequently they often contained ecological differences not seen in their constituent villages, which stood out small and compact on the landscape. Ihonoshō, the largest of the districts, extended inland from the coast across half of the peninsula's width and along most of its length on the east side, thus encompassing hills, valleys, and seashore. Great as economic differences were among districts, therefore, they were considerably less marked than among villages, which were individually homogeneous but collectively disparate.

An hour's walk in any direction would have given ample evidence of this variety. Take the case of Hirao, the most prosperous district in the county. Handsomely situated on a broad plain at the head of a bay cut deeply into the west side of the peninsula, it had a population of 1,546 scattered through fourteen settlements reaching back from the

8. There were a number of other districts consisting of small offshore islands, which have been excluded from consideration here by reason of their peculiar ecology.

bay toward the mountains, of which nine were villages, three *machi*,[9] or "towns," one a "port," and another a settlement on a small island in the bay.[10] Houses in the villages had either tile or thatched roofs, in about equal numbers; they were distinctly but loosely clustered, with open spaces between. By contrast, houses in the *machi* were nearly all tile-roofed and crowded together along townlike streets.[11] The two kinds of settlement were also occupationally distinct: villages were composed overwhelmingly of farm families, *machi* largely of shop-keepers, artisans, and day laborers.[12] Although conditions of terrain, rainfall, sunlight, and overland transport were similar throughout the district, settlements near the coast had the great advantage of water transport and the presence of the salt industry; and the predominance of dark and heavy soils inland, with light sandy soils toward the coast, made for some differences in cropping.[13]

FARM FAMILIES AND NONAGRICULTURAL PRODUCTION

Most of the population of Kaminoseki farmed. Of the county's 6,501 families,[14] 82 percent were classified as farmers and as farmers only, since each family had but one classification. The remaining 1,165, or

9. The term *machi* seems to have been used in at least two senses in the Tokugawa period: first, to designate places with a greater density of population than villages or *mura* and with more conspicuously commercial functions; and second, to designate places under the administration of a *machibugyō* (town magistrate) and to which "town" (*machikata*) rather than "village" (*murakata*) law applied. *Machi* in the first sense were not necessarily *machi* in the second or legal sense, although *machi* in the legal sense were probably almost always *machi* in the social sense. The *machi* in Kaminoseki were clearly towns in the first sense, although very small ones, but it is not clear whether they were also legal towns. Chihōshi Kenkyū Kyōgikai, ed., *Nihon no machi* (Tokyo, 1958), 306–14.

    10. *BFC* 5:279.

    11. Ibid., 288.

    12. Although there is no description of the *machi* in Hirao, it must have been very similar to the town part of Murotsu, also a port and described in detail. Ibid. 6:243.

    13. Ibid. 5:280.

    14. Excluding a total of 135 *eta*, or outcast, families and 350 samurai families that were listed as present in the districts but not included in output, expenditure, or food consumption figures. See the appendix to this chapter.

TABLE 3.1   Implied Productivity of Farm and Nonfarm Families

	Families		Income		
Place	% Farm (1)	% Nonfarm (2)	% Agricultural (3)	% Nonagricultural (4)	Productivity Ratio[a] (5)
Ōhano	96	4	77	23	7.17
Kamitafuse	96	4	74	26	8.44
Ono	93	7	66	34	6.84
Usanagi	93	7	57	43	10.02
Ihonoshō	91	9	57	43	7.62
Shimotafuse	82	18	51	49	4.37
Hano	73	27	46	54	3.17
Ogō	86	14	46	54	7.21
Ogōri	92	8	44	56	14.64
Okuni	81	19	41	59	6.14
Saga	88	12	39	61	11.47
Hirao	45	55	28	72	2.10
Sone	84	16	23	77	17.58
Befu	67	33	19	81	8.66
Murotsu	44	56	17	83	3.83
Kaminoseki County	82	18	45	55	5.56

SOURCE: Data compiled from Yamaguchi Prefectural Archives, ed., *Bōchō fūdo chūshin'an* (Yamaguchi, 1962–63), vols. 5, 6.

[a]*(Nonagricultural income ÷ nonfarm families) ÷ (agricultural income ÷ farm families).*

18 percent, were distributed through nineteen occupational categories, which were far fewer than contemporaries could have identified. Such categories as "merchant," the commonest next to "farmer," were omnibus terms that clearly covered a variety of ways of making a living. Although nonfarm families tended to be concentrated in districts with *machi,*[15] no district was entirely without them, and of course none was without farm families. Most districts had a heavy preponderance of the latter; even Murotsu and Hirao, the two districts with the largest proportion of nonagriculturalists, had nearly as many farm as nonfarm families. Occupational figures therefore give the impression of an overwhelmingly agricultural county (Table 3.1, Column [1]; see the appendix to this chapter for an explanation of some of the factors involved in preparing this and subsequent tables).

15. Districts with *machi* were Ono, Hirao, Murotsu, Befu, Shimotafuse, Hano, and Sone.

Yet the ways in which income was earned give a very different impression. Income came about equally from farming on the one hand, and industry, transport, fishing, wage remittances, and central government expenditures on the other. Nonagricultural pursuits supplied 55 percent of the income of the county, and the proportion was over 70 percent in four districts. Thus Kaminoseki's population was predominantly agricultural but earned rather more than half its income from nonfarm work.

This discrepancy was to be seen everywhere in the county in varying degree. Table 3.1, Column (2), shows the percentage of nonfarm families in the various districts and Column (4), the percentage of nonagricultural income. In every district, nonagricultural income was larger than one would expect from the proportion of nonfarm families in the population alone,[16] and in most districts between two and seven times larger. There seem to be three possibilities of reconciling the two pictures, one of a heavily agricultural population, the other of an economy rather less agricultural than otherwise.

One possibility is that farm income was grossly understated relative to nonfarm income in the district reports. Aside from the disproportion to be explained, however, there is no evidence to support such an inference and no general grounds for it. If anything, the reporting of agricultural production appears more nearly complete than that of nonagricultural production.[17] If there was any deliberate underreporting in order to minimize taxes, one would think nonagricultural production would offer the more attractive possibilities since its forms, times, and places of production were more varied, brief, and private, minimizing the chance of detection. On the other hand more was to be gained by falsifying agricultural income, which was more heavily taxed.[18] But even if farm income was underreported relative to non-

---

16. Assuming, that is, the productivity of all families in each district was the same, so that the proportion of nonfarm families and of nonagricultural income would be identical.

17. Agricultural output was listed down to the most minute quantities of fruits, nuts, and herbs, for example; the nonagricultural side contained obvious omissions, however, in nonfarm families such as *ishi* (doctor) where no income was recorded and in some items of nonagricultural income where only that part sold outside the district was recorded. See the appendix to this chapter for the treatment of these problems.

18. The weight of the land tax varied by district but ran about 45 percent of the

agricultural income by as much as 25 percent, which seems unlikely, we should still have the anomaly of an economy with 18 percent of all families apparently accounting for 50 percent of all income.

A second possibility concerns the relative productivity of nonfarm and farm families. Productivity was almost certainly higher in the former, but it cannot have been so much higher as to account for anything near the whole of the discrepancy to be explained. For that—as Table 3.1, Column (5), shows—average productivity would have to have been 5.56 times higher in nonfarm than in farm families in the county as a whole and up to 17 times in individual districts. Even the smaller differential is implausibly high. The lowest differential in any district—2 to 1 in Hirao—is probably near the actual ratio, and it corresponds fairly closely to figures from other preindustrial societies[19] and to the ratio that may be inferred from a comparison of non-agricultural wages with the average income of farm families from farming. Such comparisons suggest an average productivity ratio, on a man-day basis, of about 1.5 to 1, or on an annual basis—if it is assumed that nonfarm families worked 300 days a year and farm families 182—of 2.47 to 1.[20]

---

value of output on average. Salt production was taxed at a roughly comparable rate, but textile production was untaxed. Although the land tax was paid in rice, it was levied on the total economy of farm families and not on only their farming. Conscious efforts were made by officials elsewhere to take nonagricultural production into account in setting the land tax, and one may assume that this possibility was not overlooked by Chōshū officials.

19. Figures are difficult to come by, but we have estimates of product per worker (agriculture/nonagriculture) for Japan in 1878–99 (0.345) and in the United States in 1839–49 (0.37) and in 1869–88 (0.47). Mimeographed "Summary" of the International Conference on Economic Growth—A Case Study of Japan's Experience, September 1966, p. 2. For indirect indications of relative productivity in farming and other employments (depending on wage comparisons and the difficulty of attracting labor out of agriculture) in England during the eighteenth and early nineteenth centuries, see A. Redford, *Labour Migration in England* (Manchester, 1926), 54–69; Paul Mantoux, *The Industrial Revolution in the Eighteenth Century*, rev. ed. (London, 1948), 430–35; David Landes, "Technological Change and Development in Western Europe, 1750–1914," *The Cambridge Economic History of Europe* (Cambridge, 1965), 6: 344–47.

20. The average wage remittance per worker for the whole county was taken as an index of nonagricultural productivity, and one-half the average agricultural income of farm families in the county (assuming an average of four members per family, composed equally of workers and dependents) as an index of agricultural productivity. The per worker wage remittance was then reduced by one-third for purposes of comparison, on

Even this ratio may be too high. Few farm families could have worked less than 182 days a year, whereas craftsmen often worked less than 300;[21] and the ratio of workers to dependents in farm families may well have been higher than in nonfarm families. But at least the ratio does not seem too high and therefore may be used to estimate how much of the discrepancy between the size of the nonfarm population and nonagricultural income ought to be explained in this way. Table 3.2, Column (1), shows that differential productivity explains some of the discrepancy but leaves a good deal more unaccounted for.

This brings us to the third possibility. Farm families did not engage exclusively in farming; nearly all members worked concurrently at other occupations. In Table 3.2, Column (2), an estimate is given of how much nonagricultural income in each district was produced by farmers, on the assumption that they produced all such income not produced by nonfarmers. Several observations on these figures suggest themselves. First, farm families typically earned a large share of their total income from by-employments. Even in the most heavily agricultural districts they earned between 15 and 30 percent, as shown in Table 3.2, Column (3), and in many districts over 50 percent. Second, as shown in Table 3.2, Column (2), farm families accounted for the greater part of all nonagricultural income; in very few districts did they account for less than half and in five they accounted for 70 percent or more. Finally, confirming a statement above, nearly all farm families would have had to work at by-employments to produce the amount of nonagricultural income they evidently did.

Although these observations cannot be confirmed in detail, they are in general accord with the brief descriptions of by-employments in the questionnaire returns, which give the impression that all adults, and

---

the assumption that the nonagricultural workers who earned them worked one-third more days a year than farmers. This gave a productivity ratio of 1.5 : 1 on a man-day basis. It does not take account of the value of the food and shelter earned by the remitting workers; but this factor was probably offset by a certain amount of unreported income among farmers (including the use-value of their housing).

21. See the case of the craftsmen-farmers described in the text. For a description of a country town in another county in which it is explicitly stated that many town merchants and artisans farmed part-time, see *BFC* 16 : 123.

TABLE 3.2   Farm Families and Nonagricultural Income

| Place | Nonagricultural Income | | % of Farm Family Income from Nonagricultural Production[c] |
	% Produced by Nonfarm Families[a] (1)	% Produced by Farm Families[b] (2)	(3)
Ōhano	34	66	16
Kamitafuse	29	71	21
Ono	36	64	25
Usanagi	25	75	36
Ihonoshō	32	68	34
Shimotafuse	56	44	30
Hano	78	22	20
Ogō	34	66	44
Ogōri	17	83	51
Okuni	40	60	46
Saga	22	78	55
Hirao[d]	48	52	57
Sone	14	86	74
Befu	28	72	75
Murotsu	64	36	64

SOURCE: Data compiled from Yamaguchi Prefectural Archives, ed., *Bōchō fūdo chūshin'an* (Yamaguchi, 1962–63), vols. 5, 6.

SYMBOLS: fF = farm families; nfF = nonfarm families; Yna = all nonagricultural income; fYa = agricultural income of farm families; $fYna$ = nonagricultural income of farm families; $nfYna$ = income of nonfarm families ($nfYna = fYa \div fF \times 2.47 \times nfF$).

[a]Computation: $nfYna \div Yna$.

[b]Computation: $100 - (nfYna \div Yna)$.

[c]Computation: $fYna \div (fYa + fYna)$.

[d]In Hirao, $nfYna$ figured by using 2.47 multiplier, as indicated above, exceeded Yna, undoubtedly owing to the very high agricultural productivity of farm families. Therefore 1.00 was used as the multiplier instead of 2.47 in this district.

many children too, devoted to by-employments every working hour free from farming.[22] How much time this came to during an average year seems to have depended mainly on the terrain, which determined the relative labor-intensity of farming. Nearly all the returns mention this factor;[23] the following passage concerning Hirao is typical:

22. For some examples, see ibid. 5 : 38, 88, 136, 190.
23. See particularly the clear statement in the Ogō returns, ibid., 38.

Every able-bodied person works at salt making and other employments insofar as farming permits. The average amount of arable land per farm family is only 2.1 *tan* of paddy and 0.6 *tan* of upland, and cultivation is relatively easy since the terrain is level. In time free from farming, men make rope and rush mats and other articles by hand; and women work in the salt fields from the third to the eighth month and during the rest of the year devote themselves exclusively to weaving cotton cloth, not even taking out time to cut firewood and gather grass for compost [traditional female farm work].[24]

Such passages tell nothing about the relative size of earnings from farming and by-employments, but they leave little doubt of the importance of the latter. There is, however, a hint on this score in the wage remittance data in returns from several districts, which give not only the amount of remittances but the number of people making them and, sometimes, the kind of work they did "in other places." Per capita remittances were nearly always somewhat larger than the per capita income of the county at large. Although this difference must be discounted, since one figure refers to workers and the other to all inhabitants, it seems clear that a man could generally earn as much in a day working at a by-employment as working at farming.[25]

This impression is confirmed by data from a nearby Chōshū county that was mountainous and wholly inland, where nonagricultural employments ought to have been, if anything, less profitable compared to farming than in Kaminoseki. In this county every district calculated the income of "carpenters, sawyers, and other artisans" as income from 180 days of farming, *plus 2 monme* a day for "the remaining 180 days," which were reckoned as spent working at a craft.[26] An income of 360 *monme* for six months' work was half or more of the agricultural earnings of farm families in most districts of Kaminoseki.[27] A great deal of other scattered evidence to the same effect might be

---

24. Ibid., 296.

25. A manuscript manual on salt making from Chōshū evidently written early in the eighteenth century offers wage and other cost data to support the contention that a farm family could break even if it worked no more land than it could cultivate with family labor but would suffer a net reduction of income by cultivating additional land, owing to the high cost of hired labor. Seki, *Hansei kaikaku*, 63.

26. BFC 17:145, 377.

27. Agricultural income per farm family for the county as a whole was 562 *monme*.

cited, but one or two illustrations may suffice to make the point that by-employments often provided a major portion of farm family income.

A sericulturalist in northern Japan writing in the early nineteenth century, for example, claimed that farmers who were also sericulturalists—a high proportion of the population in some districts—earned about half of their income from sericulture. Therefore those who were skillful enough to put good years for cocoons together back-to-back became wealthy.[28] About the same time, Ōkura Nagatsune (1768–1856), an agricultural reformer with a passion for promoting by-employments, calculated that each of the adult members of a farm family could earn the equivalent of daily wages during the off-seasons of farming by domestic paper making, which he recognized as a relatively poor-paying occupation.[29] A village headman in Kawachi Province about the beginning of the eighteenth century wrote:

> My father Kajū always said that the people of this village could not prosper either by farming or by commerce (akinai) alone but must carry on both together—just as a cart must have two wheels. The importance of commerce may change from time to time so that there are years when it amounts to 60 or 70 percent of a family's living and farming only 30 or 40, and others when the proportions are reversed. Operations should be adjusted to what the times require. "Keep your eye open for the opportunity the times bring and what crops yield the greatest profit," my father always said. And I have followed his advice my whole life long and found it to be absolutely sound.[30]

Family farming was essential to the integration of farming and other occupations, since it was by the discipline and sentiment of the family that nonagricultural earnings, often the product of highly individual skills and work away from the farm, were captured for the benefit of the farmer. Almost certainly this would not have been possible in the same degree with large-scale farming using serfs or wage labor, for the masters would not then have had the same incentive to release labor for employment elsewhere. Or if they somehow managed

---

28. Yōsan suchi, MS (1794), National Diet Library, unpaginated.
29. Tamura Eitarō, Ōkura Nagatsune (Tokyo, 1944), 29.
30. Nomura Noboru, ed., Kinsei shomin shiryō (Osaka, 1955), 194. This volume consists of the headman-author's jottings over a lifetime, ranging from hints on agriculture and observations on government to brief sketches of the history of various families in the village, all of extraordinary interest.

to take the workers' earnings, the workers would have no incentive to learn nonagricultural skills and fill every minute of free time with their practice,[31] and the masters might also lose control over the workers and their labor. These problems must have been present on small family farms, but they were manageable. Labor could flow freely between farming and other occupations on and off the farm, because all earnings belonged to a group of kin[32] whose prosperity was the peasant's best guarantee in this world and his real religion.

Unfortunately, the survey returns throw little direct light on the relation of family farming to by-employments in Kaminoseki, but one may infer that family farms were the rule. The high proportion of families classified as farmers, the data given in each district return on the average amount of arable per family,[33] and the pattern of farming elsewhere—all suggest it. It is certain, too, from the descriptions of night work and of the industrial processing of agricultural commodities, that by-employments were often carried on at home. Old people, children, women, and the physically handicapped were said to work at domestic industries much of the time.[34] But much work was also done away from the farm, and there is evidence that it was typically done by family members—not for individual gain but for the benefit of the group. Many women worked in the salt fields during the summer months, returning home to resume their weaving and other work as well as their roles as wives and mothers when the salt-making season was over.[35] Men and women who left their districts to work outside for a year or more regularly sent their earnings home.[36]

31. Narita Jūhyōe, *Yōsan kinuburui* (1813), in *Sansō koten shūsei*, ed. Sansō Koten Kankōkai (Tokyo, 1930), 333. For other contemporary descriptions of the intensity of work entailed by combining farming and by-employments, see Tamura, *Ōkura Nagatsune*, 29; BFC 5:38, 88, 136, 190.

32. Thomas C. Smith, *The Agrarian Origins of Modern Japan* (Stanford, 1959), 112–23.

33. Holdings were small throughout the county; the smallest average in a district was 1.8 *tan* of arable in Murotsu and the largest 5.9 *tan* in Usanagi. (1 *tan* = 0.245 acre.) BFC 5:38, 88, 136, 190, 227, 263, 296, 338, 382; 6:75, 127, 170, 210, 245.

34. Ibid. 5:228.

35. Ibid. 5:296.

36. Ten of fifteen districts in this report listed income from wage remittances, in four cases accounting for 19, 17, 15, and 8 percent, respectively, of total income. See Table 3.3, Column (6).

TABLE 3.3   District Sources of Income
(As Percentage of Total Income)

Place	Agri-culture (1)	Industry (2)	Trade (3)	Transport (4)	Fishing (5)	Wage Remit-tances (6)	Govern-ment Ex-penditures (7)	Other (8)
Ōhano	77.0	16.0	3.0	—	—	—	3.0	1.0
Kamitafuse	73.5	22.0	2.0	—	—	0.5	2.0	—
Ono	66.0	24.0	6.0	—	—	3.0	1.0	—
Usanagi	57.0	18.0	—	3.0	—	19.0	3.0	—
Ihonoshō	57.0	31.0	2.0	—	1.0	8.0	1.0	—
Shimotafuse	51.0	28.0	20.0	—	—	—	1.0	—
Hano	46.0	21.5	29.0	—	—	—	1.5	2.0
Ogō	46.0	40.0	8.0	3.0	—	1.0	2.0	—
Ogōri	44.0	37.0	3.0	1.0	—	15.0	—	—
Okuni	41.0	22.0	7.0	9.0	3.0	17.0	—	1.0
Saga	39.0	43.0	5.0	1.0	1.0	8.0	2.0	1.0
Hirao	28.0	35.0	34.0	1.0	1.0	—	1.0	—
Sone	23.0	51.0	14.0	4.0	0.5	0.5	7.0	—
Befu	19.0	9.0	2.0	69.0	—	—	0.5	0.5
Murotsu	17.0	21.0	48.0	6.0	4.0	3.0	1.0	—

SOURCE: Data compiled from Yamaguchi Prefectural Archives, ed., *Bōchō fūdo chūshin'an* (Yamaguchi, 1962–63), vols. 5, 6.

No less important than family farming to the development of by-employments were the growth of trade, an extensive division of labor, and the elaboration of suitable commercial institutions and practices. A farm family practicing a round of nonfarm work to provide its own tools, housing, and clothing would have been short of materials much of the time and had difficulty keeping busy in off-seasons, on inclement days, and at night.[37] In any case productivity in these tasks would have been so low as to encourage leisure. A considerable degree of specialization of nonfarm work in farm families—accompanied by the buildup of special skills and capital and commercial relations—was essential to making by-employments profitable. Such a situation presupposes the extension of trade well beyond the neighboring market town.

The returns give little information on trade *within* districts, although there is indirect evidence that it was far from negligible. Not

37. Stereotyped as the *san'yo* or "three intervals" of farming free for other employments—especially for study, according to classical writers.

only were mountain and plain, coastal and inland villages complementary in obvious ways,[38] but some districts contained one or more *machi* that exchanged a constant flow of goods and services with the surrounding villages.[39] The returns describe market days on which peasants came crowding into the "towns" to sell the products of domestic manufacture and to buy raw materials and consumer goods in return; and this traffic continued at a more sedate pace on days when no market was held.[40] But the most impressive evidence of the extent of local trade is the amount of trade between districts and between the county and other regions.

Table 3.3 makes clear that a rather well-defined division of labor existed among districts, despite the ubiquity of farming and the textile industry. The income of some districts was overwhelmingly agricultural, of others as heavily nonagricultural. About three-quarters of income in Ōhano and Kamitafuse came from farming, but less than one-quarter in Murotsu, Befu, and Sone. Despite these differences most districts earned a substantial amount of income from nonagricultural production, but they earned it in notably varied ways. Industry accounted for the largest single share of income in Saga, Hirao, and Sone; trade contributed more than all other work combined in Murotsu. Wage remittances were a significant source of income in Usanagi, Ogōri, and Okuni, earnings from transport in Befu and Okuni.

These figures imply an extensive trade beyond districts. Although the questionnaire returns contain few figures on district exports and imports, estimates can be made for most products. As Table 3.4 shows, rather more than half of the output of the county was sold outside the district of origin. Exports consisted almost wholly of nonagricultural goods and services, with salt and cotton cloth alone accounting for

---

38. For example, mountain villages exported straw ropes and mats as well as charcoal and firewood to coastal villages that made salt, receiving in return the numerous services that concentrated there.

39. Hano held markets in the *machi* that were curiously bunched on the tenth, fourteenth, and nineteenth of each month, when "straw mats, hats, bamboo, cotton cloth, and other industrial commodities are brought to the market from surrounding villages for sale." BFC 5 : 229.

40. BFC 5 : 172, 218; 6 : 243. Markets (*ichi*) were few and infrequent; there were only three in the entire county as compared to at least six *machi* and perhaps more; and some markets met as rarely as twice a month.

TABLE 3.4   District Exports
(As Percentages of Production)

Place	Agricultural Exports[a]	Total Exports[b]
Ōhano	0	24
Kamitafuse	4	25
Ono	14	27
Usanagi	6	39
Ihonoshō	1	54
Shimotafuse	17	39
Hano	11	40
Ogō	1	74
Ogōri	5	58
Okuni	1	52
Saga	9	62
Hirao	39	72
Sone	1	70
Befu	1	82
Murotsu	3	81
Kaminoseki County	8	57

SOURCE: Data compiled from Yamaguchi Prefectural Archives, ed., *Bōchō fūdo chūshin'an* (Yamaguchi, 1962–63), vols. 5, 6.

[a]Because of insufficient disaggregation on the consumption side, a very imperfect method was adopted to calculate exports of agricultural products—counting as exports any items of agricultural output whose value was given in money rather than in kind. This procedure undoubtedly overstated exports since, although such commodities were probably sold rather than consumed at home, there is no way of knowing where they were sold.

[b]Estimates of exports for most nonagricultural products were made by subtracting district consumption from production, treating positive differences as exports and negative as imports. Output was added for nonagricultural families for whom no output was listed in the questionnaire (see the appendix to this chapter for further comment).

most of the total (63 percent). Indeed, the only agricultural exports worth mentioning were fruit and vegetables, which, on the most generous estimate, amounted to no more than 8 percent of all exports. Rice and other cereals were imported by every district but one; and even though cotton and indigo were widely grown and highly commercial crops, they were used mainly for textile production within districts. Nearly all salt and cotton cloth—together valued at 20 percent of the total product of the county—were shipped outside Kaminoseki, mainly to Osaka for transshipment and sale elsewhere. In return the county imported food, raw materials, fuel, and consumer goods.

TABLE 3.5   Food Surplus and Deficit

Place	Annual per Capita Food Requirements[a] (koku)	Surplus/Deficit After Taxes in Kind[b](% of food requirements)
Ōhano	1.44	+10
Kamitafuse	1.44	−3
Ono	1.44	−27
Usanagi	1.44	−35
Ihonoshō	1.44	−34
Shimotafuse	1.44	−16
Hano	1.44	−9
Ogō	1.80	−27
Ogōri	1.44	−39
Okuni	1.44	−30
Saga	1.44	−38
Hirao	1.62	−38
Sone	1.80	−59
Befu	1.44	−33
Murotsu	1.44	−58
Kaminoseki County	—	−32

SOURCE: Data compiled from Yamaguchi Prefectural Archives, ed., *Bōchō fūdo chūshin'an* (Yamaguchi, 1962–63), 5:94, 157, 207, 240, 275, 310, 353, 398, 436; 6:61, 112, 132, 182, 216, 253.

NOTE: Each district reported its food needs calculated at a certain average intake of rice and rice equivalents per person, excluding persons working outside the district, samurai, and *eta,* and translated its own food production, in its many forms, into rice equivalents.

[a]Per capita needs were specified as applying to a cross section of a population of men, women, and children. It is not clear why some districts based their calculations of food needs on a different figure from others.

[b]A few figures on food production and needs and the resulting surplus or deficit were mutually inconsistent; in these cases, the figures making for the smallest surplus or deficit were adopted.

Table 3.5 shows food imports in rice equivalents as calculated by the districts themselves. Only Ōhano, the most heavily agricultural district in the county, reported a food surplus; the remainder had deficits ranging from 3 percent of food needs in Kamitafuse to 59 percent in Sone. The deficit for the county at large was 32 percent, and required the import of nearly 14,000 *koku* of rice equivalents, enough to feed a population of approximately ten thousand people for a year. Where this immense amount of food came from does not appear, but a good guess would be across the Inland Sea from the rice-surplus region of northern Kyūshū. In any case it suggests the error of the common view that the commercialization of farming depended almost exclusively on special crops like cotton, tobacco, tea, indigo, sugar, and cocoons.

Another large group of imports consisted of raw materials, fuels, and other inputs mainly for the salt and textile industries. Coal and firewood were imported in large quantities as fuel for reducing brine to salt;[41] and most districts imported cotton and dyes, although most produced them too. Those that did not, spent enormous sums for imports. Saga annually paid for cotton and dyes alone a sum equal to one-third of the value of its total output of cloth, which was just under ten thousand bolts.[42] In addition, every district without exception imported farm tools, fertilizer, nails, bar iron, craft tools, lumber, and leather.[43]

Among the consumer goods listed as expenses by most districts were rouge, powder, hair combs, paper for tying the hair, ornamental hairpins, lighting oil, candles, bean paste, soy sauce, vinegar, writing paper, medicine, furniture, ceramics, roof tile, wooden utensils, pots, pans, rain gear, socks, straw mats, tobacco, smoking pipes, knives, razors, whetstones, buckets, needles, charcoal, and wine.[44] Nearly all these goods must have come from outside the county, since few appear as outputs in any Kaminoseki district. So many useful and attractive things to buy go some way toward explaining why, as some returns put it, farmers worked "night and day" at by-employments,[45] the chief source of money income.

The county export and import trade was closely linked to trade among districts. Quantities of labor, firewood, and straw products were sold by interior to coastal districts for salt making;[46] cloth woven

---

41. For example, Hirao produced salt worth 285,000 *monme* and imported firewood worth 14,040 and coal worth 102,525 *monme*. Ibid., 296–97.

42. Ibid. 6:185.

43. Ibid. 5:67–68, 97–98, 160–61, 210–11, 243–44, 277–78, 315–16, 357–58, 400–401, 438–39; 6:115–16, 134–35, 186–87, 219–29, 264–65.

44. Ibid.

45. Ibid. 5:88, 136.

46. For example, Shimotafuse, a district with no salt industry, produced approximately 29,000 straw mats, nearly 14,000 bundles of straw ropes, and 1,593 loads of firewood—all items used in making salt in places like Hirao, where they were imported in large quantities. Ibid. 5:136, 207–8.

in one district was often dyed in another;[47] and cloth from inland districts went out through ports in Murotsu, Hirao, and Befu, where they were carried by local boat owners to their immediate destination outside Kaminoseki. Not all interdistrict trade, of course, was so obviously tied to long-distance trade. Fishnets, tile, and wine were items of output in some districts that appear only as items of consumption in others. Still, it might be argued that the income to buy such commodities was largely generated by salt and textile production, illustrating the integration of local and regional trade and the dependence of by-employments on both.

BY-EMPLOYMENTS IN OTHER PLACES

Contemporary observers testified to the practice of by-employments in all major regions of the country, noting—usually disapprovingly—the growing tendency of farmers to become part-time merchants, artisans, and wage laborers and of some to leave farming altogether. Even in backward Mito, according to a late Tokugawa writer, not one farmer in ten lived by farming alone.[48] In the mountainous region around Kiryū, north of Edo, every peasant family was said in 1836 to practice sericulture, to weave silk cloth, or to work at paper making in the intervals of farming.[49]

Many observers claimed that more and more peasants were neglecting farming to spend additional time at by-employments because the latter were more lucrative and physically less taxing.[50] Throughout the latter half of the Tokugawa period, village headmen and writers on agriculture alike complained of the extreme shortage of farm labor for hire, attributing it to the availability to small holders and tenant farmers of other kinds of part-time employment at high wages.[51] Adminis-

---

47. In some districts income from dyeing was divided between dyeing done for people inside and outside the district; in other districts only that done for people outside was listed. BFC 6:114, 184; 5:64.
48. Kidota Shirō, Meiji Ishin no nōgyō kōzō (Tokyo, 1960), 53.
49. Ashikaga orimono (Tokyo, 1960), 1:22.
50. Yao shishi: Shiryō hen (Yao, 1960), 317.
51. Akita kenshi: Shiryō—kinsei (Akita, 1963), 852–53; Mihashi Tokio, "Edo

trative documents tend to confirm such observations. Laws concerning the regulation of village trade and industry proliferated in the eighteenth century,[52] and market towns and castle-towns were insistent in asking for protection from the competition of village merchants and manufacturers.[53]

Han authorities widely required villages to report the by-employments of each family in the village, and most village reports on general conditions routinely contained an item on by-employments.[54] Gazetteers described villages by the nature of nonagricultural production and nearness to market towns as well as by crops, terrain, and physical appearance. An early nineteenth-century gazetteer from Hiroshima, for example, listed eighty-three villages in Saeki County and mentioned specific by-employments in all but three, in some cases indicating that by-employments were collectively as important to the local economy as farming. Saeki was an unusually prosperous coastal county, but the gazetteer gave much the same attention to nonagricultural employments in other counties.[55]

Rural industry and trade were by no means uniformly small-scale and limited to work requiring little skill. Scattered around the country were hundreds of rural merchants—employers of part-time labor—whose operations rivaled all but the largest merchants in Edo and Osaka.[56] Significantly, when the Miyazu han in 1860 made an appeal for contributions to overcome a financial crisis, most large contributors came from outside its castle-town.[57] The German scientist Siebold, an inveterate number-counter who traveled widely in Japan during the years 1823–28 and knew the country better than any foreigner in the Tokugawa period, recorded the existence of a number of "grosse

jidai ni okeru nōgyō keiei no hensen," in Nōson kōzō no shiteki bunseki, ed. Miyamoto Mataji (Tokyo, 1955), 16; Fujita Yūkoku (1774–1826), "Kannō wakumon," in Nihon keizai taiten (Tokyo, 1929), 32:228.

52. Ishii Ryōsuke, ed., Hanpōshū: Tottori han and Tokushima han (Tokyo, 1961–62), 2:155–237; 3:774–927.

53. Andō Seiichi, Kinsei zaikata shōgyō no kenkyū (Tokyo, 1958), 248–335.

54. Nomura Kentarō, Mura meisaichō no kenkyū (Tokyo, 1949), 106–51.

55. Geihan tsūshi (Hiroshima, 1915), 2:741–49.

56. Thomas C. Smith, "Landlords and Rural Capitalists," Journal of Economic History 16, no. 2 (June 1956): 165–68.

57. Nihon sangyōshi taikei 7:85.

Manufakturhandlungen" making wine, soy sauce, ceramics, and iron and employing as many as seven hundred workers.[58] Most enterprises of this sort were in rural districts and worked primarily with part-time or seasonal farm labor. Small village enterprises employing between five and twenty workers were common in the sugar, salt, tea, oil, sericulture, and textile industries.[59]

By-employments often required work away from home for periods ranging from a few days up to a year or more; after all, the development of trade and industry was distributed over the landscape in patterns different from the agricultural population. In Kaminoseki, as noted earlier, farm women moved from inland villages to the coast for the salt-making season, and many other cases might be cited. A Kyūshū village reported in the late Tokugawa period that in addition to farming and making wax and sugar in the village, its inhabitants worked "at day labor in nearby provinces for periods of up to a month."[60] Peasants in Sasayama regularly migrated on hundred-day passports to nearby domains to work in breweries during the winter months.[61] In mountain villages in Hiroshima, according to the gazetteer mentioned earlier, the entire able-bodied population migrated to the lowlands for winter work, leaving the old, young, and infirm behind.[62]

Village population registers from Shinshū and Mikawa show between 10 and 20 percent of the whole population and a correspondingly higher proportion of the working population living and working outside the village on the day of compilation.[63] Although these are exceptional cases, nearly all registers from the late Tokugawa period show some village members absent for this reason.

58. Phillip Franz von Siebold, *Nippon: Archiv zur Beschreibung von Japan*, 2d ed. (Leipzig, 1897), 1:182.
59. Ibid. 7:83; *Ashikaga orimono* 1:226; Shinobu Seizaburō, *Kindai Nihon sangyōshi josetsu* (Tokyo, 1942), 15–16, 27, 64–75, 185–207; Horie Hideichi, *Meiji Ishin no shakai kōzō* (Tokyo, 1954), 194–209; Watanabe Norifumi, *Hiroshima ken engyōshi* (Hiroshima, 1960), 75–99; Hattori Shisō, *Nihon manyufakuchua shiron* (Tokyo, 1937), 3–39; Higuchi Hiroshi, *Nihon tōgyōshi* (Tokyo, 1961), 160–62; *Nihon sangyōshi taikei* 1:182–88; *Sekai rekishi jiten* (Tokyo, 1960), 22:386–92.
60. Nakamura Masao, "Amakusa no mura meisaichō," *Kiyō*, no. 12, p. 279.
61. Oka Mitsuo, *Hōken sonraku no kenkyū* (Tokyo, 1962), 152–53.
62. *Geihan tsūshi* 3:893.
63. Aichi Ken Hoi Chihōshi Hensan Iinkai, ed., *Mikawa no kuni Hoi chiho shūmon ninbetsu aratamechō* (Toyohashi, 1961), 557–64; Hayami Akira, "Shinshu Yokouchi mura no chōki jinkō tōkei," *Keizaigaku nenpō* 10 (1968): p. 70.

TABLE 3.6   Manufacturing Output of Farm Families by Prefecture, 1874

Manufacturing Output as % of Total Output		% of Manufacturing Output by Farm Families	
Percentage[a] (1)	Number of Prefectures (2)	Percentage[b] (3)	Number of Prefectures (4)
10–20	3 ⎫	1–70	5 ⎫
20–30	13 ⎬ 39		
30–40	23 ⎭		
40	Yamaguchi		
40–50	16 ⎫		⎬ 30
50–60	3 ⎪		
60–70	1 ⎬ 21		
70–80	1 ⎪	70–80	8 ⎪
80–90	0 ⎭	80–90	17 ⎭
		88	Yamaguchi
90–100	0	90–100	30
Total	61		61

SOURCE: Furushima Toshio, "Shosangyō hatten no chiikisei," *Nihon sangyōshi taikei* (Tokyo, 1960), 6:366–68.

NOTES: Labor productivity is assumed to be the same in manufacturing and agriculture. This understates relative productivity in manufacturing.

Manufacturing includes the value of processing agricultural products; forestry and marine products are not included in the value of agricultural products.

SYMBOLS: m = manufacturing output; ml = manufacturing labor force; P = total product; L = total labor force.

[a]Computation: $m \div P$.

[b]Computation: $(m/P) - (ml/L) \div (m/P)$.

Thus literary and administrative documents leave no doubt that the practice of by-employments was very common by the early nineteenth century. Their importance to the farm economy, however, is another and more difficult question. Some light is thrown on the subject by a nationwide survey in 1874 of agricultural and manufacturing production, which also reported the size of the labor force by sector.[64] If an assumption is made of the relative productivity of labor in the two sectors, therefore, an estimate can be made of the amount of manufacturing output produced by farm families (Table 3.6). Since the

64. Furushima Toshio, "Shosangyō hatten no chiikisei," *Nihon sangyōshi taikei* I:273–343.

assumption cannot be verified and figures gathered on a national scale this early were subject to wide margins of error, the results must be treated with caution.

But they should not be entirely dismissed. We are less concerned with absolute quantities than with comparisons among prefectures, and there is no reason to believe either that the survey was biased differently in different prefectures or that the relative productivity of labor in the two sectors differed significantly by prefectures. Hence the survey data are at least suggestive. They suggest, in respect to both the size of manufacturing relative to agricultural production and the proportion of manufacturing produced by farm families that Yamaguchi Prefecture (corresponding precisely with the former Chōshū *han*) stood near the median among prefectures. Thus Chōshū does not seem to have been ahead of the country as a whole industrially or in by-employments, a judgment confirmed by impressions from other sources.[65] Of course Chōshū as a whole lagged behind Kaminoseki. But in 1843 there were perhaps four or five[66] of seventeen Chōshū counties on a par with Kaminoseki, and other prefectures had their advanced and backward counties, too. One might guess, therefore, that by-employments were about as well developed in a fifth or a quarter of the country as in Kaminoseki.[67]

SPECULATIONS

Contemporaries in the latter half of the Tokugawa period were aware that trade and industry were growing and living standards among the farm population improving, and some observers explicitly linked these trends to by-employments. An Akita headman wrote in 1825 that some sixty years ago his father had begun raising silkworms, the first

---

65. For contemporary impressions of the region, see "Chūgoku Kyūshū kikō," *Satō Nobuhiro zenshū* (Tokyo, 1927), 3:699–702.

66. Ōshima, Kumage, Mitajiri, and Ogōri. "County" is used here to refer to administrative districts parallel to Kaminoseki.

67. Some entire prefectures such as Osaka, Kyoto, Tokyo, Aichi, and Hyōgo were probably economically well in advance of Kaminoseki.

person in his village to do so; after some years of technical failure his operation became highly profitable and others followed his lead. At the time of writing the headman could say, "Every family in the village without exception works at sericulture in the intervals of farming, thereby earning more income." [68]

Speculating, one may suppose that by-employments are among the most important means available of increasing per capita income in preindustrial societies, subject to two conditions. First, they must not be expanded at the cost of agricultural production (which is unlikely, anyway, since food shortages and famine would ensue). Second, an increase in total output must not result in a proportionate increase in population. Under these conditions the increase in per capita output from by-employments alone may be quite large: the number of annual working days for farm people could conceivably be doubled and the total output of the farm population more than doubled, taking into account night work and the higher productivity of nonfarm as compared to farm employments. The income effect of the growth of by-employments would seem to depend therefore, along with the amount of their growth, mainly on demographic behavior.

Whether population grows with the growth of by-employments, and if so how fast, are questions too complex for substantial discussion here, but it is at least worth noting that by-employments that use surplus farm labor may grow *independently* of any growth in population. This is not true of certain other means of increasing output under preindustrial conditions. The expansion of either arable land or urban employment, for example, would bring significant increases in output, but neither can occur without an increase in population if it is assumed that there is no radical increase in labor productivity in farming. [69]

68. *Akita kenshi: Shiryō—kinsei,* 491–92.
69. Another factor in Tokugawa Japan was that by-employments, unlike the extension of arable but like the expansion of urban population, did not necessarily give rise to an increase in food supply, so that famine continued as a population check. One might object that famine is inconsistent with a rise in per capita income, which should have resulted in a relative rise in food prices, channeling additional resources into food production. If a rise in per capita income occurred, however, it would not be on a sufficient scale to prevent the large-scale loss of life from food shortages, because (1) much of the new income would go to high income families with no desire to consume more food in normal years; (2) their added income would be used in part to bid up the prices of non-food commodities (silk, cotton, tobacco, paper, services, etc.), which competed with

The relationship between the means of economic growth and de-mographic behavior can be looked at from another angle. The expan-sion of either arable or urban employment encourages the formation of new families, therefore marriages and therefore births. The expan-sion of by-employments, on the other hand, may lead to the formation of new families by virtue of the additional income available to support them, but need not do so. Instead, existing families may choose to re-strict marriage to a single son in each generation in order to avoid frag-menting holdings (which would result in uneconomically small farm-ing units, imperil family continuity, and lower family prestige in the village), with the incidental effect of holding the birthrate well below the level it would reach without such restriction.[70]

Although this is highly speculative, it may contain part of the ex-planation of the fact that Japan's national population increased very slightly in the latter half of the Tokugawa period. Regional popula-tions were more volatile, it is true, with increases in one quarter being offset by losses elsewhere. Population grew in the southwest where arable was greatly expanded, and declined in the northeast as the re-sult of recurring famine. But in central Japan, where by-employments flourished most conspicuously and where the increase in arable was very moderate, population did not increase and may even have de-clined slightly.[71]

One may also speculate on the connection between the develop-ment of by-employments in the eighteenth century and modern eco-nomic growth.

First, much of Japan's economic growth well into this century was

---

food crops for land or labor; and (3) large annual variations in the harvest made famine inevitable intermittently even though the food supply was normally adequate.

70. There is some evidence of control over population growth in Yokouchi Village in Shinshū, whose population registers from 1671 to 1871 have been carefully analyzed by Hayami Akira. Hayami found that in the earlier half of the period (1671–1/1), the village population grew rapidly; in the latter half, when village population was stable, (1) the marriage rate for both men and women was slightly lower, (2) the average age of women at first marriage was somewhat higher, and (3) the number of children-ever of married women who lived in a married state until the age of forty-five declined signifi-cantly. Hayami, *Shinshū Yokouchi*, 59–105. For similar evidence from England, see E. A. Wrigley, "Family Limitation in Pre-Industrial England," *Economic History Re-view*, 2d ser. 19, no. 1 (1966): 82–109.

71. Sekiyama Naotarō, *Kinsei Nihon no jinkō kōzō* (Tokyo, 1957), 137–41.

achieved by the expansion of traditional industries with the aid of relatively modest technical and organizational modifications. Agriculture, food processing, fishing, lumbering, residential construction, ceramics, and woodworking are examples. This expansion was important to economic growth both for itself and for the external economies, markets, and foreign exchange thereby provided for the modern sector.[72] Nearly all such "traditional" growth was based on Tokugawa technical and organizational foundations, including by-employments. Even as they modernized, some of these industries remained substantially rural and their labor force continued to overlap significantly with that of farming.

Second, Japan's industrial labor force expanded in large part by the recruitment of workers from farm families who, thanks to by-employments, brought to their new employments usable crafts, clerical skills, and even managerial skills. Thus traditional rural weavers had no great trouble learning to operate power looms; men who had kept accounts with the abacus readily mastered modern bookkeeping; many rural moneylenders took naturally and successfully to country banking. The experience of by-employments also helped prepare the rural population, in response to market incentives, to leave their villages and to adapt to new work authorities and social groups. And by-employments contributed to spreading the ambition among rural people for more than marginal economic gains by encouraging large movements up and down the economic scale in Tokugawa villages.[73] Scores of autobiographies attest to the significance for industrialization of these ambitions, as does the high proportion of modern business leaders (as late as 1956) who were born the sons of farmers and rural landlords.[74]

72. Kazushi Ohkawa and Henry Rosovsky, "A Century of Japanese Growth," in *The State and Economic Enterprise in Japan,* ed. William Lockwood (Princeton, 1965), 66–67.

73. Smith, *Agrarian Origins,* 157–79.

74. Of the presidents of a sample of 154 of the largest companies in the country in 1956, nearly 40 percent identified their father's major occupation as "farmer"—including resident but excluding absentee landlords. Most of these men began in business in the first two decades of this century. By comparison, among American business leaders who began in business when the United States was comparably rural (about 1870), farmers' sons accounted for between 10 and 20 percent. Thomas C. Smith, "Landlords'

Third, Simon Kuznets has estimated that the leading industrial countries of the West, on the eve of industrialization, enjoyed per capita incomes two, three, or more times higher than those of presently underdeveloped countries.[75] Since these countries must at one time have been at the same low income level as today's poor countries, it follows that they reached their preindustrial eminence as the result of a long slow climb, which may have been instrumental to later industrialization. Japan may represent a somewhat similar case, since what appears to have been a long period of premodern growth, extending back at least to the early seventeenth century and possibly beyond, was followed by modern growth. If so, by-employments were an essential element of the earlier growth, permitting as they did expansion of trade and industry without any considerable growth of population.

I do not mean to suggest by this comparison that at the end of the Tokugawa period Japan reached an income level closely approximating that of eighteenth-century England; this situation seems most unlikely given Japan's subsequent economic growth and present relatively low per capita income. But just as Japan's GNP is today the third largest in the world despite the fact that she is twentieth in per capita income, so in Tokugawa times the country may have been relatively advanced in respect to technology, volume of internal trade, commercial organization, education, and number and size of cities, without— owing to a poverty of natural resources and the absence of foreign trade?—being particularly prosperous.

Yet it would probably be a mistake to think of Tokugawa Japan as a very poor country even by contemporary European standards. Western observers during the second half of the Tokugawa period were widely impressed by the amount of travel and shipping they saw, the condition of the main roads, the variety and abundance of goods for sale, the state of technology (although not of science), the spread of literacy, the size and public order of towns and cities, the excellence of

---

Sons in the Business Elite," *Economic Development and Cultural Change* 9, no. 1, pt. 2 (October 1960): 93–96.

75. Simon Kuznets, "Underdeveloped Countries and the Pre-Industrial Phase in the Advanced Countries," in *The Economics of Underdevelopment,* ed. A. N. Agarwala and S. P. Singh (New York, 1963), 143–44.

farming, and the general well-being of the population. Even as late as the 1860s Sir Rutherford Alcock, an acute observer by no means blind to the faults of the Japanese, who thought their officials were deficient in moral sense and their painting and music laughable, had high praise for the economy. He may also have explained, without knowing it, how a country in which most people farmed could generate so much trade and industry. In describing a trip through the countryside, Sir Rutherford commented, "The land seemed, for the most part, to be in very small allotments, and to furnish only one of the occupations of each household—the fisherman's net, the turner's lathe, and a little shopkeeping, all alternating with the farmer's toil."[76]

APPENDIX

The data presented in the tables of this chapter were obtained by the following methods.

Total product was derived from the district reports by totaling (1) all *listed* final goods and services domestically produced, minus the value of intermediate goods and services, valued at current prices; (2) all *listed* intermediate goods and services domestically produced, valued at current prices; (3) all *listed* "profits" (*ri*) accruing to wholesalers, merchants, peddlers, boat owners, and such, whose services were not included in (1) or (2); and (4) the imputed earnings of artisans for whom no output or earnings of any kind were reported.

Income was derived by totaling these items and deducting depreciation (the purchase cost of animals, tools, and fertilizers and the cost of house and boat repair), and adding wage remittances from outside and the expenditures in the district of the *han* government for official salaries.

Certain problems concerning the items mentioned above require comment. (1) *Prices.* The prices used in all calculations were those given for each district in its report. Prices differed very slightly from district to district and no more than could be accounted for by transportation costs. Unpriced items in a given district were valued at average prices for those items in other districts when shown; when not shown, they were dropped, since in such cases the quantities were infinitesimal. (2) *Imputed earnings.* For certain artisans (family heads) listed in the population of the district, no output or earnings of any kind were reported. In such cases income was imputed for each artisan at 2.47

76. *The Capital of the Tycoon* (New York, 1868), 1:387.

TABLE 3.7   Imputed Shares of Income

District	% of Total Income Imputed	% of Nonagricultural Income Imputed
Ōhano	4.7	19.9
Kamitafuse	6.1	23.1
Ono	9.3	27.2
Usanagi	2.6	6.1
Ihonoshō	2.3	5.3
Shimotafuse	21.8	44.0
Hano	35.4	66.2
Ogo	10.6	19.6
Ogōri	5.5	9.7
Okuni	12.2	20.8
Saga	10.0	16.4
Hirao	6.6	9.3
Sone	1.1	1.4
Befu	5.9	7.4
Murotsu	3.0	3.6

SOURCE: Data compiled from Yamaguchi Prefectural Archives, ed., *Bōchō fūdo chūshin'an* (Yamaguchi, 1962–63), vols. 5, 6.

of the average farm income of farm families in the district. (See page 80 for an explanation of the figure 2.47.) Where clearly only part of the income of an artisan was shown (for example, that part specifically stated as deriving from services sold outside the district, services sold inside being omitted), an amount was added sufficient to bring the income up to 2.47 of the average farm income of farm families in the district. The result of this procedure was probably to overstate nonagricultural income in heavily agricultural districts (where family farm income was relatively high) and to understate it in heavily non-agricultural districts (where it was relatively low). Table 3.7 shows the share of total income and nonagricultural income that was imputed in each district. (3) *Materials and services originating outside the district.* Wages paid to work-ers from outside the district were included in this category. (4) *Depreciation.* No distinction in the reports was made between investments and depreciation in listing expenditures on tools, animals, and fertilizer. In all probability the bulk of such expenditures were for depreciation, and for convenience all were counted as such.

Several groups actually living in some districts were excluded from the count of their populations for certain purposes. (1) Samurai, outcastes, doc-tors, priests, and female entertainers were excluded from income estimates since, on the one hand, no output or income information was reported for them and, on the other, the special character of their functions makes it impossible to form reasonable estimates for them. The district did not include the first two groups in its estimate of food needs, apparently considering them as distinct communities beyond the purview of the report, but it did include the other three. (2) The earnings of persons from outside working in districts were counted as production costs in those districts rather than income, since their residence in the district was of uncertain duration. Such persons were excluded from district food consumption estimates. (3) Persons from a district who regularly (or for a year or more) lived and worked outside it were included in calculating district income (wage remittances) but not in estimating district food consumption. (4) None of the categories of persons named above was included in occupational figures.

It is probable that outcastes, who evidently lived in a distinct residential and economic community and who were ignored in the reports, may nevertheless have contributed something to the listed district output in the form of labor. To the extent they did, the output of the district would appear larger in relation to the population that produced it than it was in fact; but a greater distortion would be introduced by attempting to impute income to the outcaste population. The amount of error in either case would not be large, however, since the ratio of outcastes (who must have been very low income earners) to the productively counted population was only two per hundred in the county as a whole.

Although samurai were somewhat more numerous than outcastes, they normally contributed little or nothing to the output of the districts in which they lived. Instead they lived from income paid them from the district's land taxes. They did not even contribute significantly to government services at this level, which consisted mainly of the work of village headmen who were commoners. Some of these rural samurai may have farmed. If they did, their output was not mingled with that of the population being reported, since for every category of arable land reported, the amount paid in land tax was also reported, and it is all but inconceivable that samurai were subject to the land tax and to the collection of it in common with that paid by peasants. Nor is it likely that samurai or members of their families contributed to the output of commoners by working for them as hired labor.

Doctors, priests, and female entertainers, for whom no income was listed and no reasonable estimate can be made, unquestionably performed services for the community and for travelers, but the members of this category were so few in number that the omission of their contribution is of negligible importance.

4

PEASANT FAMILIES AND POPULATION CONTROL IN EIGHTEENTH-CENTURY JAPAN

ROBERT Y. ENG &

THOMAS C. SMITH

After expanding rapidly in the seventeenth century, total Japanese population grew slowly, if at all, from the first national census in 1721 to the last census in the Tokugawa period in 1846.[1] Surprisingly, unless the evidence has been badly misread, this was a period when the econ-

Reprinted from the *Journal of Interdisciplinary History* 6, no. 3 (Winter 1976). A somewhat modified version of this article appeared as a chapter in Thomas C. Smith, *Nakahara: Family Farming and Population in a Japanese Village, 1717–1830* (Stanford, 1977).

1. From 1721 on, all jurisdictions were required to make a periodic register of the commoner population by sex, age, and family relationship; this was usually done annually but in some places at longer intervals. Also at regular intervals population by sex had to be reported up the administrative hierarchy to the central government in Edo (Tokyo), where it was aggregated by province. It is this periodic nationwide administrative count that we refer to as a "census." Sekiyama Naotarō, *Kinsei Nihon no jinkō kōzō* (Tokyo, 1957), 95–96, 123.

omy was expanding through improvements in farming, the spread of rural industry, and the growth of internal trade. Per capita income must therefore have been rising as well, and the rise by lifting income per head to an unspecifiable but critical "threshold" level and inducing institutional and attitudinal changes may have been a necessary condition of Japan's subsequent industrialization.

It has been thought that population was held in check between 1721 and 1846 by high mortality as the result of periodic food crises and a rather high level of urbanization. But recent studies of local records similar to the parish registers of Europe call this inference into question. Even though few in number these studies by Hanley, Hayami, and others consistently show low mortality and low fertility.[2] Our own study of the population of a small farming village in central Japan, which we call Nakahara, confirms these findings.[3] We intend to report elsewhere in detail on mortality in Nakahara and the reliability of the documentation. Here we are concerned with marital fertility and why it was low.

Our views are based on an analysis of the annual registers of population for the village in the period 1717–1830, which are complete except for thirteen scattered years that are missing.[4] Births in the gap-years are recoverable, however, when the child lived until the next registration. Population registers in Nakahara were made up in the sixth month of each year; they listed all residents by name, age, sex, and

---

2. The most comprehensive fertility and mortality data are crude birth and death rates, unadjusted for "infant mortality," for a group of villages in Suwa County in Nagano Prefecture between 1670 and 1860, based on a total population of more than fifteen thousand at the end of the period. See also age-specific estimates (later referred to) for Yokouchi Village, in Hayami Akira, *Kinsei nōson rekishi jinkōgakuteki kenkyū* (Tokyo, 1973), 218. There are interesting crude rates for urban populations in Sasaki Yōichirō, "Tokugawa jidai kōki toshi jinkō kenkyū," *Shikai* 6, no. 14 (March 1967): 31–41; and "Hida no kuni Takayama no jinkō kenkyū," in *Keizaishi ni okeru jinkō*, ed. Hayami Akira (Tokyo, 1969), 95–118. Crude birth and death rates for a number of scattered villages are to be found in Susan B. Hanley, "Fertility, Mortality, and Life Expectancy in Premodern Japan," *Population Studies* 28, no. 1 (March 1974): 131–35 (Tables 2–4).

3. Life expectancy in Nakahara at age 1 was 50.7 years for females and 46.9 for males.

4. *Nakahara mura shūmon oaratamechō;* these documents are housed in the library of Meiji University in Tokyo.

relation to family head, and during the year notations were made of changes in the population because of births, deaths, and migration. Unfortunately births were not normally entered until the infant's first New Year's celebration; consequently, children born after one new year who died before the next never appeared in the record. We call these omissions "infant mortality," a term not strictly accurate, and estimate their number at about 20 percent of all births.[5]

THE QUESTION OF FERTILITY CONTROL

Table 4.1 compares age-specific marital fertility in Nakahara and in a number of contemporaneous Japanese villages and European parishes for which there are estimates. To make the estimates as nearly comparable as possible, we have inflated the figures for the Japanese villages (all of which had essentially the same system of late registration of births) at an estimated rate of 20 percent in each group in order to adjust for births lost through "infant mortality."

Two things stand out in Table 4.1. First, fertility in Nakahara was about the average for the Japanese communities. Second, even after adjustment for infant mortality, fertility was distinctly low compared with all of the European parishes with two exceptions: Colyton in 1647–1719, where there is strong evidence that some form of family limitation was in force; and Thézels-St. Sernin, in the region of puzzlingly low fertility in southwestern France.[6] Fertility was much lower in Nakahara than in any of the other European communities, including Colyton at a later date. This can be seen in the column entitled

5. It is unknown whether infants were an average age of six or twelve months when first entered in the population register of the village. In estimating the number of infants who died before registration, we have assumed that the average age at registration was twelve months and so have fitted life tables for age 1 or older in Nakahara to the most appropriate Coale-Demeny model life tables ("North" and "East").

6. On the comparatively low levels of age-specific fertility in southwestern France, see Pierre Valmary, *Familles paysannes au XVIIIe siècle en Bas-Quercy* (Paris, 1965), chap. 6; Louis Henry, "Fécondité des mariages dans le quart sud-ouest de la France," *Annales* 27, nos. 4–5 (1972): 612–40, 977–1023, especially 985, 991, 1001–5; Pierre Goubert, "Legitimate Fecundity and Infant Mortality in France During the Eighteenth Century: A Comparison," *Daedalus* 97 (Spring 1968): 593–603, especially 597–99.

TABLE 4.1 Age-Specific Marital Fertility in Selected European and Japanese
Communities (Births/1,000 Woman-Years)

	Age Group							
Place and Period of Formation of Marriage	15–19	20–24	25–29	30–34	35–39	40–44	45–49	Total Fertility[a]
England								
Colyton, 1647–1719	500	346	395	272	182	104	020	6.6
Colyton, 1770–1837	500	441	361	347	270	152	022	8.0
France								
Crulai, 1674–1742	320	419	429	355	292	142	010	8.2
Le Mesnil-Beaumont, 1740–1799	542	524	487	422	329	135	017	9.6
Thézels-St. Sernin, 1700–1792	208	393	326	297	242	067	000	6.6
Meulan, 1660–1739	585	519	507	503	379	157	014	10.4
Meulan, 1740–1789	492	493	477	403	294	111	015	9.0
Germany								
Anhausen, 1692–1799	N.A.	472	496	450	355	173	037	9.9
Japan								
Yokouchi, before 1700[b]	204	382	358	266	264	164	028	7.3
Yokouchi, 1701–1750[b]	168	275	240	232	146	071	026	5.0
Yokouchi, 1751–1800[b]	188	205	226	161	116	078	010	4.0
Yokouchi, after 1800[b]	306	264	231	202	092	042	011	4.2
Kandoshinden, after 1800[b]	471	531	351	269	225	138	016	7.7
Nishijo, 1773–1835[b]	321	399	356	315	251	121	032	7.4
Nakahara, 1717–1830	214	326	304	300	221	122	034	6.5

SOURCES: E. A. Wrigley, "Family Limitation in Pre-Industrial England," *Economic History Review,* 2d ser. 19, no. 1 (1966): 89; Étienne Gautier and Louis Henry, *La population de Crulai, paroisse normande* (Paris, 1958), 105; J. Ganiage, *Trois villages d'Île-de-France au XVIIIe siècle* (Paris, 1963), 82; Pierre Valmary, *Familles paysannes au XVIIIe siècle en Bas-Quercy* (Paris, 1965), 120; Marcel Lachiver, *La population de Meulan du XVIIe au XIXe siècle* (Paris, 1969), 152; John Knodel, "Two and a Half Centuries of Demographic History in a Bavarian Village," *Population Studies* 24 (1970): 369; Hayami Akira, *Kinsei nōson rekishi jinkōgakuteki kenkyū* (Tokyo, 1973), 218; Hayami Akira, "The Demographic Analysis of a Village in Tokugawa Japan: Kandoshinden of Ōwari Province, 1778–1871," *Keiō Economic Studies* 5 (1968): 78; Hayami Akira, "Jinkōgakuteki shihyō ni okeru kaisōkan no kakusa," in *Kenkyū kiyō,* ed. Tokugawa Rinseishi Kenkyūjo (1973), 182.

[a]Computed from ages 20 to 49.

[b]Birth cohorts of mothers.

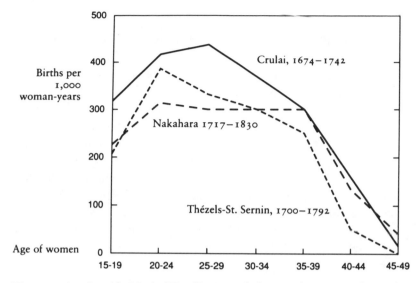

Fig. 4.1   Age-Specific Marital Fertility in Nakahara and Two French Parishes

SOURCES: *Nakahara mura shūmon oaratamechō*, Meiji Library, Tokyo; Étienne Gautier and Louis Henry, *La population de Crulai, paroisse normande* (Paris, 1958); Pierre Valmary, *Familles paysannes au XVIIIe siècle en Bas-Query* (Paris, 1965).

"Total Fertility," which shows the number of children that a woman would have if she lived in marriage from age 20 to 49 and bore children on the schedule shown by the age-specific rates.[7] Using Nakahara's total fertility as an index of 100, the ratio was 123 for Colyton in 1770–1837, 126 for Crulai, 148 for Le Mesnil-Beaumont, 152 for Anhausen, and 160 for Meulan in 1660–1739 and 138 in 1740–89.

The general contrast is brought out graphically by Figure 4.1, which compares age-specific marital fertility in Nakahara and in two French parishes representing cases of relatively high and low fertility for that country. The Nakahara curve, it will be seen, is at about the

7. It is standard practice to omit the 15–19 age group in computations of total fertility because inclusion would introduce a serious bias for two reasons: (1) the rate attributed to the whole group is usually computed from the few women who marry around the age of eighteen or nineteen; (2) in many communities early marriages are exceptionally baby-prone because of marriages forced by pregnancy.

same general level as Thézels-St. Sernin (low fertility) and much below Crulai (high fertility).

It seems unlikely that Nakahara's comparatively low marital fertility is to be explained by the practice of any form of birth control since the shape of its fertility curve is of the kind usually associated with the absence of such limitation. In these circumstances the woman's age is the preponderant factor in fertility. Fertility itself is independent of the length of marriage; it declines slowly at the early ages, and then more rapidly as fecundity declines and the proportion of infertile couples increases. This gives a convex curve. When birth control is widespread, however, couples tend to concentrate childbearing in the early years of marriage, stopping procreation when they reach the usually small number of children desired. Fertility declines with the length of marriage and may be quite low even when the woman is still young, since couples who marry young tend to bear the desired number of children at an early age. Age-specific fertility therefore falls steadily with increasing age and tends to flatten out at the late ages, giving a concave curve (Fig. 4.2).[8]

It is well known, of course, that great differences in marital fertility exist among different populations in the absence of birth control. This is probably due to the different spacing between births as a result of variations in the waiting period between birth and the resumption of sexual relations, the length of suckling, and physiological differences governing the reappearance of ovulation after confinement.[9] Fertility in Nakahara may have been low partly in consequence of some combination of these factors; we have no way of knowing. But it was almost certainly low in part because of infanticide.

There is an immense amount of legal and literary evidence of abortion and infanticide in Japan at large, although none to our knowledge places either practice specifically in Nakahara.[10] Daimyo governments

8. Louis Henry, *Manuel de démographie historique* (Geneva, 1970), 89–90; E. A. Wrigley, "Family Limitation in Pre-Industrial England," *Economic History Review*, 2d ser. 19, no. 1 (1966): 91.

9. Louis Henry, "Some Data on Natural Fertility," *Eugenics Quarterly* 7, no. 2 (1961): 90–91.

10. The most comprehensive study of this sort of evidence is the massive work by Takahashi Bonsen, *Nihon jinkō no kenkyū*, 3 vols. (Tokyo, 1941–62).

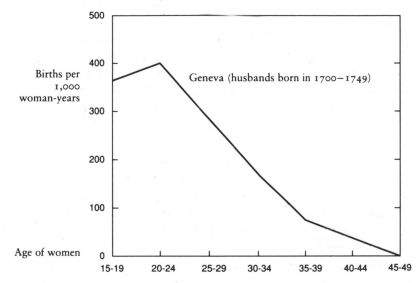

Fig. 4.2   Age-Specific Marital Fertility in a Community Practicing Family Limitation

SOURCE: Louis Henry, *Anciennes familles genevoises: Étude démographique, XVIᵉ–XXᵉ siècle* (Paris, 1956), 76.

repeatedly prohibited infanticide and abortion in the eighteenth century, attributing to these practices the stagnation of population. Moralists railed against both infanticide and abortion, frequently running these distinct terms together as if they had a common significance. Abortion was apparently more widely practiced in the towns where there were skilled specialists, but both practices were found in rural and urban locales and also, apparently, among all classes. Contemporary writers were inclined to be lenient with the poor, whose circumstances presumably drove them to these acts; their wrath was saved for families in comfortable circumstances—samurai and merchants as well as substantial farmers—who were said to limit children merely to increase their own ease or to improve the prospects of the children whom they chose to raise.

Infanticide is consistent, in theory at least, with the Nakahara fertility curve. If the act occurred at birth, as contemporary writers said, the victims would never appear in the registers. If it occurred frequently, registered fertility would be extremely low through the combined effects of eliminated births and the sterile periods of pregnancy associated with them, and at the same time the fertility curve would in all probability be convex. Infanticide is the only form of birth limitation—to equate that term with a form of abortion—that permits control over the sex of offspring, an advantage that probably no society that adopted it would forego entirely. As a result of eliminating children of the unwanted sex in various circumstances, one would expect extremely long average intervals between births. As long as there were not too many very small families, childbearing would be widely spread over the fertile years of marriage; fertility would therefore tend to vary with the woman's age rather than with the length of marriage, and so describe a convex curve.

There is no way to detect abortion specifically in the Nakahara registers but infanticide, being sex-selective, has left many traces. What follows is an analysis of this evidence, which leads us to believe that infanticide was widely practiced in the village and, moreover, practiced less as part of a struggle for survival than as a way of planning the sex composition, sex sequence, spacing, and ultimate number of children. As the evidence is complex and unfamiliar, it may be helpful to summarize the main points in advance:

1. There were few very large or very small completed families; distribution clustered heavily around the mean.
2. Small landholders had fewer children than large, and early stoppers (last child born before mother reached age 38) had fewer children than late stoppers.
3. But late-stopping small holders had larger families than early-stopping large holders.
4. The smaller the family, the younger the mother at the birth of the last child, and the more likely the last child to be male.
5. Families tended, beginning with the third child, to have a next child of the sex of which they had fewer.
6. There is evidence that children were spaced for the convenience of the mother.
7. There is also some evidence of the avoidance of an unlucky sex in the next child under specifiable circumstances.

SEX BIAS

We initially thought infanticide was practiced exclusively or mainly against females and that evidence to this effect would be found in the sex ratio at birth. We soon discovered that this was not the case. A sex ratio of 114 males per 100 females in 658 births could not be considered abnormally high. We observed, however, certain variations in sex ratio by birth order that, in time, led to the inference that infanticide was practiced against both sexes and, further, that married couples had a marked tendency to have a next child of the sex underrepresented in their present family. As may be seen below in the distribution of births by sex for births 3–10 in all first marriages, almost invariably from the third birth on, odd birth orders showed an excess of males and even birth orders either no bias or a slight excess of females:

Birth Order	Males	Females	Males per 100 Females
3	53	43	123
4	39	40	98
5	35	18	194
6	19	19	100
7	11	10	110
8	3	6	50
9	2	1	200
10	0	1	0

This tendency was evident only after the second birth; there seems to have been no general sex preference before then. The subsequent preference can be seen both in complete first marriages—first marriages for both partners that lasted through the wife's age 45—and in all first marriages, in the following way. Consider each married couple as a discrete case of marriage at each birth of a child when two or more previous children are registered in the household. Thus, a couple with six children all living and registered at home would appear four times as four different families in the sample, once at each birth after the second. Now divide these statistical families into three groups according to the sex of the previous children registered at home: those with predominantly male children (PM), those with predominantly females

(PF), and those with an equal number of both sexes ($M = F$). Then for each group calculate the sex ratio of the next children born. This test produces the following distribution for complete first marriages:[11]

Previous Siblings	Next Child Male	Next Child Female	Next Child (Males per 100 Females)
PM	30	45	67
M = F	31	21	148
PF	38	19	200

If the sex of the next child in these families was independent of that of the previous children, the ratio of male-to-female births ought to be about the same in each group of families. The ratios in the various groups, however, differ significantly from one another, and the chances of differences of this magnitude occurring independently of the sex of previous children is considerably less than 1 in 100. Also, the sex ratio in two of the groups, PM and PF, is significantly different from normal (102).[12] We must suppose, therefore, that the sex of the next child was to some extent a matter of choice, carried out by infanticide, and that families tended to eliminate infants of the sex that they had more of, and to eliminate girls somewhat more often than boys. Otherwise, it is

11. Includes all living siblings residing in the family and all of those away as hired servants but registered with the family at the time of birth of the next child; one case of births of fraternal twins of opposite sex is included.

12. We can test for homogeneity of the three groups by applying the x^2 test to a 3×2 contingency table consisting of the distribution of the sex of the next child of the three groups; the null hypothesis is that births are independent of each other and of the composition of the existing sibling set. Four degrees of freedom are lost in our assumption that the true probability of a male birth equals the observed proportion of male births in the sample (0.54) and that the expected frequency of births in each class of sibling composition equals the observed frequency. We get an x^2 of 10.6, significant at the 0.006 level on 2 degrees of freedom.

If the sex ratio at birth was 105, the expected sex ratio at age 1 (registered birth) would be 102 by Model North of the Coale-Demeny life tables (which most closely resembles the Nakahara life tables for mortality at age 1 or older). We can test for sex bias in any distribution of sex by applying the x^2 test on the null hypothesis that the true sex ratio at (registered) birth is 102. The results for the three groups are as follows:

Previous Siblings	x^2	Degrees of Freedom	Level of Significance
PM	3.4	1	0.07
M = F	1.9	1	0.17
PF	5.7	1	0.02

quite inexplicable that families with predominantly male children tended to have females in the next child by a ratio significantly different from normal; that those where females predominated tended to have males by a ratio significantly different from normal; and that those with an equal number of both sexes, although tending to have more males than females, did *not* do so by a significant margin.

When the sample is enlarged to include all first marriages, the result is the following distribution: [13]

Previous Siblings	Next Child Male	Next Child Female	Next Child (Males per 100 Females)
PM	47	65	72
M = F	42	25	168
PF	55	32	172

This sample gives a less smooth rise in sex ratio from *PM* to *M = F* to *PF;* the proportion of male births in the two latter groups was nearly identical. But in all groups the sex ratio of the next child was significantly different from normal (102), and again, the differences in sex ratio among all three groups were statistically significant ($p < 0.004$).[14] It seems likely, therefore, that parents with both complete and incomplete marriages tended to keep or "return" (as the euphemism had it) newborn babies depending in part upon the sex of the infant and on that of previous children.

SEX OF THE NEXT CHILD
AFTER THE DEATH OF A CHILD

If parents in fact selected the sex of infants generally in order to get approximately the sex mix in offspring that they wished, then with the

13. See n. 11.
14. Applying the test for sex bias as described in n. 12, we get:

Previous Siblings	x^2	Degrees of Freedom	Level of Significance
PM	3.6	1	0.06
M = F	3.8	1	0.05
PF	5.6	1	0.02

TABLE 4.2   Distribution of Sex of Next Child Born After Death of a Child
(All First Marriages)

	Sex of Deceased Male		Sex of Deceased Female	
Sex Composition	Next Child Male	Next Child Female	Next Child Male	Next Child Female
A. *All Living Sibling Sets*				
PM	2	3	6	3
M = F	3	9	8	2
PF	4	10	4	1
TOTAL	9	22	18	6
B. *Living Sibling Sets of 2 or More at Birth of Next Child*				
PM	2	3	5	3
M = F	2	9	4	1
PF	1	2	4	1
TOTAL	5	14	13	5

SOURCE: *Nakahara shūmon oaratamechō*, Meiji Library, Tokyo.

NOTES: Includes all cases where two or more children of the same sex died before the next birth but excludes three cases where two or more children of different sex died before the next birth.

Because we are primarily interested here in the relationship between the sex of a deceased child and the sex of the next child, sibship composition is introduced only as a control variable. The groups include sibling sets of one or no child, null sibling sets being counted in the $M = F$ group. As Section B demonstrates, eliminating sibling sets of one or no child does not alter the general picture.

death of a child, one would suppose that they would have a next child of the same sex as the deceased. To our astonishment, there was a significant tendency for the next child to be the opposite sex of the deceased, as the totals in Table 4.2 show.[15] Even controlling for the sex of the surviving siblings, this tendency holds. Hence, families losing a male and left with predominantly female children nonetheless tended to have a female next, and vice versa. Perhaps replacement by a child

Applying the test for homogeneity as described in n. 12, we get x^2 of 11.2, significant at 0.004 level on 2 degrees of freedom.

15. Applying the x^2 test to the 2 × 2 contingency table corresponding to all cases regardless of living sibship composition, on the null hypothesis that the sex of the deceased child was unrelated to the sex of the next child and with the assumptions that the true probability of a male birth equals the observed frequency in the sample (0.49) and that the expected frequencies of births in both classes of deceased children equal the observed frequencies, we get a highly significant x^2 statistic of 10.7 (0.001 level) on 1 degree of freedom. Moreover, for both classes of deceased children, the sex ratio of the next birth deviates significantly from 102 (0.02 level).

of the same sex was thought challenging or offensive to the powers who had taken away the deceased, but this is the purest speculation.[16]

What is certain is that this surprising behavior went against the general tendency to balance sexes. If we remove from the pool of families those with a child dying before the next birth, the sexual preferences shown above become stronger for the PM and PF groups, although not for the $M = F$ group. This tendency can be seen in the proportion of male births in the sibling sets of two or more living children. For all first marriages, the proportion of next children that are males is as follows:

$$
\begin{array}{ll}
PM & 0.42 \\
M = F & 0.63 \\
PF & 0.63
\end{array}
$$

When we eliminate first marriages where birth was preceded by the death of a previous child, the proportion is as follows:

$$
\begin{array}{ll}
PM & 0.40 \\
M = F & 0.63 \\
PF & 0.68
\end{array}
$$

LIMITATION OF FAMILY SIZE

Sex selection in the next child was probably not the unique aim of infanticide. An equally important aim, no doubt, was family limitation. Mean family size for complete first marriages was notably small, 5.1 children;[17] but by itself this fact tells us little since the small mean may

16. The objection has been made that this statement assumes an absurdity, namely, that a child of the wrong sex was killed in order to preserve it from harm. Presumably infanticide was never committed primarily in the interest of its victim but of someone else—family, mother, siblings, etc. But it is not necessarily absurd to think of an infant's being killed to protect it; one of the modern arguments for abortion is that the victim is better off than if raised as an unwanted child.

17. International comparison is complicated by the fact that the median age at first marriage of women in Nakahara was 18.5 years, about five or more years younger than in most West European parishes. However, if we restrict ourselves to cases in which the wife was younger than age 30 at the time of marriage, the mean family size for complete first marriages in Nakahara was 5.2 children, as compared with 6.1 children and 8.0 children for complete marriages in Crulai (1675–1744) and Meulan (1660–1739), respectively (calculated from figures in Étienne Gautier and Louis Henry, La population

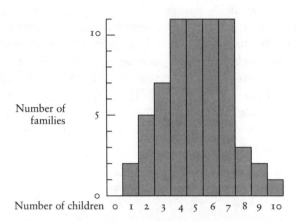

Fig. 4.3   Distribution of Completed Families by Size for All Complete First Marriages ($N = 64$)

SOURCE: *Nakahara mura shūmon oaratamechō*, Meiji Library, Tokyo.

have been the result of family limitation or, alternatively, of such factors as sex selection, infant mortality, and low fecundity. Some light is thrown on the subject, however, by the distribution of completed families by size.

As Figure 4.3 shows, there was a heavy bunching around the mean, with few families of less than four or more than seven children. The extreme bunching of this distribution can be brought out by a comparison of Nakahara with Meulan in France, using only complete marriages with the wife aged thirty or younger, a restriction explained in note 16. Only 10 percent of complete families in Nakahara had eight or more children, compared with 57 percent in Meulan in a period of no family limitation (1660–1739); only 8 percent of complete families

de Crulai, paroisse normande [Paris, 1958], 126; Marcel Lachiver, *La population de Meulan du XVIIe au XIXe siècle* [Paris, 1969] 171–72). Only two complete first marriages in Nakahara, each producing three children, are eliminated because of this restriction.

in Nakahara had two or less children, compared with 33 percent in Meulan in a period of family limitation (1790–1839).[18]

"Infant mortality," for which we have made no adjustment in the above comparison, obviously cannot account for the rarity of small or the complete absence of childless families in Nakahara. With the means at hand to achieve such families, their rarity must have been intentional. The avoidance of childless families is especially clear. As about 4 percent of any human population may be expected to be sterile, merely letting matters take their course would almost certainly have produced some childless families. But matters were not allowed to take their course: infertile brides were sent home early, as is evident from the fact that ten of thirteen divorces in the village ended childless marriages after an average of 3.0 years of conjugal living. In other words, childless marriages never became complete marriages.

Although the small proportion of large families in Nakahara, as compared with Meulan, is obviously accounted for partly by "infant mortality," a substantial difference remains even when the Nakahara figure is generously adjusted upward for "infant mortality."[19] Was the relatively small proportion of large families in Nakahara partly intentional, too?

One piece of evidence concerns the age of mothers at the birth of the last child (*MALB*), which for obvious reasons is a meaningful datum only when marriages are complete. The mean *MALB* in com-

18. The proportions for Meulan are computed from data in Lachiver, *Meulan*, 171–72.

19. To test the hypothesis that "infant mortality" accounted for the low proportion of large families in Nakahara, we inflated the size of each completed family by assigning through random drawing an unregistered infant mortality rate to each family so that:

> ¼ of the families would have a mortality rate of 100 per thousand
> ½ of the families would have a mortality rate of 200 per thousand
> ⅛ of the families would have a mortality rate of 300 per thousand
> ⅛ of the families would have a mortality rate of 400 per thousand

The size of each family was then adjusted upward according to the mortality rate assigned, with decimals rounded off to the nearest whole number. Note that the procedure implicitly assumes an overall infant mortality rate of 213 per thousand, which may be too high; moreover, some of the infants "recovered" in this way may have been eliminated by infanticide rather than natural death. Even so, the proportion of families of 8+ children in Nakahara rises only to 45 percent, still considerably lower than the 57 percent found in Meulan.

plete first marriages in Nakahara was 37.5.[20] This is rather young for a population not practicing family limitation. In this case it may be accounted for by "infant mortality"—unregistered infants dying of natural causes after the last registered birth—and, possibly, the early age of marriage for females; early marriage would have enabled subfecund couples, who in a late-marrying population would be childless, to have one or two children, presumably at an early age. However, if we divide the mothers into two nearly equal groups of late stoppers ($MALB >$ 37.0) and early stoppers ($MALB <$ 37.0), we almost rule out these possibilities for the critical early group:

MALB	Last Child Male	Last Child Female	Last Child (Males per 100 Females)
≤ 37.0	21	8	262
> 37.0	19	16	119

The early stoppers ended with a male child, by a ratio of 2.6 to 1; late stoppers on the other hand ended about as often with a female as a male. Thus, much of the early stopping was apparently deliberate; if it had been involuntary, say the result of infecundity or "infant mortality," the sex of the last child would have been randomly determined and not skewed in favor of males.

Significantly, although not surprisingly, early stoppers had fewer children than late. The mean completed family size of the two groups, respectively, was 4.0 and 6.1; although only 10 percent of early stoppers had as many as 6 children, an astonishing 71 percent of late stoppers did. No part of this difference is attributable to differential duration of marriage: the average age of marriage for the two groups of women was nearly identical—19.4 and 19.6—and all members of both groups were married through age 45. The smaller sized families were due mainly to early stopping, a good deal of which we have just

20. This is younger than one would expect if there were no limitation of (registered) births; in eighteenth-century European communities practicing little or no family limitation, mean *MALB* is about 40 or 41. On the other hand, the differential between Nakahara's *MALB* and the European norm would be narrowed or perhaps even eliminated if we could take into account infants born after the mother's last registered birth and dying unregistered of natural causes in the first year of life.

seen must have been deliberate to account for the heavy predominance of males as last children.

This leaves open the possibility that late stoppers did not practice infanticide. After all, they stopped with one sex about as often as another and had about as many female as male births in total, and abstention from infanticide would account for the late $MALB$ of the group and the normal sex ratio of both the last birth and all births.[21] But they were not abstainers from infanticide. This fact appears when late stoppers are divided into PM, $M = F$, and PF groups, as all families were earlier, on the basis of the sex of two or more children registered at home, and the sex of the next child observed for each group. Among early stoppers ($MALB \leq 37.0$) the results were as follows:

Previous Siblings	Next Child Male	Next Child Female	Next Child (Males per 100 Females)
PM	9	11	82
M = F	12	4	300
PF	15	3	500

Late stoppers ($MALB > 37.0$) produced the following results:

Previous Siblings	Next Child Male	Next Child Female	Next Child (Males per 100 Females)
PM	21	34	62
M = F	19	17	112
PF	23	16	114

In each case, the probability of a male birth increased by a large jump from PM to PF families.[22]

It would therefore appear that late stoppers continued to bear children to a relatively late age *despite* the practice of infanticide; that by infanticide they tended to keep offspring sexually balanced from one birth order to another after the second; and that the large size of com-

21. There was an exactly equal number of boys and girls among the 212 children born to late stoppers.

22. Carrying out the test for homogeneity described in n. 12, we get an x^2 of 4.6, significant at the 0.10 level on 2 degrees of freedom.

pleted families among them would not generally have been due to a need to continue procreation to a late age in order to correct a severe sex imbalance among early children. Assuming that these statements are warranted, we may add another. Both sex balance and larger-than-average family size were in all probability intentional: late stopping was the necessary means of achieving these goals.

FARM SIZE AND FAMILY SIZE

We come now to another kind of evidence for family limitation. Although there is no direct information on farm size, we have a reasonable proxy in estimates of the normal productivity of holdings in rice equivalents (*kokudaka*) of all holdings in the village, identified by holder, at ten scattered dates (1716, 1727, 1738, 1746, 1764, 1780, 1792, 1802, 1812, and 1823).[23] The accuracy and currency of these evaluations, which were made for purposes of taxation, are uncertain; they also tell us nothing about how land was distributed for farming as opposed to how it was held for purposes of taxation (roughly, ownership); nor do they reveal anything about the nonagricultural income of families. Nevertheless, we have found these data relevant in analyzing mortality in Nakahara. We use them here to divide all complete first marriages into above and below median holding families, which we hereafter call large and small holders.[24] Using twelve *koku* as the di-

---

23. *Kokudaka* expressed the productivity of a unit of land and was usually arrived at by averaging yields, estimated just before the harvest, over a period of years. Adjustments were often made to take account of differential costs, distance from market, and other factors that varied from one piece of land and one village to another. To assign a *kokudaka* to an individual field, it was necessary not only to estimate the yield per *tan* of land but also to measure the field. To estimate the yield and to survey for size all of the plots in a village, which often ran to several hundred, was an immensely difficult and politically sensitive job. It is not surprising, therefore, that assessments were not kept current.

Assessments in Tokugawa villages, it is known, tended to get out of date because of a combination of changes in productivity and infrequent and piecemeal reassessment. Also, assessments covered only land held in Nakahara, although families may have held land in neighboring villages. For these reasons assessments can be regarded as reflecting farm income, at best, only approximately; see Chapter 2.

24. First, for each family during its period of existence, we constructed a function of farming income in *kokudaka* over time, using straight-line interpolations between

viding line, the expectation of life at age 1 for large holders and small holders is 52.5 and 47.8 years, respectively, for females and 49.4 and 43.9 years, respectively, for males.

Completed family size was significantly different for the two groups. The families of the thirty-two small holders showed the following fertility pattern:

Wife's Age at Marriage	Mean MALB	Number of Children
20.5	36.1	4.5

Among the thirty-two families of large holders, the pattern was

Wife's Age at Marriage	Mean MALB	Number of Children
18.5	37.9	5.7

Large holders had an average of 5.7 children, small 4.5. This was partly because large holders' wives married two years younger on average than small holders' and ended childbearing 1.8 years older. Size of holding, however, did not affect the spacing of children; if we divide the mean number of children by the difference between mean *MALB* and mean wife's age at marriage, we get 0.29 children per year for both the large and the small holders. Thus, farm size affected family size by the age of marriage and the age of stopping, not by the spacing of children.

It is interesting that both large and small holders break down almost evenly into early and late stoppers and that size of holding and *MALB* together determine family size to a greater degree than either alone. This can be seen in Figure 4.4, where we divide completed families into four groups based on a combination of holding size and *MALB*. We have arranged the four groups down the page in descending order of average family size and have shown for each group the distribution of families by size. Notice that the order turns out to be alternately large and small holders. Each group has a strongly marked, modal family size that accounts for one-third to more than one-half of

---

registration dates and making horizontal interpolations forward and backward for the first and last dates, respectively. We then calculated for each completed first marriage the average annual income of the family over the time interval from the beginning of the marriage through the end of the wife's fecundity (age 45). Finally, we divided these marriages equally into landholding classes above and below the median.

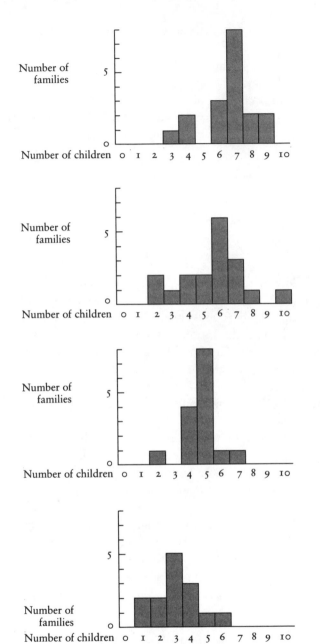

Fig. 4.4 Completed Family Size by Landholding and Mother's Age at Last Birth (Complete First Marriages)

SOURCE: *Nakahara mura shūmon oaratamechō*, Meiji Library, Tokyo.

the families, and the mode decreases neatly as we move down the page. Also, smallest family size and largest family size for the various groups decrease in the same order, although a bit less smoothly. These groups, defined by holding size and *MALB,* seem therefore to have distinct fertility characteristics.

Average family size is clearly related to holding size. Early-stopping large holders had larger families than early-stopping small holders; and late-stopping large holders had larger families than late-stopping small holders. This was probably because large holders wanted more children. They could better afford them and could use the additional labor more efficiently in farming. On the other hand, large holders' wives may have been more fertile than small holders' owing to better nutrition and shelter and less crowded quarters. In any case, holding size was not the only determinant of family size because late or early stopping, which was independent of holding size as already noted, was an equally or almost equally important factor. Its importance can be seen in the fact that late-stopping small holders had more children than early-stopping large holders, but whether accidentally or intentionally, we cannot guess.

SEX SELECTION AND FAMILY SIZE

One of the difficulties a family would have in achieving a preferred number of children was the concurrent desire for a particular sex mix and sequence of children. These objectives must have obstructed one another. Accepting or annulling births because of the sex of the infant would tend to defeat plans about completed family size, and vice versa. It is surprising, therefore, that a clear relation emerges between completed family size and the sex ratio of children. The larger the family, generally speaking, the more evenly balanced the sex of children; the smaller the family, the higher the proportion of boys. We must qualify this statement before exploring possible explanations.

Families of the smallest size used in testing the relationship—one to three children—had in fact an almost even number of boys and girls. But dividing this group into early and late stoppers reveals that early stoppers ($MALB \leq 37.0$) had nearly twice as many boys as girls:

Number of Families	Total Males	Total Females	Mean Birth Interval (Years)
10	15	8	3.8

while the few late stoppers ($MALB > 37.0$) had nearly all girls:

Number of Families	Total Males	Total Females	Mean Birth Interval (Years)
4	2	8	6.1

This difference may be due to sampling error, as the number in each group is small. But another explanation is also possible: since late stoppers with three children or fewer had long intervals between births, they may have tried repeatedly for males, failed to get them and after annulling a number of births, finally settled for females. If so, the early stoppers, who were much the more numerous group, would more accurately reflect the intentions of small families.

With the qualification then that a few small families ended up unintentionally with a high proportion of girls, the statement holds that the sex ratio of children was high in small completed families and converged to normal as family size increased. This relationship is apparent when we exclude late stoppers from families with one to three children:

Family Size	Total Males	Total Females	Males per 100 Females
1–3	15	8	188
4–5	56	43	130
6+	101	94	107

One naturally wonders to what extent the relation between family size and sex ratio was the outcome of different family strategies, and to what extent due to factors beyond anyone's control. It will be obvious to the wary reader that we cannot really hope to answer this question, but some observations relevant to an answer are possible.

Three partial explanations hinging on unintentional factors can probably be rejected. One turns on the wife's age at first marriage. Among complete first marriages, the earlier the age of marriage, the larger the mean completed family size tended to be:

Wife's Age at Marriage	Number of Families	Mean Family Size
18 or less	33	5.7
19–21	22	4.7
22+	9	3.8

Now *if* couples also tended first to have a certain number of males and then—in the event that they had more children—females, the earlier the marriage the larger the completed family would be and also the lower the sex ratio of the children. But this does not seem to have been the case. Eighty-six percent of all complete first marriages for women occurred before age 22, and the mean age of marriage for women with four–five and six or more children ever was nearly identical:

Number of Children	Number of Families	Wife's Age at Marriage	Mean MALB
1–3	14	22.9	33.4
4–5	22	18.7	36.0
6+	28	18.4	40.8

So age of marriage would seem to have no influence on family size *after* three children and, hence, none on the difference in sex ratio between families of four–five and six or more children.

Another possible explanation concerns the effects of mortality on completed family size. As large families had proportionately more deaths among children before the birth of the last child than small families had, the desire to replace deceased children conceivably prompted these families to continue procreation longer than they would have otherwise, and also to accept more female births.[25] However, when we examine the case more closely, it is by no means certain that large families really had a disproportionately high child mortality in terms of person-years of risk. Rather, they may have suffered more deaths before the birth of the last child merely because childbearing continued longer.

If we count the proportion of children born and dying before the mother's age 38, the figure in families of one to three children is 7 per-

---

25. For complete first marriages, the proportion of children who died before the birth of the last child is 17 percent in families of six or more children, 12 percent in families of four to five children, and 11 percent in families of one to three children.

cent, while it is 13 percent in families of four to five and 14 percent in families of six or more. Although there may be a real difference between very small families and the others, there is none among families with more than three children. Further, in computing mean family size, if we eliminate children who died before the last birth, we still find a significant difference among the groups (the figures in parentheses have been standardized to a base of 100):

Number of Children	Number of Families	Mean Family Size	Mean Family Size (Deceased Excluded)
1–3	14	2.4 (34)	2.2 (37)
4–5	22	4.5 (64)	4.1 (69)
6+	28	7.0 (100)	5.9 (100)

Thus, child replacement seems to account, at best, only marginally for differences in completed family size and sex ratio.

The third explanation has already been rejected in another context, namely, that even though small families practiced infanticide in favor of males, large families rarely resorted to infanticide and so ended inadvertently with approximately the same number of males as females. If we take complete first marriages with six or more children and divide the group according to the sex of the children registered at home, beginning when each family had only two children, the probability of the next child being female rises from 0.38 for PF families to 0.41 for $M = F$ and to 0.62 for PM:

Previous Siblings	Next Child Male	Next Child Female	Next Child (Males per 100 Females)
PM	22	36	61
M = F	19	13	146
PF	23	14	164

These results suggest that large families were intentionally large and intentionally sex-balanced.

THE RELATION BETWEEN FAMILY SIZE AND THE SEX OF CHILDREN

We can only speculate as to why family size and the sex of children were linked. Our guess is that all families wanted at minimum one or two male children on account of their value as labor and as male and replacement heirs. Small families were predominantly male, therefore, because they accepted male children, tended to eliminate females, and stopped procreation early. But few families wanted many more than the minimum number of males for fear of causing future competition for the family headship and creating problems about the division of property and the care of noninheriting sons. After the minimum number, therefore, female children were as desirable as males or more so, since they raised none of these problems and could perform tasks in the house and on the farm that were unsuitable for males. They were also valuable as a means of affiliation with other families, and they could inherit in the event of the failure of the male line or be used to recruit an adoptive heir by marriage. Consequently, the greater the number of children a family had, the higher the proportion of girls was likely to be. This is not meant to imply that large families first assured themselves of the minimum number of males, then added females at the higher birth orders. On the contrary, large families tended to keep the sexes in balance as they went along, which suggests an approximate notion of ultimate family size from the start.

SPACING CHILDREN

If we may cautiously conclude that infanticide sometimes enabled families to approximate the number and sex of the children that they wanted, we must then ask whether it was also of help in spacing children conveniently. For complete first marriages, let us look at the mean (registered) birth interval in years and fractions of years for intervals 0–1 (marriage to first child) to 4–5 and also for the penultimate and ultimate intervals:[26] (First birth intervals are not counted in penulti-

26. For most demographic events in Nakahara we have only the year of the event's occurrence; in computing birth intervals we have assumed that births were distributed evenly through the months of the year and occurred on average at midyear. This assumption can entail a maximum error of 0.5 year in dating a particular birth, but we can expect the error to be substantially reduced on average: for those births that can be dated by the month we found an average possible error of no more than one month by our assumption. A more serious source of error arises from our inability to account for "infant mortality," which would add to the length of the birth intervals. Thus, our birth

mate or last birth intervals; any interval for birth orders 2−5 that also happened to be the last birth of the mother is counted only in the tabulation for the last birth interval.)

Interval	Number of Intervals	Mean Interval	Standard Deviation (Year)
0−1	64	2.6	2.3
1−2	57	4.4	2.3
2−3	50	3.3	1.5
3−4	39	3.2	0.9
4−5	28	3.5	1.8
Penultimate	57	3.9	1.9
Last	62	4.2	2.4

If we keep in mind comparable data from European parishes, three features of these data stand out. First, the intervals tend to be very long; second, after the 1−2 interval they show no decided tendency to lengthen until the last interval; and third, the 1−2 interval is much longer than subsequent intervals, whereas in European parishes it seems invariably shorter.[27]

The length and uniformity of the Nakahara intervals (except the first two) would seem to result from a combination of "infant mortality" and infanticide for purposes of family limitation and sex selection, independently of considerations of spacing. This is suggested by the fact that, at almost every interval, the distribution ranges from short to extremely long with no pronounced mode. If families were

---

intervals are less accurate than and not strictly comparable with conventionally measured intervals for which exact dates of birth are available.

At first sight, the 0−1 interval looks suspiciously long compared with the European norm of about 1.5 years or less. However, 70 percent of the brides in complete first marriages married before age 20; 39 percent before age 18. As the following table shows, the mean first birth interval decreases as the age of marriage increases:

Age of Marriage	Number of Cases	Mean First-Birth Interval
16 or younger	15	3.4 years
17−19	30	2.6
20 or older	19	1.9

Thus, it seems probable that adolescent sterility, in conjunction with "infant mortality" and some infanticide, could well account for the length of the 0−1 birth interval.

27. For example, for complete marriages between 1740 and 1789 at Meulan, the mean second birth interval is 1.5 years, compared with 1.7 years for the third birth interval, 1.8 years for the fourth, and 2.1 years for the fifth. Lachiver, *Meulan*, 184.

spacing for convenience, their standards of convenience were too various to be perceptible.

But the 1−2 interval may be an exception. Its length is so idiosyncratic yet consistent, standing out clearly in every subset of families, that one suspects that there was some deliberate prolongation of this interval in some families. We speculate that the second child might differ from all others in a way affecting its timing as follows. The first child had to come as soon as possible after marriage to prove the fertility of the bride. Beginning with the third child, given average spacing, there would be one or more older children in the house to care for the new arrival. Thus, the first child would be age 7 at the birth of the third child and in many ways able to care for himself or herself and help with the baby. At later births the existing children would be still older and the mother's situation easier. But her situation might be difficult at the second birth, when with normal spacing the first child would be only 4.4, that is, unable to care for himself, let alone help with another child. Also at this time, the mother's responsibilities in the house might be greater because of the aging or decease of the husband's parents, and she might consequently be tempted to defer the second birth until the first child was somewhat older. The deferral would be less likely, however, if the husband's mother were still alive, an unmarried sister at home, or some other adult female in the house.

We therefore divided all complete first marriages into families in which another adult female was present at the time of the second birth and those in which there was none, excluding families in which the first child died or departed before the birth of the second. The mean 1−2 interval was significantly different ($p < 0.05$) between the two groups—3.5 and 5.1 years, respectively.[28] Only 18 percent of intervals in the first group were five years or more and only 5 percent were seven years or more, whereas the corresponding percentages for the second group were 47 percent and 28 percent. We suspect, therefore, some deliberate spacing for the convenience of the mother at the second

28. The number of families in these groups was twenty-two and thirty-two, respectively. A test of the difference in means yields a t statistic of 2.3, significant at the 0.05 level on 52 degrees of freedom.

birth, and possibly also at other births although for reasons that we are unable to discern.

The data on spacing bring us back to a point that we mentioned earlier: age-specific fertility in Nakahara shows a convex curve of the kind usually associated with unrestricted births, not the concave curve associated with birth control. The reasons for the shape of the curve in Nakahara, where births were limited by infanticide, would seem to be the following. First, infanticide gave rise to a pattern of births different from other forms of limitation. Because infanticide is sex-selective, the elimination of some children of unwanted sex at every birth order in the population created exceptionally long intervals between registered births. Second, the smaller the completed family, the more sex selection was likely to have taken place and, therefore, the longer the mean interval between births was likely to be:

Number of Children	Mean Birth Interval (Years)
1−3	4.4
4−5	3.8
6+	3.2

Third, Nakahara had fewer very small and childless families than populations limiting births generally have. The result of these three factors together was to spread childbearing over the fertile years of marriage, instead of concentrating it in the early years; hence, the major factor in the difference in fertility between one age group and another was declining fecundity with age and the increasing proportion of infertile women, which tends to give a convex curve.

If infanticide was practiced without sex selection, presumably it would not be used until families reached the desired size; then it would be vigorously enforced. This would make the average birth interval relatively short and give fertility a concave curve. But it seems most unlikely that any population would accept infanticide as a normal means of family limitation and yet ignore its use to control the sex composition of sibling sets.

Infanticide, common in the past in both East and West, has been seen by historians mainly as a product of social demoralization and the struggle of parents to keep themselves and favored progeny alive.[29] This interpretation may be justified generally, although it is obviously a view based mainly on literary and legal evidence with a strong moral and class bias. But it fits the Nakahara case badly. Infanticide seems to have been widely practiced there by the most respectable and stable part of the population: married couples who, at a time when divorce and early death were common, lived together through the wives' fecund years, a term completed by no more than 59 percent of first-married couples. Also, infanticide seems to have been practiced by large holders as well as small—although somewhat less frequently— and by all holders as often in good as in bad growing years. At any rate, we find no difference in registered births per thousand of population in years when rice was dear and years when it was cheap, even though the marriage rate differs significantly for these groups of years:[30]

Price Years	Births per 1,000 Person-Years	Marriages per 1,000 Person-Years
Upper third	29.1	33.7
Middle third	26.7	46.7
Lower third	27.4	60.1

Among the apparent objectives of infanticide in Nakahara were overall family limitation; an equilibrium of some sort between family size and farm size; an advantageous distribution of the sexes in children and possibly, also, the spacing of children in a way convenient to the mother; and the avoidance of an unlucky sex in the next child. These goals required foresight and the ability to carry out long-range

29. William L. Langer, "Infanticide: A Historical Survey," *History of Childhood Quarterly* 1, no. 3 (1974): 353–65; Barbara A. Kellum, "Infanticide in England in the Later Middle Ages," ibid., 367–88; Hélène Bergues et al., *La prévention des naissances dans la famille* (Paris, 1960), chap. 6. For Japan, Takahashi, *Nihon jinkō*, and Sekiyama, *Kinsei Nihon no jinkō kōzō*.

30. Prices are spring and fall rice prices for the Mitsui main store in Kyoto, over a hundred kilometers away. Mitsui Bunkō, ed., *Kinsei kōki ni okeru shuyō bukka no dōtai* (Tokyo, 1952), 67–79. Prices and demographic events were not matched by chronological years but were offset to take account of the normal lag between demographic occurrence and its recording, as well as the six-month overlap between registration year and calendar year.

The population base for marriages was taken to be unmarried adults aged fifteen to forty-five.

plans, qualities not usually associated with demoralized or desperate people. What proportion of families used the practice of infanticide to seek some or all of these goals, which tended to overlap, we cannot say. Given the degree of agreement in subgroups on completed family size, the percentage may have been substantial. Most important, we do not know how common in Tokugawa society this pattern of infanticide was. It cannot be emphasized too strongly that Nakahara was a village with a population that never exceeded three hundred, one of thousands of that size, and possibly highly deviant. No general significance can be attributed to our findings until, in some respects at least, they have been duplicated elsewhere.

At a time when the design of spades and mattocks differed from one village to the next, it would be folly to expect in villages practicing infanticide that the patterns of family limitation and sex selection would be closely similar everywhere. It does not seem improbable, for example, that there were villages that discriminated overall against males in about the same degree that Nakahara discriminated overall against females. Nor is it unlikely that the sex bias changed from one period to another in the same village, or that different strata in the same village discriminated against different sexes or against the same sex to a significantly different degree. It will be important in looking for patterns, therefore, to disaggregate data as much as possible to prevent contrary tendencies from canceling one another to give an overall appearance of normality.

And if such differences may be reasonably expected within and between villages, we should not expect continuity from one region, historical background, ecology, or economic structure to others. If variety on the basis of these variables was as great as we believe, it will take a great amount of ingenuity and patience to uncover the prevalence of infanticide, and at every stage efforts will be hampered by the small size of villages. But if in time systematic differences do appear, we may begin to be able to identify various kinds of reproductive behavior and their social correlates in preindustrial Japan.

5

JAPAN'S ARISTOCRATIC
REVOLUTION

"An aristocracy," Alexis de Tocqueville wrote, "seldom yields [its privileges] without a protracted struggle, in the course of which implacable animosities are kindled between the different classes of society." Despite our democratic partialities, most of us would add, "And why should it?" To know the exalted pleasures of power and the grace of refined taste with the means of satisfying it; to believe oneself superior on the only evidence that gives conviction—the behavior of others; and to enjoy all this as birthright, with no vitiating struggle, nor any doubt that one's privileges are for God, king, country, and the good of

Given as the Hume Lecture at Yale University in 1960; reprinted from the *Yale Review* 50, no. 3 (Spring 1961).

one's fellowman—what happier human condition, for a few, have men devised?

Yet not all aristocracies have behaved as one fancies they must. Japan's warrior class, a feudal aristocracy even though it differed from European aristocracies in crucial respects, did not merely surrender its privileges. It abolished them. There was no democratic revolution in Japan because none was necessary: the aristocracy itself was revolutionary.

Consider the bare outlines of the case. Until 1868 Japan was ruled by a class of samurai who alone had the right to hold public office and bear arms and whose cultural superiority the rest of the population acknowledged. A party within this aristocracy of the sword (and swagger) took power in 1868 and embarked on a series of extraordinary reforms. Where there had before been little more than a league of great nobles, they created an immensely powerful central government: they abolished all estate distinctions, doing away with warrior privileges and throwing office open to anyone with the education and ability to hold it; they instituted a system of compulsory military service although commoners had previously been forbidden on pain of death to possess arms; they established a system of universal public education; and much else. The result was a generation of sweeping and breathless change such as history had rarely seen until this century. I believe, although of course I cannot prove, that these decades brought greater changes to Japan than the Great Revolution of 1789 brought to France.

Why was the Japanese aristocracy—or part of it—revolutionary? Why did it abandon the shelter of its historic privileges for the rigors of free competition, which many warriors did not survive? Its behavior, like that of a man who takes cold baths in the morning, requires a special explanation.

Two general lines of explanation have been offered; although no bald summary can do them justice, even on fuller account they leave much unexplained.

One might be called the prescient patriot theory. That is, the foreign crisis—to be quite specific, the unamiable Commodore Perry and the Americans, English, and Russians who followed him—stimulated the patriotism of the warriors and demonstrated to them the inadequacy of existing institutions, prompting them to make revolutionary innovations in the name of national salvation. This I believe is quite true in a way. But it takes for granted what most needs explaining. Communities in danger do not necessarily seek safety in innovation; commonly they reaffirm tradition and cling to it more resolutely. This was the first response to the challenge of the modern West in China and Korea; it also had intelligent and patriotic spokesmen in Japan.

The other explanation may be called the Western analogue theory. It emphasizes (in the century before Perry's arrival) the improvement of transport, the growth of towns, the development of trade, and the rise of a wealthy merchant class—all important developments that add much to our knowledge of premodern Japan. But suggestive as they are, these developments would better explain—keeping the Western analogy in mind—an aristocracy being overthrown or reluctantly forced to share power with a rising new class than an aristocracy conducting a social revolution.

Differences, rather than similarities, would seem more to the point. The man who takes cold baths is made of different stuff from most of us, and the Japanese warrior differed from the European aristocrat in ways that throw light on his seemingly odd class behavior. I wish to discuss three such ways that any satisfactory explanation of the aristocratic revolution, as I will call it, would have to take into account. One has to do with the relations of the warrior to the merchant class, another with social and economic distinctions within the warrior class, and the third with the relations of the warrior class to land and political power.

My earlier statement that there was no democratic revolution in Japan because the aristocracy was revolutionary has an important corollary: had there been a democratic revolution, the aristocracy would not have been revolutionary. Nothing unites an aristocracy so quickly and firmly in defense of its privileges as an attack from below by classes in which it can perceive neither distinction nor virtue.

Unlike the Western bourgeoisie, townsmen in Japan never challenged aristocratic privileges, either in practice or theory. They were seemingly content with a secondary political role, finding apparent satisfaction in moneymaking, family life, and the delights of a racy and exuberant city culture. This political passivity is puzzling. It is not to be explained by numerical weakness (Tokyo was a city of a million people in the late eighteenth century, and Osaka was almost half that size) or by poverty or illiteracy or political innocence. Least of all is it to be understood as reflecting an absence of resentment at the warriors' smug and strutting pretensions. There was resentment aplenty and there were many instances of private revenge; but for some reason resentment never reached the pitch of ideology, never raised petty private hurts to a great principle of struggle between right and wrong. For whatever reasons, townsmen acknowledged the political primacy of the warrior, leaving him free to experiment without the fear that to change anything would endanger everything.

But, one may suppose, no ruling group ever launches on a career of radical reform merely because it is free to do so; there must be positive incentives as well. In the Japanese case these incentives were in part born of differences within the aristocracy. Such differences were not unique to Japan, of course, but they can rarely have been more pronounced.

On the one hand were a few thousand families of superior lineage and very large income, with imposing retinues and magnificent houses, who in practice, although not in law, monopolized the important offices of government; some offices in effect became hereditary. On the other hand was the bulk of the warrior class, numbering several hundred thousand families who were cut off from high office and lived on very modest incomes; many lived in real poverty, pawning their armor and family heirlooms, doing industrial piecework at home to eke out small stipends, and resorting to such pitiful tricks as sewing strips of white cloth to the undersides of their collars so people might take them to be wearing undergarments. As warrior mothers proudly taught their children, a samurai might have an empty belly but he used a toothpick all the same.

But it was not so much the contrast between his own and the style of life of his superior that moved the ordinary warrior to fury. It was the impropriety, rather, of the merchant's wealth. Surely it was a perversion of social justice that the warrior, who gave his life to public service, should live in want and squalor while men who devoted themselves to moneymaking lived in ease and elegance, treated him with condescension and even rudeness, and in the end not infrequently found favor with the lord.

The merchant himself was not to blame since he merely followed his nature. He was feared and hated for his actions, but ultimate responsibility lay with the effeminate high aristocrats who, because of idleness or incompetence, failed to use their inherited power for the proper ends of government. No secret was made of the failure, either. Political writings were full of charges of the incompetence and corruption of government, of the fecklessness and indifference of princes; and the only remedy, it was said, lay in giving power to new men—men of lower rank, who were close to the people and whose characters had been formed by hardship. This was no revolutionary doctrine: it called for a change of men, not institutions. But the men it helped to power were in fact radical innovators.

This brings me to the final difference—or rather to two differences—between the Japanese warrior class and the European aristocracy. Japanese warriors did not own land, and their political power was to a greater extent bureaucratic. I want to say more on these points, but first it will be helpful to see how a once-feudal aristocracy had come to be without private economic or political power.

We must go back to the late sixteenth century. At that time warriors were scattered over the land in villages where they were overlords, levying taxes, administering justice, and keeping the peace. To defend their territories and lessen the hazards of life, they had long since banded together into regional military organizations consisting of a lord and his vassals. The normal state among such groups was war or preparation for war, the most direct means of increasing territory and thereby increasing strength and security.

Then, about the turn of the century, Tokugawa Ieyasu (1542–1616), a man of authentic genius who had the remarkably good fortune of having two brilliant predecessors who had already half done what he intended, succeeded in conquering the country. Instead of destroying the feudal leagues or groups, however, he chose to use them to govern, taking care only to establish his own firm control over them. Seemingly a compromise between order and chaos, the resulting political structure kept the peace for two and a half centuries.

These long years of orderly government, which favored economic growth and urban development, brought profound changes to the warrior class, altering not so much, however, the fact of warrior power (which remained uncontested) as the nature of it. I would like to mention three such changes in particular.

The first was a change in the relation of warriors to the land. The lord, in order better to control his vassals and to achieve greater uniformity of administration within the territory he dominated, gradually restricted his vassals' power over their domains. He forbade them to administer local justice; he moved them from the land into the town that had grown up around his castle; he decreed what taxes they might collect and at what rates, then decided to collect the taxes himself and in return to pay them stipends in money or kind from his treasury.

There were local exceptions to the rule, but taking the country as a whole, fiefs in land disappeared. Land and the seignorial rights associated with it, once widely dispersed through the warrior class, were now consolidated in the hands of a few hundred noble families. The typical warrior had become a townsman living on a salary paid him by the lord, with the townsman's disdain for the country and country people. Both his juridical and social ties with the land were gone. If his fief was still an identifiable piece of land at all, it was rarely more than a unit of account, with other land, under the lord's administration.

The second was the resulting bureaucratization of government. The lord, having taken into his hands his vassals' political and judicial functions, now governed an average population of about one hundred thousand. To police so large a population, to collect its taxes and regulate its trade, to give it justice and maintain its roads and irrigation works, required a considerable band of officials and clerks. The lord, of course, used his vassals to perform these functions, to man the expanding and differentiating bureaucracy under him. The warriors who manned the bureaucracy exercised far more power over the rest of the population than warriors ever had before, but it was a new kind of power. Formerly power was personal and territorial: it pertained to a piece of land and belonged to a man as inherited right. Now it was impersonal and bureaucratic: it pertained to a specialized office to which the incumbent had to be appointed and from which he might be removed.

There is unmistakable evidence of the increasingly bureaucratic nature of power in the more and more impersonal criteria for selecting officials. However writers on government might differ on other matters, by the late eighteenth century they were in agreement that ability and specialized knowledge should take precedence over lineage and family rank in the appointment and promotion of officials. To this end they devised tests for office, job descriptions, fitness reports, official allowances, salary schedules, and pensions.

It was only in the lower ranks of officials that the ideal of impersonality came close to realization. Nevertheless, men of low rank were sometimes promoted to high office; merchants and occasionally even peasants with specialized qualifications were ennobled that they might hold office; and promotion in the bureaucracy became for warriors an important means of improving status. If the highest offices usually went to certain well-placed families, this was looked on as an abuse rather than a proper recognition of rank, and an abuse that struck at the very foundations of good government. Moreover, many families of high rank were without office, and office rather than rank or wealth gave power.

Thus a group of young samurai who met just after Perry's first alarming visit to Japan, to consider what they might do for their country, were exhorted by their leader to do what they could *even though none held office*. One cried out, "But what *can* we do without office!" No one, it seems, complained of the lack of age, wealth, or high rank in the group.

The third change I would like to mention followed very largely from the second. The relationship between vassal and lord was slowly, silently, and profoundly transformed. It had been an intimate, intensely emotional relationship, based in no small part on the personal qualities of the lord, a relationship that existed between men who had fought side by side and grieved together at the loss of comrades, whose safety and families' safety depended on their keeping faith. During the centuries of peace and urban living, however, the relationship lost much of its emotional significance. It became distant and formal; it was hedged by ceremonies and taboos; the vassal came to look on his lord less as a leader in war (for there was no war) than as an administrative head.

One sees this change in the changing concept of the ideal warrior. Once a strong, stouthearted fellow, quick and warm in his sympathies, generous to the weak, unyielding to the strong, he becomes a man whose native intelligence has been disciplined in the classroom, who gets on harmoniously with his colleagues, who deals with matters within his jurisdiction without fear or favor. Loyalty is still the highest virtue for him; but where once it had meant willingness to follow the lord to death, now it meant disinterested advice to the lord and personal conduct reflecting credit on the lord's administration. Qualities of the ideal bureaucrat had come to be viewed as the very essence of the warrior.

Moreover, the power of the lord as administrative head increasingly became merely symbolic; actual power passed to lower echelons of officials. Partly this transferral resulted from the growing complexity of government, but in greater measure it occurred because the lord's position was hereditary and as time passed fewer and fewer of his breed were men of force and intelligence, fit for the top job. Vassals who still looked on the lord with awe were likely to be men who regarded him from a distance; despite all outward deference, those who saw him closer could often scarcely conceal their contempt.

Indeed some hardly tried. An anonymous author, writing about 1860, calls the lords of his day timeservers. Brought up by women deep in the interior of palaces where no sound of the outside world penetrated, surrounded from childhood by luxury, and indulged in every whim, they were physically weak and innocent of both learning and practical experience. But it was not revolution that was called for, only better education for rulers, that they might choose better officials. "The secret of good government," the writer confidently declared, "lies in each official discharging his particular office properly, which in turn depends on choosing the right man for the right job."

To summarize up to this point: the two and a half centuries of peace after 1600 brought great changes to the warrior class. They brought a change in the warrior's relationship to the land, which became purely administrative; in his relationship to political power, which became bureaucratic; and in his relationship to his lord, which became distant and impersonal.

I should like now to show, as concretely as I can, the connection between these changes and some aspects of the economic and social transformation of the country after 1868—my so-called aristocratic revolution.

Consider the creation in the years immediately after 1868 of a highly centralized government. This was a brilliant achievement, which permitted the new leaders who came to power to formulate for the first time a national purpose and to call up energies that did not before exist. Political power had lain scattered in fragments over the map, each lord collecting his own taxes, maintaining his own army and navy, even following an independent foreign policy. Then with astonishing speed the fragments were pulled together, a central government created, the entire country subjected to a single will. Feudal lords and their miniature kingdoms were swept away and one bureaucratic empire emerged in their place.

This change was possible in part because warriors had long since been removed from the land and stripped of seignorial rights. Had these interests remained, the warrior must first have been dispossessed of them—the base of his power and source of his pride. Whoever might eventually have succeded in this feat would not likely himself have been a warrior, nor would he have accomplished it without a long and bitter struggle. As it was, only the great lords had to be deprived of power, and the deed was sooner done because power had come to be exercised by officials who saw the possibility of trading them for similar powers within a vastly larger organization.

But what of the vaunted loyalty of the samurai? One would think this must have prevented the liquidation of the great territorial lords by their own vassals. The unconditional loyalty to the lord as war leader, however, had shrunk to the conditional loyalty of the administrative subordinate to his chief—a loyalty valid only so long as the chief performed his duties efficiently. That the great lords had long ceased to was known to all. Meanwhile a new and higher loyalty emerged sanctioning the transfer of all power to a central government: loyalty to the emperor, in whose name the aristocratic revolution was carried out. Nor was the emergence of this new loyalty unconnected with the decline of the older one. One suspects that men brought up in the cult of loyalty to the lord, as an absolute obligation and the noblest of human ideals, needed some escape from the disloyalty they felt in their hearts.

Second, consider how the new central government used its power to liquidate the four estates of which society was legally composed. Each estate—warrior, peasant, artisan, and merchant—was theoreti-

cally closed; it was subject to detailed restrictions concerning occupation, residence, food, and dress peculiar to itself. The new government
swept away such restrictions and endowed men with extensive civic,
although not political, rights. Henceforth anything that was legally
permissible or obligatory for one was permissible or obligatory for all;
moreover, a system of free public schools very soon gave this new, legal
dispensation concrete social meaning. The warrior lost his privileges
and immunities and was forced to compete in school and out with the
sons of tradesmen and peasants. Even his economic privileges were
done away with. Warrior stipends were commuted into national bonds
redeemable in twenty years; at the end of that time warriors, as such,
had no claim on the national income.

Now how is one to explain a ruling class thus liquidating its privileges and not by a series of forced retreats but at nearly a single willing
stroke? Surely part of the answer lies in warrior privileges' not being
bound up with the ownership of land. To restrict or even abolish them,
therefore, did not arouse fears for the safety of property or stir those
complicated emotions that seem to attach peculiarly to land as a symbol of family continuity and an assurance of the continuing deference
of neighbors. Few ruling classes have ever been so free of economic
bias against change. Warrior power was based almost exclusively on
officeholding, and this monopoly was not immediately in danger because no other class had yet the experience, education, and confidence
to displace warriors in administration. The striking down of barriers
between estates, on the other hand, opened up to warriors occupational opportunities formerly denied them, a not insignificant gain in
view of the large number of warriors who, with more than normal
pride but neither property nor important office, were nearly indigent.

This brings me to a third aspect of the revolutionary transformation of Japanese society after 1868: the explosion of individual energies that followed the sudden abolition of status distinctions. Before,
opportunity was very limited: men looked forward to following the
occupations of their fathers and living out their lives in the same villages and towns and houses. Afterward, everything seemed suddenly
changed, and young men strove with leaping hope and fearful determination to improve their characters, to rise in the world, to become
something different from their fathers.

For warriors the abolition of status restrictions meant finding new occupations and new roles in society. Few had enough property after the commutation of stipends to live without work, and not all could continue in the traditional occupations of soldier, official, policeman, and teacher. A very large number were forced either to suffer social eclipse or to become merchants, industrialists, lawyers, engineers, scientists; or they saw in these occupations exciting new opportunities for wealth and fame.

In any case there was a grand redirection of warrior talent and ambition. Despite the traditional warrior aversion to moneymaking and the merchant's love of it, many of the first generation of modern entrepreneurs, above all the earliest and most daring, came from the warrior class. Nor is this to be explained merely by the occupational displacement of the warrior. Part of the explanation lies in the warrior's aristocratic background—his educational preferment under the old regime, his cult of action, and (at his best) his intense social idealism.

Okano Kitarō, a man born in a warrior family of low rank, who founded an important provincial bank, illustrates the point. He writes in his autobiography: "I lost my wife and third daughter in the earthquake of 1923. They were on their way to a resort hotel when the great quake struck, and their train plunged into the sea. When news of the accident reached me my courage failed, but after a while my sense of responsibility returned and I thought to myself, 'You are head of the Suruga Bank! You must discharge your duty as a banker in this time of trouble! Compared to that, your personal loss is a trifling matter!' My whole body trembled."

Other classes were scarcely less affected than warriors. Finding themselves suddenly free to become whatever wishes, effort, and ability could make them, with not even the highest positions in society closed to competition, they responded with a heroic effort at self-transcendence. Freedom of this kind must always be heady; but one wonders if it is not especially so when it comes suddenly in societies with a strong sense of status differences, where the social rewards of success are more finely graded and seem sweeter than in societies less schooled to such distinctions.

In a charming little anecdote in his autobiography, Itō Chūbei, the son of a peasant who became a leading industrialist, gives some hint of the poignancy of the hopes for success he shared with other peasant boys of his generation. Upon graduating from middle school not long after 1868, the first boy in his village to do so, Itō called on the headmaster to take leave. He was not surprised to meet with an angry scolding, since he had been far from the model boy. After the master finished his scolding, however, he spoke glowingly of Itō's future and predicted that, despite his rebelliousness, he would be a success. "You will make your mark in the world, I know it!" he exclaimed. And at this the young boy, unable to hold back his tears, wept aloud. Years later, in recounting this incident to a reunion of his classmates, Itō was so affected that he wept again, and his gratitude to his former teacher was no less when, after the meeting, he discovered that all of his classmates had been sent off with exactly the same prediction.

Such hopes were real because, although not everyone was equal in the competition for wealth and honor, the privileged estate under the old regime had no prohibitive or enduring advantage. In respect to income, for example, warriors were at no advantage over much of the rest of the population, and even though they were the most literate class in society, literacy was very widespread among other classes as well and it rapidly became more so through the new schools. But most important, perhaps, warriors could not for long claim a cultural superiority, compounded of superior education, elegance, and taste, to act as a bar to the achievement of others or to prevent others from the achievement of aristocratic culture. Indeed by the twentieth century one can scarcely speak of an aristocratic culture in Japan, despite the peerage created by the government in 1885. Whether a young man came from a warrior family could no longer be reliably told from his speech, manners, or social ideas; moreover, his origins were far less important to his self-esteem and the good opinion of others than whether he had a university diploma and where he was employed. I want to return to this point.

In hope of making its revolutionary behavior less puzzling, I have discussed three ways the Japanese warrior class differed from Western aristocracies—its relation to other classes, its internal divisions, and its relation to economic and political power. I should like now to suggest, very briefly, some of the ways in which Japanese society seems to be different because its modern revolution was aristocratic rather than democratic.

First, an obvious point: the aristocratic revolution, despite the civic equality and economic progress it brought, did not create a strong democratic political tradition.

Second, perhaps more than any other single factor, that revolution helps explain Japan's rapid transition from an agrarian to an industrial society. How different the story would have been had the warriors behaved as one would expect of an aristocracy, if they had used their monopoly of political and military power to defend rather than change the existing order.

Third, as there was no aristocratic defense of the old regime, there was no struggle over its survival, no class or party war in which the skirmish line was drawn between new and old, revolutionaries and conservatives. There was, of course, tension between traditional and modern, Japanese and Western, but not a radical cleavage of the two by ideology. All parties were more or less reformist, more or less traditional, and more or less modern; excepting perhaps the Communists, whose numbers were insignificant, no prewar party thought of the past as a barrier to progress. It was a barrier in some respects, in others an aid. Modernization therefore appeared to most Japanese who thought about it at all, not as a process in which a life-or-death confrontation of traditional and modern took place but as a dynamic blending of the two. I wonder if this does not account in large part for what has seemed to many people the uncommon strength of tradition in the midst of change in modern Japan.

Fourth, status-consciousness is relatively strong in Japan in part because there was no revolutionary struggle against inequality, but for that reason class-consciousness is relatively weak. These attitudes are by no means contradictory. The nervous concern of Japanese for status is quite consonant with their relatively weak feeling about classes— higher-ups to some extent being looked on as superior extensions of the self. This attitude is familiar to us elsewhere. It is illustrated in Jane Austen by the servant who fairly bursts with pride when his master is made a baronet and in Fielding's story of Nell Gwynn. Stepping one day from a house where she had made a short visit, the famous actress saw a great mob assembled and her footman all bloody and dirty. The fellow, being asked by his mistress what happened, answered, "I have been fighting, madam, with an impudent rascal who called your ladyship a whore." "You blockhead," replied Mrs. Gwynn, "at this rate you must fight every day of your life; why, you fool, all the world knows it." "Do they?" the fellow said in a muttering voice; "They shan't call me a whore's footman for all that."

Finally—and this brings me back to an earlier point about the absence of an aristocratic culture in modern Japan—since warriors were never thrown on the defensive by the hostility of other classes, they never felt the need to make a cult of their peculiar style of life, either as evidence of virtues justifying their privileges or as compensation for the loss of them. One wonders if Western aristocracies did not put exceptional value on leisure, gambling, dueling, and lovemaking as aspects of the aristocratic way of life in good part because they were a dramatic repudiation of bourgeois values.

In any case the warrior did not have the means of supporting a leisurely and aesthetic style of life. The revolution found him separated from the land, living on a government salary rather than on income from property; he therefore carried no capital inheritance from his privileged past into the modern age. He had no country estates, no rich town properties, no consols to spare him unbecoming compromises with the crass new world of business. On the contrary, warriors were the chief makers of this world and they scrambled for success in it to escape social and economic oblivion.

Then, too, this new world was irrevocably bound up with Western culture, from which came (with whatever modifications) much of its technology and many of its conventions. Success in it had very little to do with traditional skills and tastes and much to do with double-entry bookkeeping, commercial law, English conversation, German music, French painting, and Scotch whisky. Traditional arts were not forgotten, but they were never identified with a particular social class, least of all perhaps the upper class. It is significant, for example, that the prewar Peer's Club in Tokyo, located within easy walking distance of the Foreign Office and the Ministry of Finance, was a great ugly stone building with marble stairways, thick carpets, a mahogany bar, wall-

paper, glass chandeliers, and French cuisine. In respect to
all classes of Japanese, during the first generation or two
were born cultural equals. One could not learn of these thi
any more than one could learn there a foreign language or the cal-
culus. Such subjects were taught only in the schools, and the schools
were open to everyone.

6

THE DISCONTENTED

One may consider Albert M. Craig's *Chōshū in the Meiji Restoration*[1] and Marius B. Jansen's *Sakamoto Ryōma and the Meiji Restoration*[2] in a number of ways—first, although not primarily, as superb pieces of demystification.

Each follows in detail the main figures of a single great *han* through factional struggles and fluctuating fortunes on the national scene from about 1850 to 1868, a period of crisis and conspiracy. This is a very considerable feat. These years encompass a nether world of shadowy figures that flit about changing their names, appearing and disappear-

Reprinted from the *Journal of Asian Studies* 22, no. 1 (February 1962).
1. Cambridge, Mass., 1961.
2. Princeton, 1961.

ing mysteriously, meeting furtively and passing cryptic messages. To have these shades brought to the light of day, their identities and relations established, their messages deciphered, and their comings and goings charted so one knows who was where when someone else was in Fushimi, is to be given much needed reassurance that the political history of this time is, after all, intelligible.

Or one may consider each book as a series of stimulating essays and opinions on important topics in late Tokugawa history. These asides in fact overshadow the narratives in interest; among them are biographical sketches, notes on institutions, detail on social and economic conditions—much of it new and all full of interest. Jansen, for example, describes the *shishi*, a figure who looms large in Restoration history, as a distinct personality type: a wenching, impulsive, devil-may-care fellow in whose heroic view of life a single brave and sincere man could change the course of history. The reader immediately recognizes the *shishi* as an authentic figure whom he has often seen without knowing, late as well as early in Japan's past, sometimes in most unlikely dress.

Craig suggests that during the Tokugawa period samurai loyalty to the daimyo became at once more intense and more impersonal. This highly emotional but "free-floating" quality, he believes, made the transfer of loyalty from the daimyo to the emperor relatively easy, and potent besides. I can add a footnote on impersonalization that supports this suggestion: Tokugawa Yoshimune (1684–1751), writing in 1714 as lord of the Kishū domain, lamented the tendency of officials to ignore administrative precedent; henceforth, he stated, they should consult the office diaries kept by predecessors and conduct all business accordingly, calling this strict observance of precedent the "highest loyalty" (*chūgi daiichi*)—a clerk's conception that would have made the Forty-seven Rōnin turn in their graves.[3] But one wonders about loyalty to the lord becoming, at the same time, more intense. How is this to be reconciled with references in political writings to the alienation of warriors from their lords, with the cruel parodies of these unheroic men, and with charges of their incompetence or crimes? Is it not

---

3. *Kishū seijigusa*, in *Nanki Tokugawashi*, ed. Horiuchi Shin (Wakayama, 1930), 1:595.

possible that the intensity Craig rightly senses sprang, in fact, from longing for a more satisfying loyalty than to these institutionalized incompetents—the notion, although not the phrase, was contemporary.

As the titles suggest these books are mainly to be considered as interpretations of the Restoration from the vantage point of different *han*. Despite the difference in vantage point, the authors' views on the Restoration are broadly similar. Both hold that it was in no significant sense the outcome of a social struggle, either between classes or within the warrior class; both refute in particular the view, popular in some academic and journalistic circles in Japan, that members of the ruling class succeeded in turning the "revolutionary energy" of the peasants to their own ends—"distorting" what would otherwise have been a genuine class revolution with, presumably, an altogether happier outcome. Craig and Jansen are surely right: the Restoration was not a product of class struggle, although its social consequences were revolutionary.

But this is not to say that class inequalities and restraints were not important conditions of thought and action; they were—although the discontents born of them united the aggrieved across class lines more often than along them. Jansen tells us that village headmen and *gōshi* (low-ranking warriors who lived in the country), whose dissatisfactions he describes in some detail, were extremely important in the Tosa loyalist movement; that both were to be found "in generous proportion" in the Restoration armies of Tosa in 1867; and that these two groups were among the chief beneficiaries when warrior ranks were reorganized in Tosa in 1869. One is unprepared, therefore, for his negative conclusion on their significance in the Restoration: "After a promising beginning, they lost all influence in late Tokugawa Tosa."

Craig holds that "peasant participation in the *shotai* (militia) and peasant [financial] aid were crucial to the victory of the loyalists" in the Chōshū civil war, a key victory on the way to the Restoration, but he emphasizes that "such aid was largely obtained under duress." He argues mainly on the grounds that aid came from areas under *shotai* control; but may it not equally have been that only in such areas did the local population feel relatively secure against government reprisals? In any case coercion would not explain the large number of peasant recruits to the *shotai*, amounting to half the strength of some units, or why these units fought so spiritedly. Peasant recruits seem to have been motivated by a desire to improve their status by affiliation with warriors and by treatment in the *shotai* in some respects as warriors. As Craig points out, this does not suggest a class struggle; it does, however, suggest a struggle, not without political significance, to overcome the disadvantages of class in other ways. As the examples just cited show, Craig and Jansen present evidence admitting of conclusions somewhat different from their own.

To the question of what brought about the Restoration the authors give somewhat different, although not contradictory, answers. Jansen feels that in Tosa, where the Restoration was mainly the work of individuals and the *han* was largely passive, the chief factor was the overriding concern of men like Sakamoto Ryōma (1835–67) and Nakaoka Shintarō (1838–67) for the future of the nation. Craig is less concerned with individual motivation than with what brought Chōshū as a *han* first to oppose and finally, with Satsuma, to destroy the Tokugawa. His answer is admirably clear and direct: "Dissatisfactions . . . were not the sole, or even the chief, internal factor determining the course of the Restoration. On the contrary . . . the Restoration stemmed more from the strength of the values and institutions of the old society than from their weaknesses." These strengths in Chōshū were the size of the *han,* its long-standing enmity to the Bakufu, its special relation to the court, the relative well-being and high morale of Chōshū samurai, and the political flexibility of its vigorous bureaucratic cliques.

These are important points, and in arguing them Craig by implication makes a larger point that is also implicit in Jansen's book—the positive role of tradition in making modern Japan. This role is too often lost by dividing the universe into perpetually warring traditional and modern worlds. The two books suggest how superficial and misleading such a division is. Japanese modernization was and is—it seems to me—the result of a dynamic fusion of traditional and modern elements; far from being a drag on progress, mere "feudal remnants" destined in time to disappear, the traditional elements are part of the dynamic, a vital, evolving, and inseparable part of modern society itself.

Having said this, however, one must add that the dynamic aspects of tradition, taken by themselves, may be able to explain the Restoration but not the revolution that followed. Craig is quite aware of this limitation. "Yet, it is not enough," he says, "to say that Chōshū emerged preëminent because of its embodiment in the strongest form of the positive values of Tokugawa society. Having triumphed in the Bakumatsu struggles, Chōshū-Satsuma did not go on to build another Bakufu. Instead, intent on preserving or recreating the virtues of their old society, they ended by destroying it. Why? My answer is threefold."

None of the three points that follow has to do either with the weakening of the old society or the appearance in it of what might be called modern traits—for example, urban growth, the development of commercial farming, or the increasing culture, wealth, and prestige of the merchant class. The first point, the tendency of feudalism "in every known example" to greater and greater political centralization, might be taken as a strength of traditional society since the author believes, with Joseph R. Strayer and Rushton Coulborn, that "the better feudalism works, the more rapidly it generates a political structure which is not completely feudal."[4] The other two points have to do with external influences: the adoption of modern weapons, which hastened political centralization, and "the image of the West as a militarily superior power." Here we come to the nub of the matter: "It is the latter challenge that led them [Japanese leaders] to carry out the Meiji revolution."

Japanese leaders were indeed eager to make the nation the military equal of Western nations; so were the Chinese, who were no less patriotic and possibly no less quick in recognizing Western military superiority. In the one case concern for the nation seemingly led to a revolution that had at its heart the overthrow of a class system based on differential rights and obligations; in the other it did not. One reason for the difference is that the community, the object of concern in both cases, was not identified in Japanese thought and feeling to the same extent as in China with the traditional social order and its peculiar morality. Patriotic feeling—nationalism, if you will—did not, therefore, require a defense of the traditional social system in order to preserve the community's identity and its unique moral strength.

The desire to make Japan strong was thus less important, perhaps,

4. In *Feudalism in History,* ed. Rushton Coulborn (Princeton, 1956), 9.

than the conviction that the traditional social order was not itself a source of strength. Whence came this conviction? The answer in part is simple: the new leaders, and a great many other Japanese as well, were profoundly dissatisfied with the traditional social order and already groping for a legitimate alternative. They found it in the mobile yet stratified societies of the powerful West. These discontented were not limited to a single class but existed in every broad social stratum. On the whole, they were not the oppressed and exploited but the able and ascendant, capable of forming a new ruling class; they felt unjustly cut off from positions of power and respect. Although they believed emphatically that hierarchy reflected natural inequalities among men—a conviction that made their own unfortunate positions intolerable—they were for freedom of movement within the hierarchy and against birth and other hereditary restraints upon such freedom.

This attitude is unambiguously expressed in warrior writings on government. Everywhere eligibility for office was largely determined by family rank, and everywhere this practice was bitterly attacked by writers who urged that the appointment and promotion of officials be based on merit alone. Almost all of these writers, although some more pointedly than others, also expressed the belief that because of environmental factors ability was to be found especially among lower warriors—however they may individually have defined "ability" and "lower." Hardship, they agreed, fostered intelligence and character; wealth and ease, their opposites. Some writers, in a most "unfeudal" spirit, demanded that domains be periodically reassigned on the basis of merit. And a surprising number argued that officials should be recruited from among peasants and merchants as well as warriors. Nor were these writers merely making a plea for a broadening of opportunity. They championed a cause—merit over birth—and their criticisms were a wholesale attack on government by hereditary privilege. They blamed the hereditary principle for the current failures of government and predicted it could lead only to disaster; moreover they pressed the attack in anger, roundly abusing daimyo as a class and high-ranking aristocrats, the two chief targets of criticism, as "stupid," "lazy," "ignorant," "superstitious," and even "criminal."

Evidence of the class feelings of merchants and peasants, who were generally uncommunicative on such matters, is more tenuous. Something of their feelings can be guessed from their universal eagerness to wear swords, take surnames, entertain warriors, be invited to nō plays at the castle and to audiences with the lord. They attempted to transcend the disabilities of class in a society where such efforts were almost certain to fail. Nor can one mistake the evidence of their dissatisfaction with the results. This was a dissatisfaction not so much with the social hierarchy as with the special injustice of one's position within it, and it took the form of aggression against the warrior class. Merchants often maliciously affronted and humiliated warriors, making them prostrate themselves, apologize abjectly, and use honorific language in soliciting loans; teahouses, inns, and restaurants frequently refused their custom; townsmen knocked their heads and trod on their toes in the dark of the theater where, in many han, warriors had no right to be; and forever circulating were stories of the strong-armed carpenter or the noodle-maker who had disarmed an offensive warrior and beaten him with the flat of his own sword while a crowd of townsmen looked on in transports of delight.

Were such stories and behavior harmless bluster? Or evidence of deep feelings of resentment and frustration that, given the favoring circumstances of a split within the warrior class, may have taken on political significance? I cannot help thinking the latter is nearer the truth: that dissatisfaction and a desire for change account, in part, for the widespread support of the loyalist movement by commoners. This phenomenon was not confined to Chōshū. One can only speculate on the motives for such support. In some cases, at least, motives were consciously political and closely linked to class feeling. Shibusawa Eiichi (1841–1931), the eldest son of a wealthy village headman (a fact that perhaps accounts for the young man's self-confidence and quick pride), told how as a boy he was insulted by a Tokugawa official whom he considered in every way his inferior and how then and there he determined to overthrow a system that put good men at the mercy of bad.

Significantly, Shibusawa did not set about organizing a commoners' movement against warrior government: instead he joined warriors conspiring against the Bakufu and even became a warrior himself. In this course of action—which was typical—lies much of the special interest of class relations in Tokugawa Japan. Why, despite the tensions between classes, were the ties so strong between them or, rather, between elements of them? It was, as Craig emphasizes, the vertical ties rather than the class cleavages that were the guidelines of political organization at the Restoration. But was it not partly the leaven of class discontent that made possible, within these guidelines, new political combinations capable of revolutionary acts?

7

"MERIT" AS IDEOLOGY IN
THE TOKUGAWA PERIOD

Official appointments in the Tokugawa period were based mainly on social rank, although it was widely held that, as a matter of principle, they ought to be based on ability alone. This conflict between theory and practice lay near the center of both political thought and practical politics. To a considerable extent the issue was between upper and lower samurai, between those with more and those with less rank. As time passed it became more intense, creating frustration and despair and finally raising questions about the legitimacy of existing government.

The argument for appointment and promotion on the basis of

Reprinted from Ronald P. Dore, ed., *Aspects of Social Change in Modern Japan* (Princeton, 1967).

merit[1] was, of course, Confucian. Given the ruler, it was self-evident that the quality of government depended on the ability of officials, who therefore ought to be chosen on the basis of merit. Because merit was rare, moreover, the recruitment net ought to be thrown wide—although perhaps not so wide as to cover the entire population.

"Merit," it was held, was a product of natural gifts, education, and environment: all three were equally essential. Natural superiority of intellect, temperament, and physique—the potential for merit—was a rare and mysterious gift that appeared at all social levels. In fact, the largest supply was probably found among commoners because of their number. But among commoners it rarely grew into merit. They had little time for education owing to the demands of work; as their work was organized around incessant efforts for self-advancement, it engendered a crabbed selfishness inimical to the qualities merit implied. Those qualities occurred only when, in addition to natural gifts, there was time for education, proper instruction, and the freedom from want that nurtured generosity and boldness of spirit.

Thus, for all practical purposes merit was confined to samurai. But among samurai, who were minutely graded with great differences between top and bottom, it was randomly distributed. Since men fit for high office were rare and the lower ranks of samurai most populous, it followed that considerations of rank ought never to interfere, among samurai, with the discovery and employment of talent. Curiously, considering that appointments to office were largely based on rank, this proposition was generally treated as unexceptionable. No one seriously challenged it; no one developed the formidable counterargument that rank itself was an aspect of merit. What, it might have been asked, was so likely as rank to give the absolute inner assurance that made other men obey instinctively, or to give the lofty freedom from personal interests so desirable in public life. The argument, although known, was scarcely used. Tokugawa Yoshimune (1684–1751) stated it in es-

---

1. An anachronistic term that I use here to summarize all the various qualities Tokugawa writers thought fitted men for office—intelligence, wisdom, understanding, humanity, generosity, courage. They had no term with quite the omnibus meaning of merit.

sence when he held that men of high rank were less likely than others to use office for personal advantage or to endanger the ruler's power— but in the next breath, reverting to the conventional view, he spoke as if rank and merit were unrelated.[2]

The merit principle was as much a part of political polemics as of abstract speculation. Politics in both Bakufu and *han* turned largely on factional struggles between groups that were socially similar. Nonetheless, the "outs" were forever charging the "ins"—and being charged in turn when themselves in—with making official appointments based on party, rank, and other inadmissible criteria rather than merit. Since merit is a subjective attribute, this charge was impossible to refute and therefore much used. For all that, it would have been less used had it not been capable, on the right occasions, of inflaming samurai feeling.

But why was the merit principle warmly regarded if so little honored in practice? Partly because few samurai held office and all wanted it. Office gave power and prestige and was nearly the only means of advancement in income and rank. In peacetime it was also the only way of serving the lord, and the urge to serve was exceedingly strong. Besides, given the taboo on business and the special temperament required for the arts and scholarship, it was nearly the only escape from inactivity and boredom. For a large number of samurai, therefore, the merit principle held out the only hope of office, and office the only hope of self-fulfillment.[3]

Educational opportunity was also substantially equal within the samurai class; many contemporaries claimed the lower-middle ranks were better educated than the upper.[4] The *han* schools did in fact regularly register instances of lower-rank excellence and upper-rank dull-

---

2. Tokugawa Yoshimune, *Kishū seijigusa*, in *Nanki Tokugawashi*, ed. Horiuchi Shin (Wakayama, 1930) 1:592–98.
3. Yamaga Sokō (1622–85), an influential expounder of *bushidō*, held that a warrior who did not perform his role (*shokubun*) properly, including of course serving his lord, was no better than a robber because he took a living he had no right to, and that such a person would do well to become a merchant or a peasant and so make himself an honest man. *Shidō*, in *Kokumin shisō sōsho*, ed. Katō Totsudō (Tokyo, 1929), 9:5.
4. *Shōhei yawa*, in *Nihon keizai taiten*, ed. Takimoto Seiichi (hereafter *NKT*; Tokyo, 1928), 14:416, 425, and Sakurada Komon, *Kakenroku*, in *Kinsei shakai keizai sōsho*, ed. Honjō Eijirō (hereafter *KSKS*; Tokyo, 1926), 5:106–7.

ness by seating students according to achievement. As a consequence the distribution of offices according to rank was not supported by an educational system that made the people who received office appear abler than those who did not; indeed, it often seems to have had nearly the opposite effect. Although people who long for recognition often feel themselves unworthy, this was not usually the case with aspirant samurai; they yearned for office with the firm conviction that many officeholders were less worthy than themselves.

Still another reason for the strong appeal of the merit principle was that, after all, things were going badly in the country. After the late seventeenth century, the Bakufu and the *han* were in serious financial difficulties, which were perhaps the least of their troubles. Peasants were abandoning farming for trade, merchants growing so powerful they could bring all but the greatest lord to heel by withholding credit, samurai losing their martial qualities and their lower ranks being ground down by frightful poverty. To all these classic symptoms of dynastic decay was added, toward the end of the eighteenth century, the threat of barbarian domination and debauchment. If things were to be put right and the country saved, clearly the bunglers (proved so by the troubled times) must be got rid of and abler men given power.

To what extent was merit in fact taken into account or disregarded in appointments? It is difficult to know precisely since there is no certain way of distinguishing between merit appointments and other appointments; some men of high rank were appointed for ability, some of low rank despite a lack of it. To the extent that appointments *generally* corresponded to rank, however, we may say that merit, although not necessarily ignored, was subordinated to other considerations.

The voluminous samurai genealogies of Matsue *han*[5] throw some light on the question; they would throw a good deal more if carefully

5. *Resshiroku*, MS 24-H: 17-1, Kokuritsu Shiryōkan, Tokyo. These genealogies, totaling fifty-nine volumes, provide invaluable material for the study of mobility within the warrior class. They give an immense amount of data on inheritance, marriages, adoptions, income, offices, ranks, honors, and other outstanding events, generation by generation, from the Kan'ei era (1624—44) down to the time of compilation in the last year of the Tokugawa period, for each samurai family in existence in Matsue at the latter date.

studied. But even on casual examination they show clearly enough that mobility, as measured by changes in stipend, was common in the seventeenth and early eighteenth centuries. Nearly all families of direct Matsue vassals in this period moved up or down the income scale, or both up and down—often drastically and within a single generation. During the last two-thirds of the eighteenth and the first decades of the nineteenth centuries, however, there was astonishingly little mobility up or down. The majority of families went through the whole period with no change in income whatever or with only very slight changes. The last decades of the Tokugawa period brought more movement again, although nothing like the mobility of the first period.

Changes in income were usually occasioned by changes in office. Sometimes a man was promoted or demoted beyond the normal range for his rank, making an increase or decrease in stipend necessary, or deprived of office and income as punishment for an offense. On the other hand, a man was rarely given a considerable cut or increase in stipend without a roughly corresponding change in his office, if he had one. Thus income mobility reflects to a considerable extent the degree of constraint by rank on official appointment, promotion, and demotion, and it is evident that the constraint was far greater after 1700 than before. In short, although rank was always a factor in appointment and promotion, it only became the dominant factor in Matsue in the early eighteenth century. If the experience of other parts of the country was similar, merit appointment may have become a sore issue in the second half of the Tokugawa period partly because rank was a *more* severe bar to advancement than previously.

It is at least certain that over the country as a whole large numbers of samurai were barred by considerations of rank from any office of consequence, and at some point nearly all were barred by rank from further advancement up the official ladder. For one thing, fief income, an aspect of rank, was usually a formal criterion of eligibility for important offices. Thus, in the Bakufu an income of ten thousand *koku* was required for *rōjū, wakadoshiyori,* and *jisha bugyō;* five thousand *koku* for *okoshōgumigashira* and *osobagoyōnin;* and so on.[6] After

6. Yamazaki Masatada, *Yokoi Shōnan* (Tokyo, 1938), 2:805.

1723 income was theoretically irrelevant to Bakufu officeholding because provision was made in that year for supplementary grants of income (*tashidaka*) during the term of office for vassals with less than the required minimum for the various offices. But the value of this system was mainly symbolic. For financial reasons if no other, the Bakufu chose to fill offices with men who required little or no additions to fief income; and few *han* had even this largely symbolic offset to formal income requirements.

For another thing, in both Bakufu and *han* income requirements for office were fortified by the tendency of offices to become hereditary. In Daishōji *han*, a branch of Kaga, the highest group of officials, called *karō*, were chosen from a number of families of the highest rank. None of the Daishōji *karō* of the late Tokugawa period represented the first generation of his family in this office; several represented the eighth, ninth, or tenth.[7] In the lists of holders of high Bakufu offices, the same surnames, with nearly identical personal names, often recur in the same offices, suggesting dynasties of fathers, sons, and grandsons.[8]

Nor was hereditary succession confined to high offices (to which relatives of the shogun or the daimyo in the *han* may have had special claim). In Kaga, offices pertaining to finance, trade, and monetary policy were typically held by merchant families in which they were handed down from generation to generation like property. Even if a father died when his son was a child, the son succeeded to the office upon reaching a suitable age. The son even succeeded when the father was removed from the office for misconduct.[9]

Another link between rank and office was the system by which many subordinate offices, in the Bakufu at least, were filled. Numerous bureaus, and not always the least important, had no permanent staff. Each head was obliged to staff the bureau with his own vassals and, if

---

7. A total of ten *karō* served under the last daimyo between 1854 and 1870. Of the ten, one represented the third generation in this office, two the fourth, one the fifth, one the sixth, one the eighth, two the ninth, and one the tenth. Daishōji Hanshi Hensankai, ed., *Daishōji hanshi* (Kanazawa, 1938), 495–96.

8. Tōkyō Teikoku Daigaku Shiryō Hensanjo, ed., *Dokushi biyō* (Tokyo, 1935), 495–526.

9. *Chōnin yuishochō*, MS in Kanazawa City Library.

he had too few, with additional persons hired at his own expense.[10] Thus in governing the city of Edo, the *machibugyō* used their own retainers as assistants, judges, clerks, police, runners, and so on.[11] This system restricted the free use of talent in three ways. (1) It tended to limit the headship of such bureaus to Bakufu vassals who had numerous vassals of their own, that is, to men of wealth and high rank, usually daimyo. (2) It limited the subordinate positions to the vassals of such men; hence direct Bakufu vassals of middle rank were barred from staff positions as well as from the headships. (3) Moreover, since the staff changed when its head changed, the most merit-minded ruler might hesitate to replace an incompetent head for fear of losing the experience of his staff.

Primogeniture was still another link.[12] Except for very large domains, which were sometimes divided among heirs, younger sons rarely inherited property, rank, or eligibility for office.[13] The younger son of a middle- or low-ranking family was virtually excluded from office, high or low. He might hope for a small pension from the lord, especially if he excelled as a scholar or swordsman, or for adoption as an heir by another samurai family—although if this entailed marrying a daughter of the family, it could be the least happy of all solutions. If both of these hopes failed, he could either drop into the class of commoners and go to work or live off his elder brother as an unwanted dependent. This array of life chances was not likely to make younger sons the stoutest supporters of appointment by rank or of any other tenet of the establishment. If, as contemporaries thought, younger sons were especially given to rowdy and delinquent behavior[14] or, later, over-

---

10. Thus, when a certain Toda Izumo no Kami stationed at Nagasaki died in 1785, his seventy-two retainers who had assisted him in office there left the city and were replaced by the retainers of Matsuura Izumi no Kami, his successor. Takayanagi Shinzō and Ishii Ryōsuke, eds., *Ofuregakisho Tenmei shūsei* (Tokyo, 1936), 804.

11. Ogyū Sorai, *Seidan*, in NKT 9:97.

12. If, as happened frequently, a younger son inherited owing to the incapacity of the eldest son, the latter was then in the position of a younger son with respect to inheritance, the lord, and future prospects.

13. That is, after about 1700; before that the partitioning of domains was far more common.

14. Buyō Inshi, *Seji kenmonroku*, in KSKS 1:19–20; Sakurada Komon, *Keiseidan*, in NKT 16:351; Takayanagi Shinzō and Ishii Ryōsuke, eds., *Ofuregakisho Tenpō shūsei* (Tokyo, 1937), 359.

represented in the Restoration movement, their lack of prospects was probably the reason.

It would be wrong to suppose, though, that because rank out-weighed talent in bureaucratic practice, government as opposed to its critics cared nothing for the merit principle. The Bakufu persistently tried to check nepotism, bribery, and favoritism in appointments. An administrative regulation of 1787 illustrates this effort: it stated that the cardinal duty of group commanders (*kumigashira*) was to recommend from their groups for appointment to office men of outstanding ability (*kiryō*), character (*jinbutsu*), and versatility (*tagei*); shortly after, another regulation reminded the same commanders of their oath to recommend persons on the basis of ability only, threatening punishment for contrary recommendations.[15] Since these regulations did not define ability they can hardly have had any deep influence on practice; nevertheless they held up an ideal of impersonality that was widely accepted among officials.

The sensitiveness of group commanders to any imputation of impropriety in their recommendations—revealed by an incident in 1787 reported in the *Tokugawa jikki*—illustrates the importance of the ideal of impersonality among officials. According to the story, one of the commanders hinted to his colleagues that their recommendations, unlike his own, were not above the suspicion of influence by gifts. Incensed, they planned revenge for the insult and got their chance at festivities one evening at his home. One of them picked a quarrel with him, and the quarrel soon grew into a brawl during which the guests upset food and drink, broke down sliding doors, ripped up the mats, and urinated on the floor. But perhaps they objected more to his holier-than thou attitude than to the specific charge.[16]

As noted earlier, in 1723 the Bakufu instituted the system of sup-

---

15. Takayanagi and Ishii, *Ofuregakisho Tenpō shūsei,* 367–520. Other similar orders may be cited. A directive of 1793 says that sons serving as understudies to their fathers in the Bureau of Finance were to be examined, before appointment, on their technical qualifications. A directive of 1794 provided that the sons of *hatamoto* could not be enrolled in service groups (*ōban'iri*), and hence could not succeed to their fathers' fiefs, without examination as to character and skill. Ibid., 314–15, 348.

16. Narushima Motonao, ed., *Zoku Tokugawa jikki* (Tokyo, 1905), 1:37–38.

plementary income grants making it possible, in theory, for low-ranking warriors to hold all but the highest offices of *wakadoshiyori* and above, which were excluded from the system. This was going a long way toward merit egalitarianism even in theory. A similar reform about the same time concerned the assignment of residences (*yashiki*) to Bakufu vassals. Residences, which varied greatly in size and desirability of location, were assigned according to rank. One effect of this system, which was necessary to maintain the proper social distance between ranks, was to restrict eligibility for each office to Bakufu vassals with residences of an appropriate dignity. A noble fool living in a great residence enclosed with walls and garden could not be assigned to a minor clerkship nor a sage in a hovel be made a minister without exposing rank to public ridicule. The reform did nothing about the first case; but it provided for the second by stipulating that, irrespective of rank, officials upon appointment be assigned appropriate residences if they did not already have them.[17] Like the supplementary-grants system, however, this removed an obstacle to the use of ability in government without in the least assuring that ability would be used.[18]

Critics continued to claim that rank, not ability, determined appointments. Before these reforms, Ogyū Sorai (1666–1728) had charged that, because of their relatively low rank, *hatamoto* were virtually barred from high office in the Bakufu; long after, on the eve of the Restoration, Yokoi Shōnan (1809–69) was making the identical charge. *Han* practice seems to have been no more liberal than the Bakufu's and may have been less so. Hayashi Shihei (1738–93) held that in Sendai high office was restricted to upper-income families (*tairoku no mono*), with deplorable results for government.[19] An anonymous writer who may have been Murata Kiyokaze (Seifū) said that in Chōshū the size of a warrior's fief determined the offices he was eligible for; consequently men were frequently appointed to high office who

17. Takayanagi and Ishii, *Ofuregakisho Tenpō shūsei*, 465.

18. Not all *han* were willing to concede so much to talent, even in theory. The regulations concerning warrior residences in Sendai, for example, stipulated that size should correspond precisely to domain income, and they laid down a detailed schedule of income categories with their corresponding residential sizes. The intent was clearly to prevent any blurring by accidents of officeholding of the distinctions of rank based on birth. Sendai Shishi Hensan Iinkai, ed., *Sendai shishi* (Sendai, 1955), 8:404–5.

19. *Jōsho sanpen*, in NKT 20:48.

were young, inexperienced, and physically and morally unfit, while men of talent with smallish stipends had no hope of important office.[20] In his memoirs, Ōkuma Shigenobu (1838–1922) stated that in Saga official appointments were determined by rank; intelligence and character counted for little.[21]

While bureaucratic practice was coming to take more account of ability very slowly, if at all, the inability of government to cope with domestic and external problems was rapidly being revealed. This situation encouraged stronger statements on the conflict between rank and merit, and an increasing number of writers overstepped the conventional position that the two did not always go together to suggest that they hardly ever went together. For some writers it was almost as if the two were inversely related: the more of the one, the less of the other.

Although not the first to take this position, Ogyū Sorai was perhaps the first to support it with a plausible argument. When a country is at peace for a sufficiently long time, he argued, it nearly always happens that the men at the top of the social and political system have less ability than men below them.[22] War no longer weeds out the unfit; families at the top consequently maintain themselves there through political influence, enjoying by birth the positions their ancestors had to win by deeds; possessing without effort everything they could wish, they fail to develop talent—such native ability as they have is ruined. How could it be otherwise? Raised in ease and indolence, never rebuked, constantly praised by retainers who do everything for them, they grow up soft, ignorant, proud, self-indulgent. Above all, they have no feeling for or understanding of the common people, a defect making them utterly unsuited for high office. In such circumstances, the wise ruler will recruit his ministers from men of low rank whose character and talents and sympathies have been formed in harsher circumstances.[23] According to Sorai:

20. *Bōshi ikensho*, in NKT 47:48–53.
21. *Ōkuma-haku sekijitsudan* (Tokyo, 1895), 12–13.
22. Ogyū Sorai, *Seidan*, 114.
23. Ibid., 112–13.

All human ability rises from the difficulties of life. The part of one's body a person habitually uses becomes strong. If he uses his hands, they become powerful; if he walks much, his legs become sturdy. If he practices with a bow or gun, his eyes become sharp; if he uses his mind, it grows penetrating. Every difficulty and hardship refines and strengthens. This is the rule of nature and is why Mencius said that when Heaven would entrust men with great responsibilities, it first sends them troubles. Talent therefore develops below and it is essential for government to be informed of affairs below. It is the way of the sage in recruiting talent to raise it up from below. The wise and talented men of history rose from low rank; it is exceedingly rare for wisdom and talent to carry over from one generation to another in families of high rank.[24]

If, Sorai said with obvious reference to Japan, recruiting from below has been neglected for a long time, one cannot quickly set matters right, throwing down the high and raising up the low. Those who thought so were clearly mistaken; such violent change would only result in chaos, and therefore new talent from below should be introduced gradually. If even a few men of low rank were promoted to high positions, it would break the monopoly of birth; others, seeing what could happen, would suddenly come alive with hope. A rush of talent would result; the age would be reborn.

But not if able men from below were merely made advisers to high officials, as some urged. That would leave them in reality powerless, for "talent standing below" cannot speak up. The man of low rank is so overwhelmed by the rank and power of the high official he cannot look him directly in the eye but "looks involuntarily at his collar," saying not what he thinks but what the official wants to hear. Therefore the only way to use able men of low rank is to give them the power and prestige of high office.[25]

By recruiting talented officials from below, Sorai continued, the governing elite would be continuously renewed. As new men rise to positions of honor and power, they replace others who have become a drag on government and whose biological lines naturally tend to die out—"according to Heaven's rule," Sorai said hopefully. Thus the able rule the less able; meritocracy prevails and can last forever. But if tal-

24. Ibid., 114.
25. Ibid., 115–16, 121.

ent is not continuously recruited from below, if government tries to
keep the high high and the low low, as it unfortunately tends to, its
quality will deteriorate; it will lose touch with the people, and finally
men of talent will rise up from below, where they are bred, to replace
it.[26] "It is the unvarying rule of nature," Sorai wrote, "that old things
disappear and new things take their place. Everything in creation is
subject to this rule. However one may wish to preserve something forever, it is beyond anyone's power to do so. . . . To wish for this reason
for the quick demise of the old would be harsh, but to hope it may
last forever is folly. In all human affairs, the way of the sage is to
keep human feelings in mind and not outrage them, at the same time
seeing clearly what must be done and not being blinded by human
emotion."[27]

Such statements, tasteless and innocuous in China perhaps, were
taken very differently in Japan. Sorai was proposing nothing less than
the transformation of an aristocracy of birth into an aristocracy of talent, claiming that nature itself made the transformation inevitable. His
writings must have thrilled men of low rank who believed that merit
would solve the ills of the age and that merit and low rank went hand
in hand.

Kaiho Seiryō (1755–1817) spelled out the kind of economic
changes that in his view would have to accompany merit appointment.
If one presently put the ablest men in office regardless of rank, Seiryō
said, samurai income would have to be thoroughly redistributed, or it
would often occur that officials would have little income while men
with no office had a great deal. To avoid such injustice and waste, it
was necessary to establish a new system of stipends. First, all samurai
should receive a basic rank-stipend (*iden*); then, in addition, officials
should receive a salary (*yakumai*), the amount varying with the office
and rising to a very large sum for the highest offices. Fief income would
disappear. Therefore, since rank-stipends would be small, significant
income differences henceforth would depend exclusively on officeholding; families would move up or down the income scale, irrespective of

26. Ibid., 113.
27. Ibid., 112–13.

rank, as they moved up or down the administrative ladder according to the merit of family heads. Thus, for Seiryō at least, meritocracy was quite specifically an economic as well as a political order.[28]

This meritorious economic order, according to Seiryō, was essential if "intelligent and wise men of low rank are to serve in high office and foolish and lazy men not."[29] The necessary adjustments to bring this order about, he recognized, would be painful to people presently at the top, whose income would be drastically cut: a three-thousand-*koku* income would shrink to about thirty *koku,* according to one of his illustrations. There would be fierce resistance to such economic leveling unless care were taken to see that it did not entail a simultaneous social leveling. To preserve the social significance of rank, of which fief income (*chigyōdaka*) was the main indicator, he suggested that present fief income rankings, as rankings, be retained; thus the family with three thousand *koku* would remain for ceremonial purposes a three-thousand-*koku* family, even though its actual income was reduced to thirty *koku.* Then, Seiryō claimed, there would be relatively little opposition to the actual loss.[30] One cannot be sure that his optimism was misplaced, so often have Japanese eased the loss of power by preserving its forms.

Nevertheless, Seiryō was aware of the harshness of his proposals, which he took pains to justify. Heaven, he said going against the common view that men were born unequal, endowed every man with the same capacity for understanding. If, nonetheless, some men were incapable of effort, unable to use their minds, unfit for work, it was their own fault. Having squandered Heaven's gift by idle living, it was Heaven's will and simple justice that they be punished for their folly.[31]

How did the reformers suppose that merit appointment, with all its disturbing social implications, was to be brought about? Not of

28. *Keiseidan,* in *NKT* 27:75–76. The son of a *karō* of Amagasaki *han,* Kaiho Seiryō became a *rōnin* and lectured on political economy to townsmen audiences in Osaka, Kyoto, and Kanazawa, suggesting that merit ideology was not confined to samurai.
29. Ibid., 597.
30. Ibid., 75–76.
31. Ibid., 77.

course by force; not by persuading high-ranking samurai to give up their offices to the lower ranks; but by the easiest, quickest, and oldest agency of reform under monarchy—the benevolence and wisdom of the ruler. Nevertheless, just here was the catch. According to the merit reformers, rank corrupted very nearly in proportion to its eminence; hence of all men the lord must be the least able to conceive, understand, and carry through so far-reaching and difficult a program as merit appointment. How was he, who lived among courtiers, to see through social appearances to men's real worth? And if he could not, how were simple, direct, unpolished men of low rank, however able, to come to power?

The merit reformers were under no illusions about the difficulties they faced. The daimyo, said Sakurada Komon (1744–1839) scornfully, were brought up to believe that whatever nonsense they spoke was wisdom, every action a miracle of grace and dexterity. If they played chess or any other game, their companions contrived that they won, then threw up their hands, exclaiming "My, how clever the lord is!" Hence the phrase "a daimyo's skill" (*daimyō gei*), which meant just the opposite. No wonder the daimyo for generations had been pictured in comic drama as fools. By the time a young daimyo left the palace interior, his character was ruined—he was willful, weak, pompous, foolish. And the situation was not improving: "As time passes one lord is succeeded by another like himself."[32]

Sakurada's daimyo were no worse—although certainly no better—than those of many other writers. Daimyo, in the view of men like Sakurada, were scarcely fit to referee an archery contest, let alone stand as judges of other men's qualifications. Yet this was their unique function, the essence of monarchy—the only way a single man could make his influence felt over an entire country. A ruler cannot and should not try to rule directly with his own intelligence (*chi*), Oka Hakku wrote, but by letting the intelligence of others magnify his own a thousand times. Take away this capacity and nothing was left to lordship but its name.[33]

32. Ibid., 282–83.
33. *Chikoku shūshinroku,* in NKT 13:289.

Meanwhile daimyo were donkey dull and peacock proud, and Sorai and others proposed various amelioratives for this normal condition. One was to improve the education of daimyo;[34] another to secure appointments as chief minister of men of outstanding wisdom and character.[35] But none of these suggestions was very promising. All required the daimyo to rise above himself, to make appointments of a kind that were critically needed precisely because of his inability to make them in the past.

Sorai suggested four ways that a ruler could compensate to some degree for his own social biases, which Sorai took for granted: (1) deliberately favor men of low rank in appointments; (2) be careful to appoint men representing different personalities and viewpoints, to avoid a single yes-man type; (3) start all officials at the bottom and promote no one except on the basis of performance; (4) take care that high officials never gave detailed instructions to a subordinate—otherwise subordinates would slavishly follow their superiors' orders, nothing would be revealed of their abilities, and conformity would become the standard for promotion.[36]

Further than this Sorai could hardly go in hedging against the defects of rulers. He could hope they would follow his advice, he could exhort them to be wiser than they were, but he would not deny them the power to appoint even if he could. Yet if he was right about the debilitating effects of the social system on their character, nothing short of a curtailment of their power was likely to bring any lasting improvement to government.

Given the impossibility of curtailing the daimyo's power and the difficulty of living with it, it is no wonder "present-day rulers"—the usual discreet generality—came in for much abuse. Daimyo were commonly called weak, ignorant, stupid, self-indulgent, ostentatious, and a great deal else. Honda Toshiaki, Kaiho Seiryō, Yokoi Shōnan, Murata

---

34. Sakurada, *Kakenroku*, 141; Murata, *Bōshi ikensho*, 127–28.
35. According to Shingū Ryōtei, there were even people who suggested that it was a good thing if a daimyo was plain stupid since it would be easy in that case to keep him from interfering with his ministers. *Yabureya no tsuzukuribanashi*, in NKT 31: 116–17.
36. Ogyū Sorai, *Seidan*, 120–24.

Kiyokaze (Seifū), Shingū Ryōtei, and Sakurada Komon were some of the more intemperate name-callers.[37] Diatribe against daimyo was common, defense of them rare—although many writers praised individual daimyo, often to set off the others' lack of virtue.

Enmity to the daimyo was not confined to the abstraction of "present-day rulers," nor was it devoid of subversive sentiment. Writers frequently spoke of the hatred of vassals for their lords.[38] One anonymous writer predicted that in a crisis of civil strife vassals would desert their present lords, and he thought it proper they should: "Can it be virtue to help such princes rule?" he asked.[39] Sakurada thought that when the competence of government had declined sufficiently, the country would be plunged into a new civil war, and that the daimyo would be destroyed by tougher and abler men because "those who go soft cannot last long."[40] The idea of Heaven's mandate was frequently cited with a special sense of aptness to the condition of present rulers. Matsudaira Sadanobu (1758–1829), himself a daimyo, wrote that "Heaven orders what the people wish. . . . The preferences of a man, a family, or a village are a private matter, but what the masses (*okuchō no hito*) wish *is* the will of Heaven." If a ruler disregarded Heaven's will, he would eventually be destroyed and his state perish. Now "present-day rulers," said Sadanobu, becoming quite specific in his reference to Japan and repeating the customary charges against the daimyo: they were used to people approaching on their knees saying "yes, yes," and if a minister dared tell them of the people's sufferings, they clapped their hands over their ears and the minister was condemned for thoughtlessness. Such men, said Sadanobu grimly, do not know Heaven's will or rule in Heaven's name.[41]

Honda Toshiaki (1744–1821) was as explicit about his readiness for a change in Heaven's mandate as he dared be. In a long passage in one of his major works, he showed how throughout Japanese history

---

37. Honda, *Keisei hisaku*, in NKT 20:120–21; Kaiho, *Keiseidan*, 77, 274; Murata, *Bōshi ikensho*, 61, 90, 93, 121–23, 127; Sakurada, *Kakenroku*, 78–79, 82, 85–86, 138–39; Sakurada, *Keiseidan*, 309.
38. Murata, *Bōshi ikensho*, 90–91.
39. *Shōhei yawa*, 396, 398, 402, 413–14.
40. *Kakenroku*, 85–86.
41. *Kokuhonron*, in NKT 13:330–32.

Heaven had destroyed bad rulers. Then coming to his own time, he described the evils of the day, tracing them to the influence of the rulers. All of these evils would vanish, he said, if an enlightened ruler were to appear; but no such thing was likely, and he placed his hope on Heaven's intervention. "Whose fault is it that the people starve and good fields turn to waste? These evils cannot be blamed on laziness or disloyalty [in the people] but are owing to the crimes of the rulers [*kokkun no zaika*]. When I think of this I forget myself and breathe 'Heaven's punishment comes too slowly!'"[42]

After Honda's time, merit ideology was increasingly obscured by two more dramatic issues—Japan's relations with the West and the relation of the emperor to the government. Since these issues led more or less directly to the Restoration, they have usually been seen as the chief intellectual causes or antecedents of that event. But one wonders whether, on a longer view, either was more important than the merit issue in undermining the legitimacy of the Bakufu and *han* and arousing feeling against them. On no broad political principle, not even perhaps on the emperor, were the anti-Bakufu agitators so nearly united. And for the majority of the samurai, one must remember that the opening of careers to talent was not an abstract issue but a matter of the greatest personal urgency—offering hope of escape from poverty, boredom, and helplessness. One is reminded of Sir George Sansom's judgment: "There can be no doubt that, of all the causes of the anti-Tokugawa, loyalist movement which ended in the fall of the Bakufu, the ambition of young samurai was the most powerful."[43]

42. *Keisei hisaku*, 120–21.
43. G. B. Sansom, *The Western World and Japan* (New York, 1950), 254.

8

ŌKURA NAGATSUNE
AND THE TECHNOLOGISTS

Although Ōkura Nagatsune was not rich, highborn, powerful, or a genius, he is interesting to history as a representative of a large class of
Tokugawa writers who may be called *technologists*. The technologists
were mostly obscure men—farmers, merchants, and small manufacturers—who never held high office and generally lived out their lives in
villages and small towns. All had some education and therefore some
acquaintance with the classics, but none was concerned primarily with
the great problems of government and society that engaged Confucianists. Instead, they were concerned almost exclusively with material
problems, practical and earthy ones such as keeping silkworms free of

Reprinted from Albert Craig and Donald H. Shively, eds., *Personality in Japanese
History* (Berkeley and Los Angeles, 1970).

their own droppings and improving the yield of oil from rapeseed, in the solution of which they saw the means of economic progress and human betterment. By these notions, although they had no names for them, they unmistakably meant a broadly shared increase in what we would now call national income.

Such ideas could hardly have been more at odds with those of orthodox Confucianists, who were far from thinking economic welfare an end in itself and indeed were suspicious of too much of it as bad for morals. In any case, they thought that welfare flowed uniquely from the quality of government, never from mere technique, independent of politics. Unorthodox as the ideas of the technologists may have been, however, to judge from the number of books that were published expressing them, they were widely held among educated commoners by the early nineteenth century. This chapter seeks to describe the characteristic features of this literature and to suggest its meaning for the history of the Tokugawa period.

Very little is known about the lives of the technologists. More is known about Ōkura Nagatsune's than most, yet only the barest outline can be pieced together from the few letters that survive and occasional autobiographical asides in his technical writing.[1] Nagatsune was born in a substantial farm family in north-central Kyūshū in 1768. His grandfather, whom he clearly admired, was an expert cotton-grower and took great pains to train the servants in this demanding specialty. The house name *wataya*—"cotton shop"—suggests that the family was engaged in buying, selling, and processing cotton,[2] but this business, along with the family's prosperity, seems to have disappeared with the grandfather's death when Nagatsune was eleven. Shortly afterward, Nagatsune and his father went to work for a relative who was in the business of manufacturing wax from the juice of the lacquer tree, an important domestic industry in Kyūshū, and Nagatsune continued in this employment as long as he lived in the village.[3]

1. The letters are reprinted in Hayakawa Kōtarō, *Ōkura Nagatsune* (Tokyo, 1943), 289–394.
2. Ōkura Nagatsune, *Menpo yōmu*, in *Nihon kagaku koten zenshū*, ed. Saigusa Hiroto (Tokyo, 1944), 11:252–53.
3. Tamura Eitarō, *Sangyō shidōsha Ōkura Nagatsune* (Tokyo, 1944), 5.

In his early teens, according to a friend who knew him later, Nagatsune had already learned to read and write, essential skills in a commercial household. When he developed an ambition to be a scholar, however, he came into conflict with his father. Books were not only useless to a farmer but positively harmful, the father insisted, since they led to pride, to dissatisfaction with farming, and so eventually to economic ruin. He forbade Nagatsune to study and, on discovering the boy going secretly to the village schoolmaster for instruction, cautioned the teacher against helping him. This episode appears to have changed Nagatsune's life. In obedience to his father, he gave up the classics but found a way of compensating: "Even if I could not study the classics and thus learn the secrets of ruling a country, I refused to spend my life doing nothing of value; so I concentrated my ambition on learning the art of farming and studied it for many years."[4]

Indeed, he studied it until the end of his life, although when he began is uncertain. He left home at twenty-four, possibly to advance his studies, and spent the next five years traveling in Kyūshū, stopping now and then to work at paper making and sugar refining, no doubt learning something about local farming practices in the process. Whether he made notes of his observations this early is uncertain, but it would not be surprising. Miyazaki Yasusada (1623–97), one of the earliest and greatest of the technologists, whose classic *General Treatise on Agriculture* published in 1697 was still being read, had made travel, observation, and note taking established methods for students of farming.[5]

At twenty-nine, Nagatsune's travels took him to Osaka, where he lived for many years, first working as a calligraphy teacher and later selling lacquer-tree seedlings imported from Kyūshū. An advertisement in the back of one of his books stated that, although most seedlings sold in Osaka were imported from Shikoku, Nagatsune now offered to send the Kyūshū variety to buyers anywhere on request.[6] This business allowed him to continue his study of farming by taking him to villages all over the Kinai, where the most advanced and highly

4. Ibid., 6.
5. Ibid., 8–10; Miyazaki Yasusada, *Nōgyō zensho* (Tokyo, 1936), 376ff.
6. For text, Tamura, *Ōkura*, 13.

commercialized farming in the country was to be seen. By this time he was observing systematically; wherever he went, he asked questions of skilled farmers about local soils, seeds, fertilizers, irrigation, and tools, taking down what they had to say and making detailed sketches of plants, tools, and operations.[7]

Nagatsune published his first book in 1802, about twenty years after leaving home. It dealt with the cultivation of the lacquer tree and wax making, the subjects he knew best; and its title, *Farm Family Profits* (*Nōkaeki*), sounded what was to be a major theme of nearly all of his work. The books kept coming after that: his last book, if not posthumous, appeared when he would have been eighty-eight. Not counting five unpublished manuscripts, there were twenty-eight books in all: one on ethics, two dictionaries, two on nutrition, two on government policy, one on education, and all the rest on the technology of farming and farm by-employments. The agricultural writings, which covered a great range of subjects, were among the best of their kind for clarity, range, and pertinence of detail. They eventually brought him a certain amount of recognition, including employment as an adviser to the Bakufu and several *han*, which encouraged him to give up his seedling business and move to Edo. He lived there for many years, traveling through the Kantō and the northeast and continuing to write books until his death about 1856.[8]

Nagatsune's motives as a writer were undeniably strong and probably mixed. It seems likely that he was not insensible to the possible financial rewards of writing, and he used his books to advertise his seedling business. He himself insisted that he was moved by the wish to make a difference in the world by his scholarship.[9] He also may have been moved by the hope of official preferment; in his first book he expressed the hope that officials would read it and spread its ideas, and when preferment came he seemed to welcome it. In any case he passionately wanted to improve existing farming methods, which he regarded as generally lamentable. Almost every page he wrote testified to this wish, which explains why he addressed himself to farmers rather

7. Ōkura, *Menpo*, 253, 261; Ōkura Nagatsune, *Nōgu benriron*, in *Nihon kagaku koten zenshū* 11:45.
8. Tamura, *Ōkura*, 23–26.
9. Ōkura, *Nōgu*, 49; Ōkura, *Menpo*, 253; Tamura, *Ōkura*, 5.

than officials, discussed seeds, fertilizers, and farm tools rather than government policy, and consciously wrote in language farmers could understand, knowing it would strike some as inelegant.

As to the meaning of agricultural progress (although he did not use the term himself), Nagatsune never had the slightest doubt. It consisted in substituting more for less efficient methods of farming—substituting methods that either increased yields, reduced costs, or took less skill or strength than those supplanted. Whenever he recommended a technique or tool, it was for one or another of these reasons. Thus the *eburi,* a light hoe for raking up soil around the roots of plants, he claimed not only did a better and cleaner job than the heavier *kuwa* but could be handled with ease by a ten-year-old girl. Often he expressed the superiority of one method over another rather precisely, in terms familiar to farmers. The *kusakezuri,* a specially designed weeder, permitted work to be done in two hours that normally required a full day; the *tenokuwa* made it possible for a woman to make as many furrows in a field as two men working with spades for the same length of time.[10]

Some techniques offered a constellation of advantages. In recommending a potato planter consisting of a spiked wheel run along the ground at the end of a handle in order to drill holes for the seed, Nagatsune noted that it was faster than making holes by hand and also made straighter and more evenly spaced rows, and that it thus facilitated weeding and economized both seed and land.[11] Efficient methods sometimes entailed disadvantages, however, and he implied that in such cases no invariable rule concerning efficacy could be laid down. The balance could be struck only by the individual farmer taking particular local conditions into account.[12] In Bingo Province, for example, dried sardine was used as a fertilizer because it was relatively cheap in this Inland Sea region and because its rapid effect shortened the growing season, minimizing the danger of crop damage from fall typhoons. By using it, Bingo farmers could average some sixty *kanme* of cotton per *tan* of land compared to forty in the Kinai, where the cultivation of

10. Ōkura, *Nōgu,* 53, 79, 88, 90.
11. The device was called an *imoueguruma;* ibid., 91–92.
12. Tamura, *Ōkura,* 245; Ōkura, *Menpo,* 261.

cotton was highly developed with more varied fertilization. On the other hand, the exclusive use of sardine fertilizer resulted in an inferior fiber that brought less in the market than Kinai cotton. The lower price apparently was offset in Bingo by surer and larger yields, but elsewhere it might not be—depending on the local cost of sardines and the degree of vulnerability to typhoon.[13]

In his travels Nagatsune met many skeptics who were quick to point out that the superiority of a method was no guarantee at all of peasant acceptance. Peasants were wedded to received methods, whereas anything novel contained an element of risk.[14] Nagatsune admitted this difficulty, frequently stating that peasants could never see for themselves the inefficiency of inherited methods.[15] But they could be shown, and once shown, they would no more reject a superior method than a sick man would refuse the help of a doctor.[16] Farming was evidently like an illness that could be cured by proper treatment, and Nagatsune fancied himself the doctor.

There were two ways, he said, to show farmers the superiority of a new method. Both were the opposite of exhortation and command, the chief resort of government. In trying to promote improved methods, he said, the government typically called the peasants together in their villages and made them listen to the reading of a document stating the lord's wish that they farm this or that way or plant this or that new crop. They typically listened respectfully and, predictably, did nothing. Peasants would never try what they had not seen for themselves, merely on the advice of a remote if awesome authority.[17] But

13. Ōkura, *Menpo,* 286.
14. Ōkura, *Nōgu,* 129–30.
15. "Peasants are simple and prejudiced. No matter how much you instruct them, they are not easily persuaded to grow a crop they have no experience with." Ōkura, *Menpo,* 252.
16. Nagatsune used the rapid spread of the *senba-koki* to illustrate this principle; Ōkura, *Nōgu,* 131.
17. Arthur Young, the English agricultural reformer and a near contemporary of Nagatsune, thought that farmers could not be induced to try a new crop without the payment of a bounty to cover the possible loss from the experiment. He thought not "one farmer in twenty thousand will [otherwise] venture the attempt. A certain premium for every acre is the only thing which, I apprehend, will ever spread the culture." *The Farmer's Letters to the People of England* (London, 1786), 214–15.

send an expert into the village, give him several *tan* of land to work with the new method, and the peasants would come to observe; if he got good results, they would adopt the method of their own accord. Why? Because they had seen it, and seen that it worked, and "in this age everyone is out for a profit." The key to developing a country's economy, he said, lay in "profiting the farm household" (*nōka no eki*).[18]

The other way of improving agriculture was to persuade village leaders of the superiority of a method, and let them teach and persuade others by example, which would be the more influential because of their local standing.[19] How such men were to be persuaded in the first place, Nagatsune did not say, but he clearly thought they could be reached through the written word without concrete demonstration, presumably because they were better educated, in a stronger economic position to take risks, and more accessible to abstract ideas than ordinary peasants. He and other technologists wrote for this class of men and saw them as potential leaders of reform. "What I pray for," one of them wrote in expressing hope for the improvement of sericulture, "is that the skilled of the world will teach the unskilled, and that the unskilled will learn from them."[20]

Nagatsune hoped that "the leading men [*osataru hito*] of villages will experiment with specialized tools so that they will see for themselves their advantages and will then teach others to use them."[21]

If the question had been put to Nagatsune, "You say that agricultural progress depends on the adoption of more efficient methods. But where do these improved methods come from and what assures that they will keep coming?" he could have answered the first part of the question but possibly not the second. He certainly would have pointed out, first, the importance of invention, using the modern word *hatsumei* and meaning the same thing by it that we do now—the discovery, inadvertently or by study and experiment, of any method that was

18. Tamura, *Ōkura*, 34.
19. Ōkura, *Nōgu*, 52.
20. Baba Shigehisa, *Kaiko yōiku tekagami*, in *Sansō koten shūsei*, ed. Sansō Koten Shūsei Hensankai (Ueda, 1927), 60–61.
21. Ōkura, *Nōgu*, 521.

new in some important respect.[22] And he could have illustrated such discoveries.

In his book on farm tools, he credited a farmer near Osaka named Imamiyamura Kyūzaemon with inventing a new plow, called a *nichō-gake*, with two parallel blades. The two blades permitted rows of a growing crop to be straddled and the rows between to be plowed, making it easier to plant a winter crop while the summer crop was still ripening and thus giving both crops a longer growing season. Because of the overlapping of the peaks of labor at the harvest and the planting, this procedure was difficult without the new plow, which Nagatsune claimed would turn eight times as much land in a day as could be turned with a spade. The new plow had a special advantage in the Kinai, where winter wheat overlapped summer cotton, a particularly labor-intensive crop, and where it was often necessary to avoid the overlap by removing cotton plants from the fields before they had finished blooming, with a consequent loss of yield and an adverse effect on the color and quality of the cotton.[23]

Not all important inventions could be attributed to particular persons. In the same book, Nagatsune cited the case of one anonymous invention, the *senbakoki* (or *mugikoki*, as he called it), one of the most important farm tools developed in the Tokugawa period. It consisted of a waist-high frame fitted with bamboo or iron teeth through which stalks of rice or other cereal were pulled to strip away the heads of grain. According to Nagatsune, it worked ten times faster than the older method of using one hand to pull the stalks between two sticks held in the other like chopsticks, which was slow and wasteful of grain and could not be used by children and old people since it required great skill and arm strength. Because the new thresher eased the usual shortage of labor at harvesttime, it reduced the danger of loss from bad weather and made easier the planting of a winter crop hard on the fall harvest.[24]

---

22. Ōkura, *Menpo*, 278. In *Nōgu benriron*, Nagatsune included a biography of an inventor and correspondent of his who had made important innovations in hydraulic engineering. For other references to invention, see Den Tomonao, "Yōsan suchi" (1794), MS, National Diet Library, Tokyo, vol. 2; and Narita Jūhyōe, *Yōsan kinuburui*, and Tsukada Yoemon, *Shinsen yōsan hisho*, in *Sansō koten shūsei*, 90, 322.

23. Ōkura, *Nōgu*, 96.

24. Ibid., 130–32.

Whether invention was potentially a process in which new discoveries forever succeeded one another was a question Nagatsune never seriously entertained. His first reaction might have been to dismiss it. Practically, he might have argued that there already existed an inexhaustible store of "inventions" not widely or universally known. This was the result of centuries of adaptation of farming—of tools, seed, crops, tillage—to local conditions of climate and soil. These adaptations varied endlessly, with the result that although the spade was used everywhere, for example, its size, design, and heft differed almost from village to village.[25] Because this kind of microadaptation suffused all aspects of farming, the country constituted a vast network of local agricultural experiment stations—not Nagatsune's words, but a concept he would have understood—and in any one of the stations there were likely to be inventions that could be applied advantageously elsewhere. To seek these out and spread knowledge of them was the object of Nagatsune's endless travels and voluminous publications. Such adaptations were to be found in backward as well as advanced regions, and scarcely any element of technology could be safely overlooked. What seemed clumsy to an observer might be perfectly suited to the problems of a particular agriculture. Consequently, Nagatsune explained, he included in his book on tools many sketches of implements whose value outside their own localities was unknown to him, and he exhorted readers to try out any tool that looked useful.[26]

It was obvious to him that enormous improvements in agriculture could be made by the diffusion of the innumerable "inventions" that existed. Miyazaki Yasusada had described the most advanced methods of cotton cultivation a century ago, and those methods, Nagatsune said, were backward compared to methods now in use. Even so, cotton was still grown properly in only half a dozen provinces; in others it was poorly fertilized or grown on the wrong kind of soil, even where the right kind was available.[27] In parts of the country all farming operations were done with a few basic tools, whereas in the Kinai specialized tools were used, with a substantial gain in efficiency, for weed-

---

25. Nagatsune stated that, in general, the same *kuwa* was not used beyond a radius of 3 *ri*, or 7.33 miles, mainly because of local differences in soil. *Nōgu*, 66.

26. Ibid., 5.

27. Ōkura, *Menpo*, 251–53.

ing, mulching, fertilizing, furrowing, aerating, raking, transplanting, thinning—even different spades were used for different soils.[28] Again, in the southwest, whale oil was commonly used to great effect against rice borer, whereas in the northeast crop losses from this insect were enormous.[29]

Still the question remained, in theory at least, of what would happen when all existing techniques were perfectly diffused. Would agricultural improvements come to a halt, or would new and more efficient techniques appear and keep appearing? Quite possibly Nagatsune would have come down on the optimistic side of this question. He obviously believed that farm technology was not stable and never could be, for no element of it could be applied in precisely the same way on two farms. Each farmer had to adapt each technical element to the unique combination of soil, climate, and terrain on his farm, trying first this and then that to get the best results. For this reason, contrary to the usual opinion, said Nagatsune, farming was the most subtle and demanding of all occupations, and there was all the difference in the world between the intelligent and the stupid farmer. By making constant adjustments and observing their results, the intelligent farmer would make "discoveries" or "inventions" (hatsumei).[30] Other technologists also seem to have believed that there would always be intelligent farmers who would improve on the most advanced techniques. The author of a book on sericulture, who clearly thought his book represented the best knowledge of the time, explained,

> What is written here is for persons without experience and by no means explains everything. The reader should keep firmly in mind the distinctive coloring of the worm upon sleeping and waking as explained earlier. Then with a few years of experience at raising worms he will master the technique, and there will be no such thing as failure. Moreover, in this way the number of experts (kōsha) will increase, and they will discover

28. Ōkura, Nōgu, 52. Nagatsune described the significance of tool design graphically: "If tools are ill adapted to their uses, even a strong young man working with them wastes a vast amount of strength (chikara) and effort (rō) and yet gets poor yields; whereas efficient tools can be used by a delicate young girl and yet give good results at the harvest." Ibid., 49.
29. Hayakawa, Ōkura, 75–86.
30. Ōkura, Menpo, 261, 278; Tamura, Ōkura, 245.

(hatsumei) excellent new methods, and the people who may be considered treasures of their localities will become numerous.[31]

Nagatsune gave an example of the kind of "inventions" an intelligent farmer might make. If he had on his farm both sandy and heavy soil, he would note that cotton grew more luxuriantly in the latter, but that, because the plants had to be placed farther apart, the yield from a given area of land was less than with the former. He might therefore try mixing the two—by no means an improbable idea, given the constant working of grass, leaves, ashes, and other matter into the soil and the practice of transferring soil from river bottoms to hillside terraces— thereby discovering how to improve the yield of either soil alone.[32]

Nagatsune seemed to believe that by virtue of the need for constant adaptation to local conditions, farming entailed experimentation and discovery. This process of adaptation, presumably what had produced the present stock of techniques, might go on indefinitely. But neither he nor any other technologist actually raised the problem of sustaining the process. For them, the real problem was the diffusion of existing techniques. They were quite familiar with the idea of experiment in the limited but important sense of deliberately trying alternative methods and comparing results.[33] Although he did not give all the details we would wish, the author of the oldest extant Japanese book on sericulture, published in Edo in 1712, appears to have described just this process when he recounted, "One year I tried various kinds of eggs and also early, middle, and late cocoons, and by this

31. Den, "Yōsan suchi," vol. 2. Most writers stressed the need for adaptability on the part of the farmer, since no rule of thumb for fertilization, planting dates, and so on applied equally to any two places. For a statement of the principle by a village headman in the mid-Tokugawa, see Nomura Noboru, ed., *Kinsei shomin shiryō* (Osaka, 1955), 187. The writer cited in the text claimed women made poor sericulturalists because, although they could learn a routine by rote, they were confused by any change in weather requiring adaptation. The reason, he said, was that "although there are women who are naturally intelligent, their understanding is inferior to that of even a stupid man." Den, "Yōsan suchi," vol. 1.

32. Ōkura, *Menpo*, 278.

33. Arthur Young used the term *experiment* to mean merely try or test. Thus, for example, it was an experiment to grow parsley on a farm for the first time for use in feeding sheep; when Young speaks of something "experimentally," he means knowing from having tried it oneself. *Farmer's Letters*, 219, 220, 224, 234, 236, 241, 244, and especially 246.

means discovered the reason that the worms' sequence of sleeping and waking is sometimes delayed."[34]

It was characteristic of the work of writers like Nagatsune that they described in great detail the technology they sought to disseminate. On the subject of fertilizing cotton, for example, Nagatsune told the reader, among other things, the kinds of fertilizers—dried sardines, oil cakes, urine, night soil, manure, ashes, river muck—to be used at particular stages of growth; the proportions of water to fertilizer in making liquid fertilizer; how the proportions should be varied with growth of the plant; the advantages and disadvantages of fast-acting fertilizer; how close to the stem to drill holes for fertilization; what types of fertilizer to avoid in certain kinds of soil; the appropriate quantity and probable cost of fertilizer per *tan* of land.[35] His book on tools contained drawings, with measurements, for each part of each tool, so they could be made easily by a village carpenter or blacksmith; usually he also gave information on where a tool could be purchased and the probable price. A passage from a book on sericulture will illustrate this attention to detail:

> On the third day following the emergence of the larvae from the eggs and their placement in trays, the now-young worms should be moved to new trays and placed in them with twice as much space as before. This is called *hekikoku*. Then, after the transfer, the center part of the leaves of the mulberry should be prepared for feeding, taking care to chop them cross-hatch. One must be careful not to use leaves too close to the stem at this time; such leaves are tough and the young worms cannot eat them well and therefore become thin. But if the tender center part is fed them, the worms grow fat and their sleeping and waking will be regular, so that they sleep and wake in unison. In feeding the worms from this time until the first sleep, it is necessary to pick and chop the mulberry leaves separately for each of eight feedings. For if the worms are fed with leaves left from even the previous feeding, the leaves will have dried out, and the worms will be unable to feed sufficiently and will starve.[36]

Or again:

> In choosing cotton seed, pick a bush of medium height with luxuriant shrubbery and no dead branches, and take cotton bolls in full bloom with

34. Baba, *Kaiko yōiku tekagami*, 60.
35. Ōkura, *Menpo*, 270–76.
36. Den, "Yōsan suchi," vol. 1.

heavy fibers from a branch three or four branches from the bottom. Do this when half the bolls on the tree have opened. The choice of the seed is extremely important and should be made by the family head and not entrusted to servants. In buying seed from other districts, examine it in the palm of the hand. Good seeds have a slightly black look, bad ones a reddish hue. Also knead the seed with the fingers. Round seeds generally are poor; pointed seeds generally are good. For storage, remove the seed from the surrounding cotton and dry it in the sun. Then take it out from time to time to expose it to the sun in order to keep it absolutely free of moisture.[37]

Passages like this, on nearly every page of every book, suggest the enormous importance these writers attached to technical proficiency in farming. Indeed it would hardly be an exaggeration to say that, in their view, success depended on this alone. If it were achieved, success was assured; if not, nothing would help. Other factors tended to be ignored or rejected outright. Little mention was made of frugality or industry in the farmer, qualities that orthodox Confucian writers harped on (to the neglect of technical skill), clearly not because these virtues were thought unimportant by the technologists but because they were taken for granted. No mention was made of the rate of taxation, the quality of justice, and other political and administrative factors that Confucian writers regarded as crucial, again not because they were deemed insignificant but because the technologists and their readers could do nothing about such matters.

However, the technologists vehemently attacked religion and the idea of fate in its effect on farming. Results were determined by skill, they insisted, not luck or divine help, and they insisted no doubt because contrary beliefs were widespread. Passages like this one from a book on sericulture by an egg-grower in Shinshū are typical:

> It is true that luck is not wholly absent from sericulture, yet in the final analysis results depend on skill. There are good and bad years depending on the weather, but one man gets better results than another because of his methods. Let two men be equally lucky, one will succeed and the other fail by reason of differences in skill. Even in good growing years when everyone prospers, yields vary with skill. Although everyone is the same distance from Heaven, it is plain that there are differences in ability (*jinriki*). People who do not recognize this fact stupidly pray to Buddha and *kami*, or they blame the eggs for their bad results and envy the success of others.

37. Ōkura, *Menpo*, 18.

Buddha and *kami* may help ever so much, but if one's sericultural methods are slipshod (*orosoka*), one is not going to get good results. But if one's methods are made sound by inquiring tirelessly about methods from experts, one will get good results even in bad years.[38]

Some sericultural writers seem to have excluded the possibility of failure with proper methods. "Sucesss with silkworms is not a matter of luck but depends entirely on skill."[39] "People who know [the five errors to avoid] will not have one bad year of cocoon production in a hundred."[40] "If one takes this book out before the worms hatch and thereafter reads the [appropriate section] every day and further follows the methods outlined, he will never suffer failure."[41]

Amid such assertions, however, notes of a different kind were occasionally struck. The author of an influential book on sericulture, first published in 1803 and translated into French in 1884, quoted a number of Chinese sayings of dubious value about sericulture, such as the one that burying silkworm dung on the northeast of a house would assure the prosperity of the family's sericulture.[42] In the middle of a sober technical discussion of the feeding of silkworms, another work paused to warn against raising more worms than one could feed, on the ground that this condemned part of the worms to starvation, an offense against nature (*shizen*) punishable by the ruin of the family and the sickness and death of its head.[43] Or again, an author deduced the love of the silkworm for warmth from the fact that these insects originated from the ear of a horse and therefore shared its *yō*, or male, sunloving character.[44]

The welfare of farm families was the principal objective of improved farming in Nagatsune's view. Indeed, he thought that one without the other was impossible, for farm families would change their

38. Shimizu Kinzaemon, *Yōsan kyōkō roku,* in *Sansō koten shūsei,* 409.
39. Den, "Yōsan suchi," vol. 1.
40. Narita, *Yōsan kinuburui,* 299.
41. Tsukada, *Shinsen yōsan hisho,* 70–71. This book, published in 1801, was a revision of a book (or manuscript) completed in 1757, and the language of this passage is almost word for word the same as a passage on page 25 of Baba, *Kaiko yōiku tekagami,* published in 1712.
42. Uegaki Morikuni, *Yōsan hiroku,* in *Sansō koten shūsei,* 9–10, 232.
43. Den, "Yōsan suchi," vol. 1.
44. Satō Tomonobu, *Yōsan chawaki,* in *Sansō koten shūsei,* 95.

ways only when they saw an advantage for themselves. In recommending particular reforms he was careful to point out advantages that would appeal to them—higher yields, lower costs, higher prices, full employment.[45] From some of the reforms he advocated farmers alone could benefit, such as improved tools to ease the physical strain of farm work or leather shoes to keep the farmer's feet warm as he went about his chores in cold winter weather. "If anyone sees this book and discovers in it methods that prove profitable," Nagatsune wrote in a treatise called *Hōkaroku*, "my many years of collecting information will not have been wasted."[46] Moreover, he was primarily interested in economic advantages. When he spoke of "profits," he meant monetary profits, as his writing mainly about cash crops and cottage industries, his concern with yields and costs, and his extensive citation of prices make clear. Even when apparently talking of other benefits, he was likely to have monetary profits in mind, as when he spoke of saving labor, which easily translated into lower wage bills or (alternatively) larger family earnings from by-employments with the labor saved.

Nagatsune and the sericultural writers laid great stress on the long-run significance of small increases in output or savings in costs, as the following examples show:

> Cotton seeds selected in this way [by suspension in water to pick the heaviest] may be sown sparingly, one-half *kanme* per *tan* of land being used instead of the normal *kanme* and a half; and because of their superiority these seeds will root well, grow vigorously, and require little thinning.[47]

> *Tsuranuki* [leather footgear worn in winter by Kinai peasants] have other advantages over straw sandals. One can go into the fields earlier in the morning and work better because they keep the feet warm and supple, and they eliminate the need for hot water to wash the feet daily. These are not great advantages in a single day, but day after day over a lifetime they become significant.[48]

> The utmost care should be taken not to let a single silkworm die: every worm represents a potential profit.[49]

45. Ōkura, *Nōgu*, 52, 63, 72, 75, 79; Ōkura, *Menpo*, 266, 267, 270, 276–77; Ōkura Nagatsune, *Seikatsuroku*, in *Nihon kagaku koten zenshū* 11:316, 332–35.
46. Tamura, *Ōkura*, 240.
47. Ōkura, *Menpo*, 270.
48. Ibid., 100–101.
49. Den, "Yōsan suchi," vol. 1.

Farm family profits—to use Nagatsune's phrase—were the primary aim of all technologists. The author of "Yōsan suchi," who was raised in a sericultural family, told how he came to write his influential book. Dissatisfied with the prevailing methods of sericulture, he read all the Chinese and Japanese books he could get on the subject and put their wisdom to the test; then he traveled about the country studying the methods of others; finally, he experimented with ideas of his own and made several "discoveries" (hatsumei). Then, he stated none too modestly, he understood sericulture thoroughly and, thinking it a shame to use his knowledge to benefit a single family, decided to share it with others as widely as possible. He pointed out how important the decision might be, for "families that raise silkworms earn half of their income from this source, so that those that are successful year after year become wealthy; those that fail are impoverished." [50]

Again and again, in different ways, the theme of wealth and family survival recurred in writings on sericulture. One author called sericulture "an occupation that creates wealth" (tomeru waza) because from egg to silk filament takes only a little more than a month; therefore, where sericulture flourished, wealth accumulated in every household. A single family known to this author had an income of 376 ryō (worth about 400 koku of rice at the time of writing) in ordinary years (reinen) from raising eggs; small operators (koie) in the same district made one-tenth that on average.[51] Another writer pointed out that sustained success with silkworms would permit a family "to multiply its wealth a hundredfold," and he offered an edifying example. There was a young boy in his district who lost his father, and the boy and his mother were so poor that they could not afford to light a fire morning or evening. Then the boy began raising silkworms, inquiring of expert growers throughout the neighborhood about method, working night and day to improve his technique. After five or six years he became expert himself and his profits began to increase; he invested them in farmland and forests and in time became the wealthiest man in the re-

---

50. Ibid. "I was able," the author writes, "to discover things that are in no modern or ancient book on sericulture."

51. Narita, Yōsan kinuburui, 319, 326–30.

gion. Thus, said the author, was *toku* (virtue, in this case filial piety) rewarded by *toku* (profit).[52]

Despite such dramatic illustrations of the efficacy of proper method, however, it is clear that the technologists were more interested in general improvement than in the enrichment of a few gifted or lucky farmers. Nagatsune spoke of ameliorating the labor of the "masses" (*banmin*) by improving farm implements; he and others hoped exceptional men in each village would instruct the ordinary men around them in better farming. One of the writers cited in the previous paragraph thought sericulture could increase the income of tens of thousands of little people (*saimin*) and declared that his book was intended "to make sericulture easy" and "to prevent the novice from falling into error."[53] Technologists conventionally apologized for their literary style, pointing out that they wrote so that, with the aid of phonetic signs alongside the characters and illustrations, even women and children could understand.[54]

In aiming at improving the income of the generality of farm families, these writers came very close to a crude notion of economic development. "If everyone will follow this book," said the preface to a sericultural manual published in 1810, "not only will it enrich individual families but the wealth of Heaven and Earth will increase like the sea coming in at full tide. Tomorrow we see the results of what we do today." Very often the technologists used the word *kaihatsu*—development—to describe the spread of an industry or technique over an entire district. Sometimes they implied *kaihatsu* without using the word, citing examples that make the meaning unmistakable.[55]

Narita Jūhyōe, a practicing Ōmi sericulturalist, estimated that the production of silk yarn had doubled between the beginning of the

52. Uegaki, *Yōsan hiroku*, 216, 289.
53 Narita, *Yōsan kinuburui*, 299.
54. Ibid., 297; Baba, *Kaiko yōiku tekagami*, 25; Uegaki, *Yosan hiroku*, 196. Although humble about their literary accomplishments, technologists were often far from modest about their technical knowledge: "This text contains many mistakes in characters, *kana*, and composition; but concerning the principles [*kotowari*] of sericulture, there is no doubt of its usefulness in all of the many provinces." Tsukada Yozaemon, *Teisei yōsan hisho,* in *Sansō koten shūsei*, 193.
55. Tsukada, *Shinsen yōsan hisho*, 63.

Tokugawa period and the early eighteenth century, then quadrupled between that time and the date of writing in 1813. Nor was this necessarily at the cost of other production. Sericulture, many writers pointed out, could be carried on entirely with female labor so as not to displace male labor from farming. Narita said that in all parts of the country, the prosperity of sericultural villages was obvious to anyone. He thought that the production of many other commodities had developed (*kaihatsu*) in the same way as silk yarn in the last one hundred or even fifty years. He illustrated from his own province, where a certain kind of weaving had been invented in the Meiwa era (1764–71) and half a century later, "ten thousand" families made their living by it.[56]

The technologists were not alone in grasping, although crudely, the idea of economic development; officials and orthodox Confucians were familiar enough with the idea of an increase in output from a given population.[57] But they had a very different notion of the benefit that ought to accrue from such development. For most of them its significance lay mainly in the increase in government revenue or an improvement of a domain's balance of payments; any increase in popular welfare was incidental.[58] For the technologists, the aim of development was clearly "to enrich" farm families and its effect on government finance was secondary. Indeed the latter subject was rarely mentioned. It is true that they occasionally used the word *kokueki*, a term meaning "benefit to the country" that was popular with officials; but the term was a vague one and it is by no means clear that, in using it, the technologists meant the interests of government rather than those of the people of the country or, where the stress was on government, that they meant increased revenue rather than the general political benefits that might be expected to flow from a prosperous population. The sericulturalist Narita, who used the term frequently, went out of his way to explain that by *kokueki* he did not mean increased government in-

56. Narita, *Yōsan kinuburui*, 211, 325, 343.

57. Fujita Teiichirō, *Kinsei keizai shisō no kenkyū* (Tokyo, 1966), 31–60.

58. Not everyone took this view. The author of *Kakinoki dan* wrote, "People who nowadays advocate profiting the nation (*kokueki*) strive only for the lord's profit. But if one would enrich a country, the best method is to make the people prosperous first." In Takimoto Seiichi, ed., *Nihon keizai taiten* (Tokyo, 1928), 15:132.

come, which entailed increasing taxation and was therefore like gambling in a family—taking from one to give to another—implying that
true *kokueki* was an increase in total welfare.[59]

This stress on private interest to the neglect of the government was
natural. The technologists wrote for the edification of farmers and
other producers whose exertions and innovations they saw as the main-
spring of economic progress, the only kind they were concerned with.
They were convinced, judging from Nagatsune's explicit statements
and the implicit assumptions of others, that farmers and artisans could
be moved only by self-interest. Moreover, as practical men of affairs,
they did not question the propriety of this egoism but accepted it as a
datum. Their view was radically un-Confucian, for if there was any
proposition that united Confucians it was that the social good required the curbing of selfish interests and could not conceivably be
built on them.

A considerable audience for technological information and views
on the propriety of selfishness emerged only in the eighteenth century
with the spread of commercial farming and farm by-employments.
These developments spread literacy, put cash in the hands of farmers
for buying books, and gave them a new appreciation of the importance
of increasing yields and cutting costs. How pure the appreciation could
be is shown by notes on agriculture made in Kishū about 1700. It is
clear that the author was speaking of an agriculture devoted mainly to
the cultivation of cereals, one with no major cash crops such as cotton,
indigo, or sugar. Yet, astonishingly, he not only listed and quantified
the costs and income of a typical farm for a year but also calculated the
cost of producing one *koku* of rice, breaking the cost into seventeen
inputs including the labor of separate operations (planting, weeding,
harvesting) and the cost of wear and tear on tools.[60]

The author of these notes was no ordinary peasant. But he came
very early; later there were many farmers with such attitudes scattered
about the country who could be reached by books. One book on se-

59. *Yōsan kinuburui*, 324.
60. Ōhata Saizō, *Saizōki*, in *Kinsei jikata keizai shiryō*, ed. Ono Takeo (Tokyo,
1932), 2:414.

riculture had a first printing of three thousand copies, and many books went through several editions.[61] The spread of literacy through rural Japan, without which the technical literature on farming could not have flourished, is a fascinating story not yet fully known;[62] clearly it was linked to closer ties between town and country and increased rural income. Rural schools usually were locally supported, and it is impossible to believe that this voluntary expenditure on education was at the expense of other forms of consumption, given the general austerity of rural life. At any rate, by the late eighteenth century, villages without several literate members were rare enough that Nagatsune could complain of farmers reading tales and stories rather than his books.

The developments that produced the audience—commercial farming, by-employments, rising income, literacy—produced the technologists themselves. Few came from the samurai or official class or even from castle-towns; they were typically from villages and small towns, where they were commercial farmers or merchants of the kind thrown up by the eighteenth-century changes in agriculture and the growth of rural industry. Miyazaki Yasusada was a farmer and, as his far-flung travels, citation of Chinese books, and surname suggest, a man of some means, education, and status.[63] Nagatsune's grandfather was a cotton-grower and merchant; he had relatives who were wax-makers on a sufficient scale to hire labor. He himself became a seedling merchant. Nearly all of the writers on sericulture were sericulturalists, egg-growers, or silk merchants, and several were at the same time village teachers and doctors.[64] Commercial occupations operating in highly competitive markets where profit margins were narrow, where the difference between 18 and 25 percent oil yield from rapeseed was the difference between bankruptcy and prosperity, turned some men's attention to improving technology.[65]

61. Sansō koten shūsei, 7; several books carried the word revised in their titles, such as Shinsen yōsan hisho and Teisei hōsan hisho.
62. Ronald P. Dore, Education in Tokugawa Japan (Berkeley and Los Angeles, 1965), 252–90.
63. Miyazaki, Nōgyō zensho, 6.
64. Sansō koten shūsei, 5–13.
65. Seikatsuroku, 316.

The travel that the more commercial of these occupations required of their followers also underlined the importance of technology by permitting the observation of local technical differences and their economic consequences. Significantly, nearly all writers on technology told of extensive travels either in the course of business or for study.[66] One is struck, moreover, by how easily these men, who were commoners and without office, seemed to have moved about the country; they spoke matter-of-factly of going from one province or region to another. Rarely did they mention going from domain to domain—as if these jurisdictions did not exist. Such apparent ease of movement did not exist until the eighteenth century. It was the result partly of improved transport and partly of the relaxation of administrative barriers because of the routine issuance and acceptance of passports in order to facilitate the movement of labor required by the geographically uneven growth of industry and trade.[67] Travel did not become legally or administratively free; but by the late eighteenth century no severe restrictions were put on the movement of individuals as opposed to families (the units responsible for the cultivation of land), as can be seen from the very high percentage of legal residents of villages who actually lived and worked elsewhere.[68]

The eighteenth-century improvement of the mails, largely because of the development of private postal companies, also facilitated the work of technologists, who depended on them to reach readers and to communicate with one another. Because technologists were widely scattered about the country, the mails must have been crucial to morale as well as to the substance of their work. Nagatsune knew farmers interested in agricultural improvement all over central Japan, no doubt partly from his travels but also from acquaintances made through the mails. In his book on tools he made a plea for readers to send him

66. Miyazaki, Nōgyō zenshu, 24–28.
67. Oka Mitsuo, Hōken sonraku no kenkyū (Tokyo, 1963), 152–53, 158. Twice serious efforts were made to return to their villages rural migrants to Edo and other cities, but even the more severe of these, in 1843, applied only to migrants who were without passports issued by their village headmen. Kōda Shigetomo, "Edo no chōnin no jinkō," Shakai keizai shigaku 8, no. 1 (April 1938): 13.
68. Hayami Akira, "Shinshū Yokouchi mura no chōki jinkō tōkei," Keizaigaku nenpō 10 (1968): 70.

sketches of any implement they found he had overlooked.[69] The preface of the *Shinsen yōsan hisho* reveals what appears to have been a three-cornered correspondence among sericulturalists, since the two authors of the preface lived in different provinces from each other and from the author of the text. How the three communicated does not appear; but the preface states that the book's author, after finishing the manuscript, had sent it to the preface writers, asking each for criticism in the light of the sericultural practices of his district.[70]

Two other factors help explain the rise of the technologists in the eighteenth century. It was one thing to improve one's own farming or sericulture, another to collect and collate information at great effort, and possibly expense, for the benefit of others. This civic spirit probably was partly due to the Confucian notion, which went with the spread of education, that the highest function of knowledge was public service, together with the inability of most technologists to hold public office. The other factor was the availability of technical books in Chinese as models, without which this particular substitute for office might not have occurred to so many. However, the technologists do not appear to have been greatly indebted to Chinese authors for their technology. They constantly cited their own observations and experience, rarely the Chinese; and when they did cite the Chinese it was often to establish the originality of their own views or the inappropriateness of Chinese experience to Japanese conditions.[71] Nagatsune did not mention China in the four books I am most familiar with; and except in historical passages the Chinese were only passingly mentioned by the sericulturalists. The one extended discussion of Chinese practice by any of the sericulturalists to the best of my knowledge was a passage discussing the fact that silkworms normally slept three times in China and four times in Japan and attributing this difference to environment. The proof was as follows: Three-sleep worms occasionally occurred in Japan as a result of mutation (*hensei*), and they were typically small and yielded silk of inferior quality. Some years ago the au-

69. Ōkura, *Nōgu,* 5.
70. Tsukada, *Shinsen yōsan hisho,* 63.
71. Boastful statements were fairly common; for example: "No one in China or Japan has previously explained these five prohibitions in such a way as to make sericulture easy [as this book has done]." Narita, *Yōsan kinuburui,* 299.

thor bred eggs from a number of three-sleep worms, discovering that in the second and third generations they slept four times and made excellent cocoons; but in following generations they reverted to three sleeps and again gave poor thread. "Hence, it is clear that our country is suited to four-sleep worms, and people should not be misled by a liking for novel things and Chinese books into thinking that three-sleep worms are profitable."[72]

How much influence the technologists may have had on practice is a matter of conjecture. Technology made slow but cumulatively important progress during the Tokugawa period; few branches failed to receive significant innovations, and the best existing techniques were greatly extended geographically, sometimes with powerful effects. In the course of the eighteenth century, for example, the *taka* loom, until then confined to Kyoto, displaced the simpler, smaller, and less versatile *izari* loom all over the country, increasing output and quality and variety of textiles.[73] If technological progress cannot be attributed to the technologists, it is at least certain that it could not have occurred without the commercial interest in technology these writers reflect.[74] Any influence on practice they may have had very likely continued beyond the Tokugawa period. Improvements in agriculture in the early decades after 1868 came largely from the better dissemination of Tokugawa technology by the efforts of private reformers who may have been influenced by their Tokugawa precursors.[75] The latter's books continued to circulate and to be reprinted after the Restoration, whereas new and better ones accumulated slowly. Private agricultural reformers, as well as the government officials who around 1900 became the

72. Den, "Yōsan suchi," vol. 3.
73. Sanpei Kōko, *Nihon kigyōshi* (Tokyo, 1961), 197–210.
74. The case of Russia underlines the importance to technological improvement in agriculture of a large class of commercially oriented farmers. During the latter half of the eighteenth and the first half of the nineteenth centuries, there appears to have been no significant general improvement in Russian agriculture, despite the proliferation of societies among the nobility for the improvement of farming. One of the reasons seems to be that the Russian serf was largely cut off from the market by lordly exploitation. Jerome Blum, *Lord and Peasant in Russia* (New York, 1964), 404–13; and Michael Confino, *Domaines et seigneurs en Russie vers la fin du XVIIIe siècle* (Paris, 1963).
75. Shūjirō Sawada, "Innovation in Japanese Agriculture, 1880–1935," in *The State and Economic Enterprise in Japan*, ed. William Lockwood (Princeton, 1965), 338–44; Ronald P. Dore, "Agricultural Improvements in Japan, 1870–1900," *Economic Development and Cultural Change* 9, no. 1, pt. 2 (October 1960): 69–91.

chief agents of reform, may have found inspiration in the example of men like Nagatsune.

But, surprisingly, politics was the sphere in which the technologists were perhaps most important. Although they said virtually nothing explicitly political, they gave expression to views radically subversive of a political system in which a hierarchy of inherited status, occupation, and economic reward was thought to represent a natural moral order. This order was profoundly disturbed by economic and technological change that altered occupations and status, and much of the political writing of the period attacked such change as arising from moral turpitude, as the assertion of selfish interests and ambitions over the public good, which had to be suppressed at all costs. The technologists, on the other hand, applauded it. They exhorted peasants to make themselves prosperous and indeed rich, and the richer the better, by improving their farming, expanding income from by-employments, and exploiting market opportunities.[76] How antagonistic this advice was to the orthodox conception of society can be seen by a glance at agrarian legislation in any part of the country; everywhere it was mainly concerned with suppressing the engrossment of land, high rural wages, the diversion of agricultural land and labor from staple to cash crops and from farming to trade and industry, and "luxurious" habits among the peasants—all manifestations of the kind of economic individualism encouraged by the technologists.[77]

Not only were the technologists saying, by implication, that men with enough intelligence and enterprise to alter their status and style of life might ignore the limitations placed on them by birth; they were also saying in effect that the pursuit of private interest by enough people would change society for the better by adding to the sum of

76. A village headman in Kawachi Province writing about the beginning of the eighteenth century warned that, for villagers, attempting to become too rich would almost inevitably lead to ruin; he gave many examples from his village to prove his point. These were mainly families who had tried to engage in long-distance trade with Nagasaki and the northern provinces. But his point was that there were great dangers in overextending oneself, not that there was anything wrong with such ventures if successful. Nomura, ed., *Kinsei shomin shiryō*, 194–95.

77. For example, *Akita kenshi: Shiryō—kinsei* (Akita, 1963), 2:852–53; Oka, *Hōken sonraku*, 152–60; Ishii Ryōsuke, ed., *Hanpōshū Tokushima han* (Tokyo, 1960), 921.

human welfare and therefore that the good of society was not uniquely determined by the moral quality of the ruler but might in part well up from the selfish strivings of the masses. It is not surprising that these implications were not drawn out, for they were directly contrary to the ideas of the ruling samurai class, namely, that the egoism of ordinary men could be held in check and kept from ruining society only by the constant example, admonition, and resolute power of the rulers. Almost certainly the technologists were largely unaware of the full implications of what they wrote.

But because every society, even Japanese, has its cranks, the technologists can be said to have been politically important only insofar as their ideals were shared by others. Fortunately the evidence, although circumstantial, suggests a tentative answer. The technologists spoke for a large number of people. First, they were not abstruse, precious, or even speculative thinkers. They were practical men who addressed themselves to the most concrete and widespread problems imaginable. Second, they wrote for a fairly large readership, considering the limitations of literacy. Third, they came from a large class of commercial farmers and rural merchants and manufacturers whose concerns they seem to have reflected, and these men were leaders in their own communities. Finally, in the increasingly commercial environment of the countryside, a considerable proportion of the peasants sought to maximize returns and enlarge their holdings and income at the expense of neighbors. Surviving land registers in districts not cut off from market influences by distance or geography show land continually changing hands by purchase and foreclosure,[78] confirming observations to this effect by contemporaries. Competitiveness within the rural population helps account for its extraordinary responsiveness after the Restoration to the opportunities of industrialization, public education, and freedom of residence and occupation. Altogether, therefore, the technologists appear to have reflected aspirations and strivings that were

78. Hasegawa Shinzō, "Kinsei kōki minami Kantō nōson no kōzō," *Shichō*, no. 99 (June 1967): 62–68; Imai Rintarō and Yagi Akihiro, *Hōken shakai no nōson kōzō* (Tokyo, 1955), 50–54; Inoue Kazuo, ed., *Mikawa no Kuni Hoi chihō shūmon ninbetsu aratamechō* (Toyohashi, 1961), 557–601.

widely shared, and if Ōkura Nagatsune had historical importance, it was as a spokesman not for novel but for commonplace ideas.

How commonplace has by no means been shown, but if the ideas of the technologists were as widespread as they seem, even though never expressed as an ideology, they help to explain the transition from Tokugawa to Meiji society. Great historical structures are not brought down until the popular beliefs and behavior supporting them are deeply eroded, and this long process is not always accompanied by the beating of ideological gongs. Unless some such process was at work in Tokugawa Japan, the Restoration and its social consequences become nearly unintelligible, and we are thrown back on speculations that pose greater problems of understanding than they would solve.

9

PEASANT TIME AND
FACTORY TIME IN JAPAN

If the farm family would escape poverty, it must treat time as precious [*kōin oshimubeshi*]. By rising early and shortening the daily rest period, two additional hours a day can be worked. That is seven hundred and twenty hours a year: the equivalent of sixty days, or two months, when no food is consumed, no wage paid, no oil required for lighting. . . . Thus can the farm family escape the pain of poverty, raise itself up, illuminate the deeds of ancestors, and confer blessings on descendants.

Nōgyō mōkun, a farm manual (1840)

In "Time, Work-Discipline, and Industrial Capitalism," E. P. Thompson describes how factories changed the time sense of English

Reprinted from *Past and Present*, no. 111 (May 1986).

common people, concluding that the "first generation of factory workers were taught by their masters the importance of time."[1] Workers of
that generation brought to the factory an inappropriate inner sense of
time that Thompson, following others, calls "task-orientation" and
identifies by three characteristics. First, the peasant or laborer pursues
an accustomed round of activity that appears to be a necessity imposed by nature's rhythms. Second, social intercourse and labor inter-
mingle, blurring the division between "life" and "work"; there is little
distinction between labor and "passing the time of day," and life alter-
nates between bouts of intense effort and idleness. Third, this attitude
toward labor appears wasteful and lacking in urgency to men used to
living by the clock.[2]

To illustrate, Thompson quotes descriptions of task-orientation in
nonmarket societies. Evans-Pritchard is quoted on the Nuer of the
Sudan: "The daily timepiece is the cattle clock, the round of pastoral
tasks, and the time of day and the passage of time through a day are to
the Nuer primarily the succession of these tasks and their relation to
one another."[3] And Pierre Bourdieu on the Algerian peasant:

> Submission to nature is inseparable from submission to the passage of
> time scanned in the rhythms of nature. The profound feelings of depen-
> dency and solidarity toward that nature whose vagaries and rigours he
> suffers, together with the rhythms and constraints to which he feels the
> more subject since his techniques are particularly precarious, foster in the
> Kabyle peasant the attitude of submission and nonchalant indifference to
> the passage of time which no one dreams of mastering, using up, or saving.[4]

1. *Past and Present*, no. 38 (December 1967): 86.
2. Ibid., 60.
3. Ibid., 58.
4. Edward E. Evans-Pritchard, *The Nuer* (Oxford, 1940), 100–104; Pierre Bourdieu, "The Attitude of the Algerian Peasant Toward Time," in *Mediterranean Countrymen,* ed. Julian Pitt-Rivers (Paris, 1969), both cited in Thompson, "Time," 58–59.
Jacques le Goff describes a similar attitude in fourteenth-century Europe: "On the
whole, labor time was still the time of an economy dominated by agrarian rhythms, free
of haste, careless of exactitude, unconcerned by productivity—and of a society created
in the image of the economy, *sober and modest,* without enormous appetites, unde-
manding, and incapable of quantitative efforts." *Time, Work, and Culture in the Middle
Ages* (Chicago, 1980), 44. David Landes holds that before the railway task-orientation
was characteristic of rural societies everywhere. *Revolution in Time: Clocks and the
Making of the Modern World* (Cambridge, Mass., 1983), 25, 72.

Over the centuries task-orientation had been modified in England, but not so far as to avoid a severe conflict over time when industry developed. The struggle to impose time discipline on English working people began in the domestic manufacturing districts long before the appearance of the factory. Nevertheless, it was in the textile mills and engineering workshops, where time discipline was most rigorously imposed, that the contest became most intense. Victory came hard; it took employers a generation of fines, money incentives, bells, preachings, and schoolings to teach workers the importance of time.[5] Nothing less was required than the creation of "a new human nature upon which . . . incentives could bite effectively."[6]

Thus the struggle over time discipline reveals with special clarity and economy the deep cultural conflict Thompson sees in the industrial revolution in England. The English transition to modern industry was peculiarly protracted and fraught with difficulty. England's was the first industrial revolution—there were "no Cadillacs, steel mills, or television sets to serve as demonstrations as to the object of the operation"—and all cases of industrialization are unique.[7] Yet Thompson appears to see in time discipline a universal element of conflict, illustrating at length that "what was said by the mercantile moralists as to the failures of the eighteenth-century English poor to respond to incentives and disciplines is often repeated . . . of the people of the developing countries today." He concludes, "Without time discipline we could not have the insistent energies of industrial man; and whether this discipline comes in the forms of Methodism, or of Stalinism, or of nationalism, it will come to the developing world."[8]

This seeming prediction of universal cultural conflict over time discipline describes Japanese industrialization poorly. Although early Japanese factories were deeply troubled by strife between workers and management, difficulties over time do not appear to have been particularly acute. Tokugawa peasants, who by Thompson's reckoning should

5. Thompson, "Time," 83, 85, 90.
6. Ibid., 57.
7. Ibid., 80.
8. Ibid., 91, 93.

have been the most task-oriented of people[9] and whose progeny provided a major part of the early factory labor force, had a lively appreciation of time. Not, of course, of clock time: that would have required
the habit of timing critical work independently of night, day, and
weather—impossible in farming, with or without clocks. Nevertheless, time was regarded as fleeting and precious, and great moral value
attached to its productive use. Farmers made elaborate efforts to coordinate work and to stretch nature's constraints by the skillful use of
early and late varieties, between-row planting, straw-covered planting
beds, fast-acting fertilizers,[10] and other time-saving devices. None of
this ingenuity, however, was for the benefit of individuals. Time was
not a personal possession but belonged primarily to families and,
through them, to kin, neighbors, and villages.

These two aspects of Tokugawa peasant time, the economic value
placed on time and the social value placed on its group control and
use, call into question the implicit assumption that all preindustrial
people have so casual a sense of time that they must be taught its value.
They also suggest that a high economic evaluation of time need not be
accompanied by its individualization but may instead be combined
with a high degree of time socialization. This combination in Japan not
only survived the coming of the factory but became the basis of a formidable time discipline within it. Indeed, it appears that time thrift in
the Japanese factory was not imposed unilaterally by management but
was a joint creation with workers.

PLANNING TIME

Basic to task-orientation is the given sequence of work set by nature's
rhythms so that "the day's tasks . . . seem to disclose themselves, by

9. Thompson attributes great importance to the development of wage labor in
farming in bringing a shift from task-orientation to timed labor. Ibid., 61. In the latter
half of the Tokugawa period, Japanese farming was carried on almost exclusively with
family and family exchange labor.

10. "It is characteristic of cotton that if fertilization is late, the branches and leaves
grow luxuriantly but the blossoms are sparse. . . . After midsummer a fast-acting fertilizer [ashi-hayaki koe] may be used. Although all plants require fertilizer, in the case of

the logic of need."[11] The only urgency is to do the task indicated; no one need pay close attention to time or to plan it. It bespeaks a certain attitude toward time, therefore, that one of the earliest Japanese books on farming, the *Hyakushō denki*, a compilation of current knowledge of crops, soils, and farm management dating from about 1680, insisted on the necessity of planning: "Things that must be done during the year ought to be planned and prepared for at the beginning of the year; otherwise everything will bunch up at the end and cause trouble. What must be done during the month should be planned on the first day. . . . If each moment of each day is not properly used, the peasant cannot escape a lifetime of poverty."[12]

If the author is not quite saying that time is money (as in fact he seems to be), he asserts unambiguously the need for planning. The assertion is not unusual; many of the several score of Tokugawa farm manuals that have been published strike the same theme. They warn the farmer to start preparing for the spring planting immediately after New Year's: to make straw mats and rope, repair tools, see that the animal gear is in order, clear ditches and weed paths, cut wood, trim windbreaks, make home repairs so that time need not be taken for such work later, and select and treat planting seed to be put away carefully and intermittently exposed to the sun to keep dry.[13] A much-

cotton the timing of the application is particularly important in determining profit and loss for the farmer." The author also states that in Bingo Province dried sardines were used as fertilizer because they were "fast-acting," helping to bring the plant to maturity before the typhoon season. Ōkura Nagatsune, *Menpo yōmu* (1833), in *Nihon kagaku koten zenshū*, ed. Saigusa Hiroto (Tokyo, 1944), 11:270, 286.

11. Thompson, "Time," 59. Landes also makes the point: "We have already noted the contrast between the 'natural' day of the peasant, marked and punctuated by the *given sequence* of agricultural tasks, and the man-made day of the townsman. The former is defined by the sun. The latter is bounded by artificial time signals and the technology of illumination and is devoted to the same task or an array of tasks *in no given sequence*" (italics mine). *Revolution in Time*, 72.

12. *Hyakushō denki* (Tokyo, 1977), 1:46.

13. For representative statements explicitly or implicitly advocating planning: Miyanaga Shōun, *Shika nōgyō dan* (1789), 6:43, 238; Fuchizawa En'emon, "Keiyū kosaku shō" (1847), 2:12; Takamine Yoshitada, *Nōmin no kinkōsaku no shidai oboegaki* (1789), 2:291; Onuki Man'emon, *Nōka shōkei shō* (1822), 22:20; Ozeki Masunari, *Kashoku kō* (1821), 22:113. Volume and page numbers refer to the collection of agricultural treatises *Nihon nōsho zenshū*, 31 vols. (Tokyo, 1977–81); hereafter cited NNZ. The books cited above come from the provinces of Etchū, Rikuchū, Iwashiro, and Shimotsuke; all except Shimotsuke were relatively backward economically.

quoted proverb advised, "Plan for the year in the first month; for the day, in the morning."[14]

Some purists recommended planning the day's work the night before, making ready any special food and gear that might be needed. Characteristically, the advice is detailed. *Saizōki,* a book written about the same time as the compilation just cited, stated: "If five people are to go the next day to cut grass on the mountain, sickles and carrying poles should be prepared the night before so as to be ready in the morning. Matters should be arranged so that the group can work the upland fields as it returns, and spades should be carried to the fields to be ready. . . . Thus each day's work should be planned the night before with great care."[15]

Time horizons were by no means limited to the year. Peasants were exhorted to economize at all times and especially to save in bumper years for the inevitable bad years, when even a wealthy peasant could lose his land, see his family driven onto the highways by destitution, and find himself another man's servant.[16] There was much discussion by farm writers of measures to improve soils (a notoriously long process), and many crops were held to do best at intervals of some years.[17] "If you grow eggplant, do not grow it again on the same field for five or six years. It dislikes short intervals and languishes if repeated within two or three years."[18]

From the eighteenth century on, writers of farm manuals were enthusiastic advocates of sericulture, vaunting its profitability and citing cases of whole villages and districts transformed by its adoption.[19] But

14. Miyanaga, *Shika nōgyō dan,* 208.

15. Ōhata Saizō *Saizōki* (ca. 1700, author from Kii Province), in *Kinsei jikata keizai shiryō,* ed. Ono Takeo (Tokyo, 1932), 2:410.

16. Sunakawa Yasui, *Nōjutsu kanseiki* (1723, author from Awa Province), in NNZ 10:333; Miyaoi Yasuo, *Nōgyō yōshū* (1812, author from Shimōsa Province), in NNZ 3:17; Miyanaga, *Shika nōgyō dan,* 166, 201, 270.

17. Yoshida Tomonao, *Kaikō suchi* (1795, author from Kōzuke Province), in NNZ 3:99–215.

18. Fukushima Teiyū, *Kōsaku shijō sho* (1839–42, author from Musashi Province), in NNZ 22:253.

19. Narita Jūhyōe, the author of *Yōsan kinuburui* (1813), tells how since the 1760s the development of sericulture and weaving had transformed the economy of his home district in Ōmi. As a result tens of thousands of people now made their living

silkworms were delicate creatures requiring constant and expert care; the beginner could not hope to master the art of raising them for some years, and in the meantime there would inevitably be losses from disease and poor-quality cocoons.[20] Since sericulture required special equipment, a major reallocation of time, and often a reallocation of land for mulberry as well, peasant households were not likely to take it up without thought of the long term. But many did take it up, since there was a dramatic spread of sericulture to new districts in the last half of the Tokugawa period.[21]

Like other Japanese, peasants thought of the family (*ie*) as a corporate entity with a transgenerational life of the highest moral value. Farm manual writers were overwhelmingly concerned with the details of farming, but amid the discussion of soils, tools, and plant varieties they often touched on themes of larger significance. An eighteenth-century farmer from Hokuriku who wrote on farming closed a discussion of the rice harvest with instructions on the rituals to be performed. Make a *torii* of bamboo in the field, he advised, and celebrate the Gods of the Five Grains; then husk the rice left over and present it to the ancestors of the family.[22]

Comments on the relation of the family to farming were sometimes more abstract:

> The farm family consists of the fields, wealth, and heirlooms handed down from ancestors. This property does not belong to us, the living members of the family. We must not imagine it does even in our dreams. It belongs to the ancestors who founded the house; we are only entrusted with its care and must pass it on to our descendants. . . . There may be events beyond our control, such as flood, fire, or illness, as a result of which the sale

from weaving and "the wilderness around these mean villages has been developed." He believed that whole provinces could be enriched in this way. In *Sansō koten shūsei,* ed. Sansō Koten Kankōkai Hensankai (Tokyo, 1930), 2:221, 323.

20. Den Tomonao, "Yōsan suchi" (1794), MS, National Diet Library, Tokyo, vol. 1.

21. Shōji Kichinosuke, *Kinsei yōsan hattatsushi* (Tokyo, 1964), 29.

22. Miyanaga, *Shika nōgyō dan,* 216. Elsewhere the author explains the connection among the gods, farming, and the family. Heaven assigned all occupations, including the backbreaking work of farming. Persons who did this work "sincerely" would accumulate "hidden virtue" (*intoku*) and would someday receive the "rewards" (*yōhō*) of the gods, which "reach even to descendants" (pp. 61–62).

of property becomes unavoidable. In that case, we must make every effort by saving and planning to recover what has been sold, make the
property whole again, and pass it on undiminished to our children and
grandchildren.[23]

LAND FORMS, CROPPING DECISIONS, AND PLANNING

Cropping decisions raised difficult problems of work scheduling, which
were in some degree different for each farm family. The idiosyncratic
nature of such problems resulted mainly from land forms and patterns
of land transfer over long periods of the past. By Tokugawa times,
farms were typically composed of a number of small and scattered
fields, usually on uneven terrain, where even adjoining fields (according to one writer) were likely to be different in respect to soil, drainage,
sunlight, access to water, or exposure to wind. Consequently most
farmers grew a mix of crops and crop varieties, and the mix tended to
differ from neighbor to neighbor. Manual writers insisted that the
most important factor separating the quality of one man's farming
from another's was skill in matching crops and varieties to the growing
conditions of individual fields.[24]

And cropping decisions required anticipating work flow. Each
crop[25] entailed a number of narrowly timed tasks: seed treatment, soil
preparation, planting (and often transplanting), repeated and num-
bered weedings and fertilizations, and so on. Hence cropping decisions
set a work schedule for an entire growing season.[26] Since most families

23. Miyaoi, Nōgyō yōshū, 15–16.

24. NNZ 22:335.

25. In Kōsaku shiyō sho (1839–42), Fukushima Teiyū of Musashi Province dis-
cusses over thirty crops grown in his village, in most cases listing several varieties of
each: twenty-five for rice, twelve for potatoes, six for wheat, fourteen for buckwheat. In
NNZ 22:203–80.

26. Frederick Barth describes a somewhat similar need to plan cropping among the
Fur-speaking agriculturalists in central Africa: "Every individual needs to obtain plots
of several kinds, suitable for different crops and uses. A configuration of sizes and types
of farm implies an allocation of labour to alternative products: millet, and some onions,
for basic subsistence, and readily marketable crops such as tomatoes, wheat, garlic,
onions for cash needs. . . . In the course of the year, every person will need to cultivate at

had few adult workers and little or no access to work animals, careful thought had to be given to the scheduling implications of crop choices. Critical and labor-intensive tasks could not coincide or overlap too broadly;[27] otherwise a planting would be ten days late, a weeding skipped, a fertilization half-done.[28] Since there was no way of controlling weather, scheduling problems were likely to be serious even with the best of planning and some manual writers gave advice on which tasks to skip in specific cases of time conflict.[29]

The coordination of work on crops grown during the same season was complicated by the widespread practice of double-cropping. Winter and summer crops tended to overlap and crowd one another. A standard problem in manuals was how to get winter wheat planted early enough to stand the onset of cold weather but not so early as to interfere with the fall rice harvest. Authors universally advised staggering the fall harvest by a mix of early, middle, and late rice varieties;[30] however, staggering complicated the summer work schedule and at times required compensatory changes in other crops.[31] Another technique for summer-winter combinations was to start the new crop be-

least one farm [plot] in each category. One may choose to distribute the labour more equally between summer and winter crops. Individual skills and preferences, and established usufruct rights to irrigated land, will influence these allocations." "Economic Spheres in Darfur," in *Themes in Economic Anthropology*, ed. Raymond Firth (London, 1978), 189.

27. "From the spring plowing through planting, transplanting, and weeding to the fall, every task has its proper time. Even a single day's delay of a task may result in crop failure in a bumper year." Miyanaga, *Shika nōgyō dan*, 208–9.

28. The diary of the Noguchi family in modern Fukuoka Prefecture provides concrete illustrations of how one operation's getting off schedule affected others. "Noguchi-ke nikki" (1847–65), in NNZ 11:225.

29. *Satokagami* (ca. 1830–40, by an unknown author from Hizen Province), in NNZ 11:105; Fukushima, *Kōsaku shiyō sho*, 206.

30. The importance of varieties is suggested in Miyanaga, *Shika nōgyō dan*, 79–81. The author listed only those varieties used in his and neighboring villages: nine early, twenty-four middle, and thirty-three late varieties.

31. Deciding the optimum proportions of different varieties was a complicated matter. Varieties often had particular soil preferences and so were not perfectly interchangeable. Also, although early varieties relieved pressure on the fall planting, they yielded poorly and tended to interfere with the spring wheat harvest; late varieties yielded well but required more labor to protect them from birds and animals, pressed on the fall planting, and were subject to damage from early winter weather. Although middle varieties alleviated these strains and yielded well, they concentrated labor at the busiest time of year for other crops.

tween the rows of the maturing crop, which changed work schedules by advancing planting dates and raised an additional delicate problem. The new crop had to be up, firmly rooted, and clearly visible by the time the old crop was ready to harvest, but not yet of a size to interfere with harvest work or suffer damage from it.

Planning strategies must have been standardized to some degree, but for a variety of reasons routinization was limited. Fields frequently changed hands because of purchase, foreclosure, and rental, and each transfer changed the labor requirements and cropping possibilities of two farms. Cropping rules themselves decreed year-to-year changes. Rice varieties were not supposed to be planted continuously on the same land, and crop records in fact show frequent changes of variety on particular fields.[32] A surprising number of common crops required rotation intervals of more than one year: safflower two years, eggplant five, peas six, Chinese yams seven.[33] Then there was always the wild card of weather, upsetting the most carefully laid plans and forcing complex readjustments. The farm diary of the Noguchi family of Kyūshū, running from 1847 to 1865, is a saga of struggle against weather. Far from being entranced by nature's rhythms, the Noguchi were ever fighting to overcome its irregularities: flood one year, drought the next, too much rain early in the summer, too little later.[34]

Many authors insisted on record keeping as an aid to planning—otherwise who could remember how long it was since yams had been grown on "Front Field"?—and some authors had very exacting standards of the art. In his treatise on cotton, Ōkura Nagatsune (1768–1856) advocated standardizing the time for recording yields: "After picking the cotton each day, return immediately to the house, weigh the cotton, and enter the results in a notebook at so-called picking-weight, since the weight will vary later on."[35] No doubt such record keeping was exceptional, but farm records nonetheless survive in con-

---

32. For examples: Nakamura Satoru, "Kinsei senshin chiiki no nōgyō kōzō," *Kyōto Daigaku Jinbun Kagaku Kenkyūjo chōsa hōkoku*, no. 12 (March 1965): 83; Yokosen'i Mitsuaki, "Kinsei kōki minami Kantō no nōgyō gijutsu," *Nihon rekishi*, no. 96 (June 1956): 56–57.

33. *NNZ* 22:331.

34. "Noguchi-ke nikki," 211–84.

35. Ōkura, *Menpo*, 281.

siderable number and from widely scattered places. The Noguchi family diary gives rice yields annually for each field and records the average yield per *tan* of land for each variety.

TIME IN THE ISHIKAWA FARM DIARY

We get a realistic, as opposed to a theoretical or cautionary, view of the use of time in the diary for 1867 of the head of a family named Ishikawa[36] that lived in the hilly country southwest of Edo, where farming was less commercial and technically advanced than in some parts of the country. For every day of the year, Ishikawa notes his activities, although not what others in the family did, and unfortunately his notations are terse—"worked wheat," "went to market"—often leaving the reader with an imperfect idea of what he did. Yet the 354 entries, accounting for every day of the lunar year,[37] give us as close a view of the actual use of time by a Tokugawa farmer as we are likely to get. There is also a helpful year-end summary of crop yields, attesting to Ishikawa's interest in productivity and to the fact that the family grew twelve crops and also raised silkworms. To coordinate so many operations took expert timing, and it was not unusual for Ishikawa to go on successive days from cutting one crop to seeding another, on to milling a third, then back to threshing the first.

In Ishikawa's case coordination was complicated by status. As a low-ranking samurai and a man of importance in his village, he was obliged to spend 39 days during the year on public and ceremonial functions, some of which by their nature could not have been timed for his convenience. The remaining 315 days were distributed broadly

36. This family diary, covering the period 1720–1942, was discovered in 1942 by Toya Toshiyuki, a young scholar of agricultural history who later died as a soldier in the Philippines. The Ishikawa were owner-cultivators with approximately one *chō* of land in the late Tokugawa period and therefore may be thought well-off but not rich, although they had in addition a modest income as low-ranking samurai. Toya Toshiyuki, *Kinsei nōgyō keiei ron* (Tokyo, 1949), 157–68. The diary for four years—1728, 1804, 1840, and 1867—appears in ibid., 169–228.

37. There were 354 days in the ordinary year in the lunar calendar, making it 11 days short of the solar year. To compensate, an additional month was inserted every 33 or 34 months.

among 222 outside workdays, 35 inside workdays, 2 market days, 38 mixed workdays (part inside and part outside, including 16 part-day trips to market), and 18 rest days. What was meant by "inside work" is uncertain but evidently not "rest," which was named separately. In addition to the usual chores recommended for slack seasons, such as rope making, tool repair, and the treatment of seeds, inside work may have included help with the silkworms, for which the women of the family were responsible, and the record keeping necessary for the year-end summary of yields. Outside work is invariably specified, providing the diary's most detailed information on the use of time.

Three things stand out in these detailed entries: the extraordinary variability of tasks from day to day, the steadiness of the work flow, and the general infrequency of rest days. One hundred twenty-seven different field tasks (many frequently repeated) are recorded during the year. Often two or three appear in a single day, and each day's tasks tend to vary from those of the previous day. The entries give an immediate impression of this variability, but it is made clearer by some simple counting. If we classify each of the 260 outside workdays (including 38 mixed workdays) by the degree of correspondence between the work done on that day and the work done on the next previous outside workday, we get the following breakdown:

Type of Task	Number	Percentage
Tasks completely different	158	60.7
Tasks partly different	61	23.4
Tasks same	41	15.7
TOTAL	260	99.8

Such variability does not necessarily mean continuous and radical improvisation. Within broad limits the round of work was implicit in the cropping pattern. But the cropping pattern itself was not a given; it was a considered plan to which there were possible alternatives, as is clear from the important changes in cropping on the Ishikawa holding between 1720 (for which there is year-end summary) and 1867. At the same time, with so many crops and tasks the detailed and final ordering of work on many days must have waited until the last minute. Unforeseen events also occasioned adjustment in plans: the village celebration of a much-needed rain in the eighth month; trips to market (possibly linked to price movements); emergency construction that required several days of timber cutting followed by irregular visits from a carpenter who had to be assisted. There is some indication of agricultural rhythms in the tendency of public work to fall early in the year before the spring planting. But some duties continued at regular intervals during the year, and rest days show little seasonal variation. The most rest days in any month is five in the first; and astonishingly no month after the third has more than one except the seventh month, with three. The alternating bouts of intense work and leisure that Thompson emphasizes are not easily discernible, but the Ishikawa family may have been exceptional.

FARM MANUALS AND
STRUCTURAL CHANGE IN AGRICULTURE

It is impossible to know how many Tokugawa peasants followed the advice of the manuals, but we have some clues. Many manual writers were farmers themselves: so they wrote, and their knowledge of local crop varieties, soils, and problems of weather and terrain confirms their claim. Others based their writings largely on interviews with *rōnō*, old and sage farmers. But neither farmer-authors nor *rōnō* were a cross section of the farming population. Authors were literate at a rare level; *rōnō* sought out for their exceptional knowledge were usually local notables and otherwise exceptional men. Often both were idealistically committed to improving Japanese farming.[38]

But what set these men apart also gave them influence. *Rōnō* played a semiofficial role in spreading agricultural improvements in their home districts in early and middle Meiji,[39] and it is likely that they performed a similar if less organized role earlier. Ōkura Nagatsune, who

---

38. "So that farmers can read this book easily I have avoided the use of difficult characters, in the hope of being widely understood [*zoku ni tsūzuru*]." Ōkura Nagatsune, *Nōgu benriron*, in NNZ 15:136.

39. Ronald P. Dore, "Agricultural Improvement in Japan, 1870–1900," in *Economic Development and Cultural Change* 9, no. 1, pt. 2 (October 1960): 77–82.

from his extensive travels and interviews had as good a knowledge of rural society as any late Tokugawa writer, believed that agricultural innovations were typically spread by demonstration: local experts first demonstrated them, and then others followed their lead. Peasants, he wrote, would no sooner turn their backs on an innovation shown to be useful than refuse a doctor when ill.[40] A village headman, writing in Akita in 1825, might have been illustrating Nagatsune's text in telling how his father introduced sericulture to his district: "At first he suffered losses, but as he gained experience the undertaking became extraordinarily profitable. The entire village without exception took it up as a by-employment, and it now makes a great contribution to our property."[41]

Nagatsune's own book *Nōgu benriron*, published in 1822, was immensely popular. The aim of the book, "to reduce the people's labor," is evident on nearly every page.[42] The specialization of tools, Nagatsune argued, was the secret both of proper cultivation and of the saving of labor. He held up Kinai farmers as models to the rest of the country, since they had a different tool for each task and felt that with anything but the right tool "they waste time and effort and get poor results."[43]

Nagatsune had collected information from all over the country on efficient tools developed to meet special local conditions but not widely known elsewhere. He included drawings and descriptions of those that seemed most promising to him and accompanied the drawings with comments on the tool's efficacy. The *daikoku* would "cut through roots as if they were tofu." The *eburi*, a cunning rake for mounding up the soil around plants, did a better job than the hoe and was easy to

---

40. Tamura Eitarō, *Sangyō shidōsha Ōkura Nagatsune* (Tokyo, 1944), 31. Nagatsune was very much aware of the great progress that could be made by using improved technology. He praises *Nōgyō zensho*, a book on agriculture by Miyazaki Yasusada completed in 1697, adding, "But that was over a hundred years ago and methods were backward then compared to today." Ōkura, *Menpo*, 253.

41. *Akita kenshi: Shiryō—kinsei* (Akita, 1963), 491.

42. Ōkura said that his ambition to reduce the people's labor was motivated by a desire to repay *kokuon*, the blessings conferred by the nation on Japanese. This sentiment, saving time and labor for the nation, should be understood in connection with notions about the ownership of time discussed in the section of this essay entitled "Time, Family, and Community." Ōkura, *Nōgu*, in *NNZ* 15:133–34.

43. Ibid., 52.

use. The thousand-tooth thresher could thresh ten times more grain in a given time than the old chopstick thresher.[44]

Village opinion tended to enforce the farming standards set by *rōnō* and manual writers like Nagatsune. Even in backward Hokuriku neighbors watched one another's farming with a critical eye. The Hokuriku author quoted earlier on harvest ritual spoke of a fad in his district for the latest farm tool, saying that if a family did not have one, neighbors talked.[45] (His book, incidentally, had illustrations of over fifty farm tools.) He also warned about carelessly getting grains of early rice varieties mixed with the seed of middle varieties because, aside from other disadvantages, the field would present a motley appearance when the plants matured. "People will then take the field to be neglected and think it disgraceful."[46]

The manual writers' concern for the productive use of time was the result of the continuous tightening of the labor market during the second half of the Tokugawa period, a tightening that drove home the manuals' lessons to the farmer. Trade, industry, and farm output were all expanding during this period, while overall population growth was almost nil for reasons that are poorly understood but may include widespread family limitation. As a result, real wages rose steadily and large holders who depended in critical part on nonfamily labor (mainly servants and tenant labor services) found costs rising and labor less reliable. Increasingly they were unable to compete with the smaller family farm. Slowly, over an ever-larger part of the country, they found it prudent to transfer fields to small farmers by sale or rental.[47]

This shift in land management altered the context of decisions about time. First, farming now took place within smaller and more

44. Ibid., 90.
45. Miyanaga, *Shika nogyo dan*, 335.
46. Ibid., 46–47.
47. For an overall view of economic growth during the Tokugawa period, see Susan B. Hanley and Kozo Yamamura, *Economic and Demographic Change in Preindustrial Japan, 1600–1868* (Princeton, 1977), 66–90; also Nakamura Satoru, *Meiji Ishin no kiso kōzō* (Tokyo, 1956), 164–208. An outline of Tokugawa population trends can be found in the first chapter of Thomas C. Smith, *Nakahara: Family Farming and Population in a Japanese Village* (Stanford, 1977). The shift away from large holdings is described in Thomas C. Smith, *The Agrarian Origins of Modern Japan* (Stanford, 1959), 108–56.

solidary units, where work more directly and obviously benefited those who did it. Second, as farms (as opposed to units of ownership) came more nearly to match average family size, the larger farms decreasing and the smaller increasing in size, less reliance could be placed on hiring labor from neighbors at peaks of workload.[48] Labor might not be available at all and was certain to cost more if it was. For that reason writers repeatedly warned farmers that working more land than they could with family labor was the way to ruin.[49] Third, the family farmer was able to integrate farming with by-employments in trade and industry in a way large farmers working with an array of servants and tenants never could.

The discipline of the small family made it possible to move labor back and forth from farming to by-employments, not only seasonally but from day to day and within the day, and also to use the off-farm earnings of individuals for the benefit of the farm and the family. This flexibility encouraged the spread of by-employments and thus put even tighter time pressure on agriculture. A sericulturist describes the result:

> Spring cocoons overlap both the spring wheat harvest and the rice transplanting. It is just before the rice transplanting is completed that the worms require the most care. Then comes the reeling of filament from the new cocoons, and after that, when it is time to weed the rice and the weather is unbearably hot, the summer cocoons come on and the reeling starts again. At these times, when a single day's neglect means the loss of worms from death, the sericulturist is so busy he cannot tell night from day.[50]

48. This situation persisted into the period after World War II. At the end of the war, 70 percent of farm families worked less than 1.0 hectare of arable land; the proportion of hired labor used on holdings up to 0.5 hectare was 2.7 percent, and on holdings of 0.5 to 1.0 hectare, 2.4 percent. These figures are national averages and do not include labor received in exchange for labor. Ōuchi Tsutomu, Nihon nōgyōron (Tokyo, 1978), 154.

49. One writer, using figures on output and wages, demonstrated that the year a solvent farm family added to its holding and hired labor to work the additional land, "that year will it suffer a deficit and begin to borrow money." Seki Jun'ya, Hansei kaikaku to Meiji Ishin (Tokyo, 1956), 63. Others made the same point without the aid of figures: Itō, Nōgyō mōkun, 248, and Ōnuki, Nōka shōkei shō, 28. The author of the latter stated, "It is well to cultivate an amount of arable land proportionate to the number of persons in the family or slightly less. If the amount is greater, labor will be insufficient and the quality of care will suffer."

50. Narita, Yōsan kinuburui, 333.

All these developments encouraged attention to the use of time; indeed, the penalty for inattention could be extreme, since farming was highly competitive. Small plots of land moved continuously from family to family by sale and mortgage, shifting holders up and down the social and economic ladder of the village. Substantial holdings frequently melted away while small and medium ones grew; and holdings that grew in one decade commonly shrank in the next.[51] This turbulence was inherent to family farming with little or no use of animals. Relative farming efficiency—and hence the ability to retain and expand holdings against competitors—was powerfully affected by family size and age and sex structure in proportion to holding size; and family size and structure perpetually changed as a result of birth, marriage, aging, and death.[52] No farming family, therefore, had any sort of long-term security, and families with a nonchalant attitude toward time were certain to be short-lived.

Families were continually disappearing from their villages, and new ones appearing because of the segmentation of families successful enough to divide land between heirs. Biological failure was not the reason for family demises; heirs could always be adopted if there was land and other property to inherit. Families died out or dispersed or migrated because they failed economically.[53] In striving to manage time and energy efficiently, therefore, families were struggling for corporate continuity in the community.

Failure in the struggle had unhappy consequences: "If a family sells off the buildings and homesite handed down from ancestors, neglects its fields and sees them dispersed to others and so loses its rights (*kabu*) in the village, then it may flee to the most distant place in the land, but it cannot escape Heaven's punishment for the crime of unfiliality."[54] Or again: "Let us pray to the gods and Buddha that our

51. For examples. Imai Rintarō and Yagi Akihiro, *Hōhen shakai no nōson bōzō* (Tokyo, 1955), 50–53; Smith, *Nakahara*, 118–22; for a twentieth-century case, Ronald P. Dore, *Shinohata* (New York, 1978), 32.

52. There were ways to mitigate cyclical effects: methods such as adoption in and out of the family, delay or hastening of marriages in and out, and possibly infanticide. See Smith, *Nakahara*, 59–85, 122–46.

53. Ibid., 127–30.

54. Ōnuki, *Nōka shōkei shō*, 20.

children surpass others and make their way in life. For if they disregard the wishes of their parents, live idly, and bring ruin to the family, the effects of their crime will last for generations to come."[55]

CONCEPTS OF TIME AND PRODUCTIVITY

Where farmers had to ponder the duration, order, and potential interchange of tasks, they were not likely to find difficulty in thinking of time abstractly relative to their work. This abstraction occurred, in fact, before the shift of land from large to small holders was far advanced. The earliest Japanese book on farming, the *Shinmin kangetsushū*,[56] dating from the first half of the seventeenth century, lists the man-days per unit of land required for various farming operations on both paddy and upland.[57] Such estimates were a standard feature of later farm manuals and became more refined with time. They soon included not only man-days per unit of land for all the major crops of a district but an increasingly detailed breakdown of labor-time for each crop by task, requiring figures in tenths of man-days, with adjustments if the work was done by women or children.[58]

In addition to yields and labor requirements, the manuals often listed for the major staples the cost per *tan* of land for fertilizer, tools, wages, animal hire, taxes, and so on. The difference between yields and these costs may be taken as the return on family labor. (Costs were sometimes cited in kind but could be readily converted to money at market prices.) Thus the monetary return on family labor on a man-day basis was theoretically calculable for major crops.[59] Rough esti-

55. Ōhata, *Saizōki*, 399.
56. Compiled in response to questions concerning agriculture by Doi Seiryō (1546–1626), the lord of a small domain in Iyo Province. NNZ, vol. 10.
57. Ibid., 109–20. Also included are estimates of labor for a great variety of ancillary tasks: twenty days a year for house repair, twenty for cleaning wells and ditches, three for cutting and shaping wood for the handles of farm tools, and so on.
58. Takamine, *Nōmin no kinkōsaku no shidai oboegaki*, 293–308. To the best of my knowledge, farmers generally had no way of measuring these values precisely. Few Western-style clocks can have been present in peasant villages, although it is possible that fire clocks and sand clocks were used.
59. For example, Fukushima, *Kōsaku shiyō sho*, 286–94, gives (a) the cost of each item of expense for a married couple without children cultivating six *tan* of paddy and

mates of this kind must have informed shifts in cropping when farmers, in great number and often illegally, took significant percentages of land out of rice to grow cotton, mulberry, indigo, sugar, tobacco, and rush for tatami.[60]

TIME, FAMILY, AND COMMUNITY

Time was one of the two major productive resources of Japanese peasants; like its counterpart, property, it belonged to the family, a condition reflected in law. Families were punishable for the transgressions of individual members and therefore expected to control them. In population registers—the basic documents of administrative and legal control—individuals were always entered by family membership, never autonomously, although sometimes of necessity they were listed as one-person families. The rights to sit in the village assembly, to draw water from the irrigation system, to participate in the management of the shrine, even to reside in the community: all were lodged in families, never in individuals. If all living members of a family died, the family's name and rights (*kabu*) in the village would continue to exist if there were property to inherit; relatives or the village itself would then appoint an heir, whether kin or not, to inherit the family name, house, ancestors, and tax burdens.

The primacy of the family over its members is seen in the language of farm manuals. If by "farmer" we mean an individual man or woman managing a farm, agricultural writers had no equivalent. Of course they had several common words for peasant—*nōmin, hyakushō,* and *nōfu*—but none that necessarily suggested a managerial role. When they had need to express the idea of a decision-making agent in farm-

---

six *tan* of dry fields, and (b) the value of the crops produced. Each item of expense and production is given in both physical and monetary values. These figures therefore yield the return on an unknown number of man-days of work; and a reasonable estimate of the number of man-days can be derived from the number of man-days for various operations required on three *tan* of paddy and four *tan* of dry fields given elsewhere in the book, making possible the calculation of return per man-day.

60. Ōhata, *Saizōki,* 401; Furushima Toshio and Nagahara Keiji, *Shōhin seisan to kisei jinushisei* (Tokyo, 1954), 23, 32, 36; Ōkura, *Nōgu,* 212.

ing, they used the word *nōka*, or farm family. Thus the *nōka* was said to ponder, decide, plan, harvest, and succeed or fail, and to have ancestors and descendants.

Some manual writers were concerned with assuring the high degree of individual compliance with *nōka* decisions required. Compliance was urgent, since it was a "principle [*ri*] ever to be kept in mind" that the *nōka* could not move in unison (*sorotte*), hence farm successfully, without "a complete harmony of wills." The utmost care should be taken, therefore, to raise children not to be self-willed (*wagamama*) or self-indulgent (*hoshiimama*), so that they might grow up to be frugal and forbearing and "modestly give way to others": "Children must be warned from an early age against extravagance and willfulness and self-indulgence. Their clothing and the other articles they use must be kept below the family's status and means. If out of too much love children are indulged with fine things, they will come to love extravagance, and this extravagance will grow with age. Restraint becomes difficult if it is not taught early."[61]

Time, which belonged to the family, also belonged through it to the village and neighbors on whom the family depended for access to water, common land, the village shrine, and mutual aid. Villages laid down complex rules on the use of time: the proper number of days' mourning for family members of different status; the kind and number of courses to be served guests at weddings and funerals, and hence the time spent preparing them; the occasions on which sake could be brought to the fields and served during work breaks; whether villagers could leave the village for work outside.[62] Many villages set standard wage rates for various kinds of farm work, by sex, at various levels of skill.[63] Leaving work for New Year's greetings was forbidden in some villages except between parents and children.[64]

As the bylaws of village youth groups (*wakashu*) show, communal regulation of time was by no means a strictly utilitarian concern. These

61. Miyanaga, *Shika nōgyō dan*, 218.
62. *Nihon shomin seikatsu shiryō shūsei* (Tokyo, 1979), 21:757, 760, 762–68; Oka Mitsuo, *Hōken sonraku no kenkyū* (Tokyo, 1962).
63. Andō Seiichi, "Kinsei zaikata shōgyō no tenkai," *Kishū keizaishi kenkyū sōsho* 5 (July 1956): 4–5.
64. Maeda Masaharu, *Nihon kinsei sonpō no kenkyū* (Tokyo, 1952), 44.

documents are moral protocols having little or nothing to do with procedural matters within the group. They enjoin frugal, decorous, sober, and industrious behavior, which is identified with filial piety and winning the favor of the "gods of Heaven and Earth" (*tenchi kamigami*). They illustrate and warn against self-indulgence, avarice, licentiousness, quarrelsomeness, and other kinds of immorality associated with the misuse of time. Spending "leisure with young friends may result in unseemly events and unfiliality toward father and mother."[65] Thus members are warned never to miss a meeting of the youth group (where they are under the sway of elders); always to be present in the group on festival days; to rise early, work fiercely, and devote themselves single-mindedly to family occupations; to spend their spare time studying, reading, and writing; not to leave the village for entertainment or festivals; not to drink or gamble; not to sing popular songs; not to play the samisen or use slang. To disobey such injunctions would disgrace their parents and the village and invite the punishment of the gods.[66]

No doubt because the village was considered a single moral sphere, efforts were made to monitor and improve the use of time in the community. A youth group in Wake County in Bizen Province felt impelled to designate certain days only that could be observed as holidays in the village, and to mete out punishment (*ishugaeshi*) to evil persons violating this dispensation. The Hōtokusha, a society inspired by the teachings of the late Tokugawa agrarian moralist Ninomiya Sontoku (1787–1856), gave much attention to the proper use of time and to the abolition or curtailment of singing, dancing, and theatrical performances in villages. A certain follower of Ninomiya's named Furuhashi made up a time schedule (a "work-rest table") and exhorted fellow villagers to follow it; another made the rounds of the village each morning wakening people to the sound of a wooden clapper.[67]

The language of Tokugawa agriculture was rich in vocabulary expressing work in a context of obligation to others. *Suke* was labor given by a dependent to a protector in return and gratitude for benefits

65. *Nihon shomin seikatsu shiryō* 21:782.
66. Ibid., 769–73, 777–78, 781–82.
67. Yasumaru Yoshio, *Nihon no kindaika to minshū shisō* (Tokyo, 1974), 20–21, 63–65.

such as the loan of land, animals, and a house.[68] *Yui* was an equal exchange of like labor such as mutual help in transplanting rice. *Hōkō* was service while living as a servant and quasi member in another's family. There were numerous words for work apart from social relations, but these refer to the physical act or effort of work (*shigoto, hataraki, kasegi*). It is difficult to find any word that suggests work in a social context without carrying a sense of obligation to others.

After the Meiji Restoration in 1868, this limitation of vocabulary became an inconvenience. None of the words mentioned could properly be used for factory employment, which in both theory and law was held by the new Westernizing government to result from a contract freely entered into by autonomous and equal parties. So foreign to social experience was this notion, however, that no satisfactory general term for worker was found until the 1930s.

Meanwhile the word *shokkō*, coined in middle Meiji, became the standard word for factory worker. From the beginning it was marked by the stigma of poverty and unattached status. It soon became a term of opprobrium, and workers vigorously objected that its use branded them as outcasts. Companies responded by coining new words for worker in company documents, but none came into general use. *Shokkō*, despite its heavy pejorative overtones, continued to be the usual word for factory worker through the 1910s. The long and unsuccessful search for a satisfactory word suggests the great difficulty of combining in the same word both the idea of honor and the idea of working for oneself without respect to social obligation, a combination uncongenial to Tokugawa peasants and early industrial workers alike.

TIME AND MODERN INDUSTRY

Two general propositions have been advanced in this paper: that late Tokugawa peasants had a lively, morally rooted sense of the preciousness of time, and that they thought of time as socially rather than indi-

68. Shiozawa Kimio, "Iwate ken Kemuyama mura no ichi nōka keiei," *Keizaigaku*, no. 28 (July 1953): 92–133.

vidually controlled. This is, of course, a matter of degree. Tokugawa peasants were far more sensitive to the value of time than populations that have been described as task-oriented, but they were no doubt less so than modern Japanese factory workers.[69] In addition, a wide variation in attitudes must be assumed in so large a population. Nevertheless, owing to the near universality of family farming among peasants, the importance of labor intensity to successful farming, and the frequent movement of farm families up and down the landholding and social scales of their villages, it is difficult to think that any large part of the farming population was casual about time or its social control.

Tokugawa peasants did not, of course, go into modern factories in any significant number, and their children and grandchildren, who did, had different formative experiences. Farming itself changed remarkably little from the grandparents' time to the grandchildren's. The structural features of agriculture of the previous century—small farms, overwhelming dependence on family labor, the integration of farming and by-employment—persisted beyond World War II. But during this time the environment of farming was transformed, and in few ways so remarkably as by the spread of schools, railroads, and public offices, all of which increased the awareness of clock time among country people. It was a slow process, however. Until 1900 a significant proportion of children did not attend school, especially in country districts, and at that date even in the largest and most modern factories the vast majority of blue-collar workers had four years or less of schooling. The influence of the railway came yet more gradually. Tokyo was not joined to Osaka by continuous rail until 1889, to Aomori in the north of Honshū until 1891, and to Shimonoseki in the extreme south until 1901.[70]

The first two generations of Japanese factory workers, covering roughly the years from 1880 to 1920 (when Tokugawa influence would

69. David Landes makes a persuasive case that Western city people developed an acute appreciation of the value of time before mechanical clocks became available; hence, "The clock did not create an interest in time measurement; the interest in time measurement led to the invention of the clock." *Revolution in Time*, 51, 58, 71–72.

70. Nakanishi Yō, "Daiichi taisen zengo no rōshi kankei," in *Nihon rōshi kankei shiron*, ed. Sumiya Mikio (Tokyo, 1977), 86; Kōgakkai, ed., *Meiji kōgyōshi*, 2d ed. (Tokyo, 1929), 3:190–92.

have been most direct and discernible), were marked by troubled and occasionally violent labor relations. Problems, moreover, were clearly most intense in large and heavily capitalized enterprises, where time regulation was the strictest. Yet time does not seem to have been a critical issue between workers and managers. Neither group spoke passionately of problems of time; indeed, government statistics show that relatively few labor disputes before World War II originated in part over working hours and even fewer primarily over them.[71]

The workers' relative lack of interest in a shorter working day may partly reflect the Tokugawa peasant's preference for income over leisure up to a level near the limits of physical endurance. In 1889, when Tokyo's tramcar workers demanded a ten-hour day, they did not ask for a reduction of their eighteen-hour working day but only for "proportional" overtime pay after ten hours. Many observers noted the eagerness of workers to work overtime. Yokoyama Gennosuke (1870– 1915) wrote in 1897 that, despite a normal working day of twelve to fourteen hours, most workers worked several additional hours of overtime daily. Masumoto Uhei, an engineer with many years of factory experience, said in 1919, when the regular working day was ten to twelve hours, that workers judged the attractiveness of a factory by the amount of overtime available in it and that employers stole skilled workers from one another with promises of overtime. In the early 1920s letters from workers to the plant newspapers at the Yawata Steel Works complained about favoritism in the assignment of overtime,

71. Agriculture and Commerce Ministry figures show 234 strikes in the period 1897–1907; in a total of 6 (2.99 percent) of them, "shortening working hours and so on" was an issue. There are no relevant data for 1908–13. Home Ministry figures for the period 1914–30 give two slightly different totals for the number of "strikes and factory closings" resulting from labor disputes (5,741 and 5,965). Working hours and holidays were an issue in 4.20 percent and 4.14 percent of these, respectively. Even these low figures exaggerate somewhat the importance of time as an issue, owing to the exceptionally large number of strikes involving workers' hours in the single year 1921. This was a year of unusual labor turbulence, and workers tended in the course of labor disputes originating over other issues to exploit the International Labor Organization's recent endorsement of the eight-hour day. For the period 1922–30 there were 8,829 labor disputes of all kinds, and for each dispute the ministry assigned one issue as primary and others as secondary. Working hours and holidays were classified as the primary issue in 2.3 percent of all disputes. Nihon Rōdō Undō Shiryō Iinkai, ed., *Nihon rōdō undō shiryō* (Tokyo, 1959), 10:424–534.

stating that senior workers got all the overtime. No worker's letter complained of excessive overtime.[72]

Equally important in easing early problems of time in industry was the workers' conception of the employment relationship as properly governed by hierarchical ethics. Workers' criticism of employers was couched in moral language calling for loving concern for workers and condemning its absence as cruel and unrighteous. Even in labor disputes entailing work stoppages, before 1918 workers put their demands to management in the form of a "petition"; in talks to settle disputes, workers cooperated with management to avoid even the appearance of a negotiation between equals.[73] Workers clearly observed these forms in order to preserve the integrity of their moral claim to hierarchical justice. They may have been similarly constrained from making prime issues of working hours, holidays, and fines for tardiness, believing that if they did, they would call into question the moral basis of the relationship.

On the understanding that the employment relationship was not or ought not to be strictly impersonal, managers often tolerated a certain tardiness and absenteeism. In some factories there was a customary leeway between official and actual starting times.[74] Punishments for tardiness set out in company regulations in the early part of the century do not seem particularly harsh, and efforts to discourage absenteeism placed more emphasis on bonuses for attendance than on penalties for absence. As late as 1900, the Yokosuka Naval Arsenal did not automatically discharge a worker for absenteeism until three weeks had gone by without word from the offender.[75] Commonly after the settle-

---

72. *Rōdō sekai*, no. 44 (15 September 1899); Yokoyama Gennosuke, *Naichi zak-kyogo no Nihon* (Tokyo, 1959), 32–33; Masumoto Uhei, *Kōjō yori mitaru Nihon rōdō seikatsu* (Tokyo, 1919), 128; *Kurogane*, 1 September 1920 to 15 March 1924, especially the letters of 1 March 1921, p. 1, and 1 September 1921, p. 3.

73. See Chapter 10.

74. Strikes pertaining to time often seem to have resulted less from the enforcement of precise schedules than from changes in the margin of latitude allowable. For examples: *Rōdō oyobi sangyō*, September 1916, pp. 57–58; March 1917, pp. 26–27.

75. At Yokosuka workers reporting on time but leaving work early received half a day's pay if they had worked half of the normal hours. Considerably severer was the provision that workers who were fifteen minutes or less late but thereafter worked the full day received only 70 percent pay. *Yokosuka Kaigun Kōshōshi* (Tokyo, 1935), 1:99, 141.

ment of work stoppages, the workers apologized for their actions and
the employers granted pay to workers for the time lost in striking—
gestures on both sides aimed at healing a breached moral relationship.

Managers felt free, on the other hand, to demand workers' time
whenever and in almost whatever amounts required. Even the most
firmly established holidays were routinely canceled when work flow
was heavy.[76] Daily working hours were only nominally fixed, and in
busy periods work began well before the prescribed hour and continued long after quitting time. Company rules commonly provided
for occasions on which workers would work an entire night of overtime following the regular working day.[77]

How alert and energetic workers could have been during such
marathons is doubtful, but they rarely complained loudly. In fact no
time-related issue seems to have aroused worker indignation as much
as the appearance of favoritism in promotions and raises and invidious
distinctions between white- and blue-collar workers did. *Rōdō sekai*, a
turn-of-the-century magazine promoting unions, complained, "Don't
our workers know the value of work time?"[78] In 1914 *Yūai shinpō*,
the official organ of a nascent labor union, ran an editorial purporting
to voice workers' demands of "capitalists." Included were demands for
treatment with parental love (*oyagokoro*), profit sharing, equal treatment with white-collar employees, promotion based on ability (*jitsu-
ryoku*) and character (*jinkaku*) rather than on personal connections
(*enko*), and bonuses for outstanding performance—nothing about
working hours, pace of work, holidays, or penalties for tardiness.[79]

Significantly, the spread of discussion among employers in the
1910s about shortening working hours was based not on workers' demands but on the growing belief, supported by experimental evidence,

76. Workers, who were paid by the day, were not paid for holidays and therefore
viewed them as a mixed blessing. In 1923 the Yawata Steel Mill instituted four paid
national holidays a year, so that workers' patriotic appreciation of these festivals would
not be dampened by the cost to them in lost earnings.

77. *Kōjō oyobi shokkō* (Nōmushō Kōmukyoku, 1900), 24–26; *Kōjō chōsa yōryō*
(Nōshōmushō Kōmukyoku, 1897), 75–76; Yokoyama, *Naichi zakkyogo no Nihon*,
32–33, and *Nihon kasō shakai*, in *Yokoyama Gennosuke zenshū*, ed. Sumiya Mikio
(Tokyo, 1972), 1:221–33; *Yokosuka Kaigun Kōshōshi*, 1:139, 141, 144–45.

78. *Rōdō sekai*, no. 26 (15 December 1898): 256.

79. *Yūai shinpō*, no. 28 (15 May 1914): 215.

that excessive working hours lowered labor productivity and so under-mined Japan's competitive position in the world.[80] Workers themselves cited this argument in letters to the press, claiming that shorter hours would permit them to work more efficiently,[81] and Suzuki Bunji, the most influential spokesman for labor at the time, made the same point forcefully.[82] Rarely if ever did workers argue for shorter hours on explicitly selfish grounds. Their insistence on seeing issues of time in the context of social and moral relations is suggested by their reaction to the call of the Paris Peace Conference in 1919 for worldwide reform of working conditions. Japanese employers were alarmed at the inclusion in the call of a demand for the eight-hour day, claiming compliance would raise their labor costs prohibitively. Japanese workers, on the other hand, paid less attention to the eight-hour issue than to the provision that labor was not a commodity.[83] Workers took this as international validation of their demand for recognition of worker *jinkaku* (moral personality) and hence for the improvement of their status both in companies and in society generally.

Still, time discipline in Japanese factories in the early twentieth century was unquestionably lax by present standards, and laxness was not overcome for some decades.[84] The gradual improvement was in part the result of a more finely calibrated sense of time that came with the increased use of clocks and watches generally and from cumulative experience with factory time. But more important than either was the

80. For an early expression of this view, see the Mitsubishi personnel handbook for the Nagasaki Shipyard, *Rōdōsha toriatsukaikata ni kansuru chōsa hōkokusho* (Mitsubishi Zōsenjo, 1914), 1:51–53. Even among intellectuals extraordinarily sympathetic to workers the discussion of working hours emphasized the productivity effect of the shortened hours. See the answers to the questionnaire on working hours in *Rōdō oyobi sangyō*, July 1917, pp. 14–25.

81. Ibid., January 1919, p. 35.

82. Ibid., March 1918, pp. 176–77.

83. This attitude is suggested by workers' letters to *Rōdō oyobi sangyō*, but it is perhaps most clearly illustrated by the statement in October 1919 of the Yūaikai, Japan's leading labor organization, endorsing the nine principles concerning labor adopted by the Paris Peace Conference. The Yūaikai statement strongly emphasized the principles dealing with the dignity of workers—that workers were not articles of commerce, not appendages (*fuzokuhin*) of the machine, not to be treated as mere things (*busshitsuka*)—but said nothing about the eight-hour day, the forty-eight-hour week, or the one-day-off-a-week principle. Ibid., October 1919, p. 1.

84. Japanese returning from study or work in Western factories typically extolled

gradual legitimation of the factory by company reforms that raised worker status; increased job security and real wages; gave some measure of protection against sickness, injury, and old age; shortened working hours; and institutionalized worker-management consultation. From the beginning, there had been a certain presumption in favor of the factory's legitimacy because of a seeming parallel of the factory to family and community authorities. When employers and managers undercut the hopes stirred by this parallel, they demoralized and angered workers. But as the treatment of workers slowly improved, so did their time discipline. Workers may not have been always happy with the resulting disposition of their time (and may not be today), but they came to recognize its legitimacy.

The acceptance of factory time seems to be a result not of the transcendence of the preindustrial time sense, as Thompson suggests it was in England, but of the more or less untroubled adaptation of the older time sense to the requirements of the factory. Let me suggest three reasons for this view. (1) Something like the revolution in time sense that

---

the time discipline found there and made comparisons disparaging Japanese workers, who were said to work at an unhurried pace, loaf when not directly supervised, and generally take several times the number of persons required to perform a given task in "advanced Western countries." One cliché had it that "unlike Western workers, Japanese sell time, not labor." These comparisons were perhaps exaggerated with the intention of shaming and exhorting Japanese workers, but they also contained a substantial element of truth. At the same time, however, critics of Japanese workers increasingly recognized that long hours and infrequent holidays had much to do with poor performance. Men and women who day after day worked twelve to fourteen hours, barely managing to feed their families and under constant threat of layoff, could not reasonably, it was argued, be expected to work with élan. Employers acknowledged the problem but were loath to risk reducing hours in the expectation that productivity would offset higher labor costs. Little therefore was done to reduce hours until the depression following World War I, when the government, the public, and employers began to feel international pressure for the eight-hour day at the Paris Peace Conference and subsequent ILO conferences. The *Nihon rōdō nenkan* for 1920 described the reaction of employers to these pressures: "If we examine the so-called eight-hour system, we discover that it is eight hours only nominally and in fact eight-hours-plus-overtime. Overtime is normally two hours a day but sometimes as many as four. Japanese workers generally want only to maximize their earnings and are not concerned with the eight-hour day, and employers have taken advantage of their attitude to contrive a stopgap policy. Since the depression began in March, however, industry has been forced to curtail operations and shorten working hours. Some companies with eight-hours-plus-overtime systems have no shortened overtime as to establish a true eight-hour system." *Nihon rōdō nenkan* (Osaka, 1921), 2:104.

Thompson speaks of had already taken place. No doubt elements of task-orientation remained, as they do today, but it seems unlikely that they were so pervasive as to pose a major obstacle to modern industry. (2) If they had posed such an obstacle, early Japanese industry would have been accompanied by an ideological attack on workers' time behavior, and there is little evidence of anything of the sort. (3) The feature of preindustrial time most closely linked to social processes—the notion that in significant social relationships time does not belong unconditionally to ego—not only survives today but has become a central element in time discipline in Japanese business and industry.

It is well known that workers' restriction of output was a major problem in U.S. industry from early in the history of the factory.[85] Underlying the practice were (and are) beliefs about what constituted a fair day's work, the fear that exceeding a certain rate or "stint" would result in the elimination of jobs, and the worry that any increase in the pace of work in order to boost piecework earnings would quickly lead to a reduction in rates. Japanese managers must have been aware of these problems, since a Japanese translation of Frederick W. Taylor's *The Principles of Scientific Management* (1911) was published in 1913[86] and since Western views on management generally were widely discussed. Yet I have never encountered mention of the problem specifically with reference to Japanese industry in the period before 1920 (which I know best and in which such a reference would most likely be found); nor have I discovered an indigenous word for "stint." Managers often complained about the slow pace of Japanese workers, but they attributed this pace to bad work habits, to individual laziness, or even to overwork—never, that I know of, to a collective effort of workers to control time against an employer.[87]

Employers did adopt U.S. pay schemes that based individual pay

85. Daniel Nelson, *Managers and Workers: Origins of the New Factory System in the United States* (Madison, Wis., 1975), chap. 4; Frederick W. Taylor, *The Principles of Scientific Management* (New York, 1967), 9–29.

86. Hazama Hiroshi, *Nihon rōmu kanrishi kenkyū* (Tokyo, 1964), 18.

87. From an early date, it was a common worker tactic, called *taigyō*, or slowdown, to come to work but do little or nothing during labor disputes. This, however, was an undisguised dispute tactic, not an everyday and more or less covert work rule.

rates on output per unit of time, with workers who produced more getting a higher hourly rate. In the United States such plans represented an effort by employers to overcome group restrictions on output by appealing to the individual worker's wish for higher earnings. These plans appealed to the same desire in Japan but were evidently not inspired by the problem of output restriction. On the contrary, when production processes permitted, management frequently adopted incentive plans that used the group rather than the individual as the unit of account. The earnings of small work groups were calculated as a whole: groups that produced more in a given time earned more, and individuals shared according to some prearranged allocation.[88] Somewhat similar schemes had been tried in the United States and were poison to Taylor. In his view, they were bound to fail because they gave the individual no significant incentive: why should a person work hard when he would share any group gain whether he worked hard or not?[89] Japanese managers were apparently not anxious about this possibility and relied on the wish of individual workers to be seen by their workmates as doing their utmost to increase the earnings of the group.

From personal experience managers were sensitive to the effect of hierarchic relations on the control of time. Autobiographies of businessmen are full of passages about youthful periods of heroic sacrifice and hard work for a company or patron. Satō Kiichirō (1894–1974), who went from Tokyo University to the Mitsui Bank in 1917, explained that he worked day and night without holidays after joining the bank, and that he did so not so much because he liked the work as because he wished to help his superior obtain his objectives.[90]

Takahashi Korekiyo (1854–1936), who joined the Bank of Japan under the protection of its president Kawada, is a classic case of conceding control of time to a patron. Sometime after he started work at the bank, he received an invitation from Gotō Shōjirō, Minister of Agriculture and Commerce, to join the ministry. Takahashi replied that

---

88. For an early example of such a scheme at the Mitsubishi Nagasaki Shipyard, see *Rōdōsha toriatsukaikata ni kansuru chōsa hōkokusho*, 41–42. A detailed example of a group incentive plan can be found in Andrew Gordon, *The Evolution of Labor Relations in Japan: Heavy Industry, 1853–1955* (Cambridge, Mass., 1985), 165–66.

89. *Principles of Scientific Management*, 70–77.

90. Yamada Katsundo, ed., *Watakushi no shūgyō jidai* (Tokyo, 1957), 125.

he could do so only at the direction (*osashizu*) of President Kawada Koichirō (1836−96), explaining that he had entrusted his fortunes to Kawada. Gotō said in that case he would send a telegram to Kawada (who was traveling at the time) asking for Takahashi's release. The next day one of Gotō's assistants asked if the telegram could quote Takahashi as saying that he would join Gotō if Kawada approved. "No," said Takahashi, "I have no idea of joining or not joining. In this matter I have no will of my own." Now, however, he became uneasy about the telegram and wrote Kawada explaining what had transpired, quoting himself as saying "Korekiyo has entrusted himself wholly to President Kawada. He has no will of his own. What he does is entirely up to President Kawada." As things worked out, Kawada refused Gotō's request, settling the matter.[91]

Control of one's time by another was often a painful experience, and it is not surprising that the theme was a subject for humor. A cartoon in a major Tokyo daily in the 1920s shows a group of male office workers sitting at desks facing one another in Japanese office fashion (Fig. 9.1). At the far end of the group, with his back to the wall, sits the section chief, deep in the scandal page of an afternoon newspaper and unaware that the wall clock behind shows an hour past quitting time. The others, acutely aware of the clock, exchange helpless glances as the chief reads happily on. No one calls his attention to the hour: no one can. To do so would suggest that the obligations of the group are limited to a fixed amount of time sold to the company, after which employees are free of responsibility. The cartoon may have amused readers because it depicted a preposterous imposition on time by a thoughtless superior whom the victims could not correct without violating norms—a situation ordinary men and women knew all about.

Thomas Rohlen has given us a valuable description of a neighborhood branch bank where he worked as a participant-observer for a year in 1968−69. Work at the branch began with a meeting of all per-

---

91. There was a certain disingenuousness in Takahashi's reply to Gotō, since in his letter to Kawada he made it clear that he did not want to accept Gotō's offer. So he did not really leave the matter to Kawada, but it is significant that he did not feel he could on his own reject the offer from Gotō, a man of great eminence and power, and instead pretended the decision lay elsewhere. Takahashi Korekiyo, *Jiden* (Tokyo, 1976), 2:28−29.

Fig. 9.1   Quitting Time

NOTE: The caption to the cartoon reads: "Quitting time has come and gone, but the section chief shows no sign of leaving. Everyone goes through the motions, turning the pages of a ledger, writing aimlessly, while keeping an eye on the clock. Alas, the section chief does not look up from the scandal page of the afternoon edition. Truly, to work in a company is no picnic."

sonnel at 8:30 in the morning, presided over in rotation by a different person daily. Although there was a nominal quitting time of 5:30, the actual quitting time depended on work flow. There was "no set time when work ends, no time clock, and a reluctance to leave before the rest. Staying late is a common quality of office work. In some instances, the whole office will stay until the last person is finished." Rohlen's "conservative" estimate of the average week at the bank was fifty-six hours, plus an additional four to six hours of obligatory socializing with officemates. Office parties combined with meetings and Saturday afternoon group recreation consumed yet another four to six hours a month, and two overnight trips sixty hours a year. The total comes to sixty-two to sixty-four more or less compulsory hours a week. Behind this regime were the enforcement powers of the office group, in which "a failure to lend a hand, or an unusual reserve receives immediate notice and often leads to interpersonal problems that take a long time to resolve."[92]

It is widely known that Japanese workers are legally guaranteed a certain number of holidays a year, depending on seniority. Commonly, they do not use all the days they have coming. Ronald Dore describes how this comes about among blue-collar workers at Hitachi:

> Workers take their holidays one or two days at a time as occasion arises. It is almost universally the practice to ask that days taken off for sickness should be counted as part of one's annual holiday. . . . The next, more or less legitimate, claim on holidays is for attending weddings and funerals. Those who do not use up their ten, fifteen or twenty days' holidays in these ways, may take other days off—with the foreman's agreement. . . . Foremen are reluctant to have people take leave because they have a stake in a high attendance record and high production figures, and when order books are long they are likely to be under considerable pressure from enthusiastic managers. One can, of course, insist on taking one's holiday entitlement. . . . but insistence on one's rights to a holiday *merely for one's own personal pleasure when everyone else is working his heart out can well earn the foreman's displeasure*—at the expense of one's merit rating and so of one's wage.[93] (My italics.)

CONCLUSION

To return to Thompson, he was surely right that the values attached to time by preindustrial people profoundly affect the nature of worker adaptation to factory time discipline. He would appear to be mistaken

---

92. Thomas R. Rohlen, *For Harmony and Strength: Japanese White-Collar Organization in Anthropological Perspective* (Berkeley and Los Angeles, 1974), 97–111.
93. Ronald P. Dore, *British Factory—Japanese Factory: The Origins of National Diversity in Industrial Relations* (Berkeley and Los Angeles, 1973), 187–88.

in predicting (insofar as he did) that the preindustrial time sense is necessarily a source of resistance to the factory.

For Thompson these features seem to be at or near the heart of worker resistance to early capitalist industry, since he speaks of time measurement "as a means of labor exploitation." The idea sounds Marxian: the employer pays the worker for only part of his working time, taking the remainder without compensation. Such a practice would indeed be exploitive and would sufficiently explain worker resistance. But that is not what Thompson means by exploitation;[94] the issue, instead, is the loss of human values and a way of life associated with task-orientation: presumably the blurring of the distinction between life and work, the capacity for play, the comforting sense of necessity in the round of tasks appointed by nature's rhythms. These preindustrial values were obliterated by the enforcement of factory time with the aid of puritanism. "Puritanism, in its marriage of convenience with industrial capitalism, was the agent which converted men to the new valuations of time; which taught children in their infancy to improve each shining hour; and which saturated men's minds with the equation, time is money." The conversion entailed "the most far-reaching conflict" and was marked by "exploitation and . . . resistance to exploitation."[95] Exploitation then appears to consist in the loss of vital inner freedoms, submission to machine time, and acceptance of a crabbed time-is-money view of life. None of these things could have happened except for task-orientation, without the grace of which there could have been no fall. Moreover, this loss of grace is an experience that "the developing world must live through and grow through."[96]

Japanese do not seem to have had such a fall. Tokugawa peasants had a time sense strikingly different from task-orientation. They cannot have had a fine sense of clock time, of course, and the resulting initial awkwardness with the factory regime might have developed into a serious issue. But it did not; the prolonged period of conflict with management was mainly over other matters. One of the reasons it did not would seem to be that workers also had significant views on the

94. "Time," 80, 93–94.
95. Ibid., 91, 93–95.
96. Ibid., 95.

ownership of time—an aspect of time sense that Thompson does not treat directly. Time for workers *and* managers was enmeshed in social structure: an aspect of social relations that could only in marginal cases be disregarded so that time could be bought and sold like rice cakes. The simultaneously high economic and social evaluations of time seem to have been crucial in facilitating the establishment of time discipline in Japanese factories. The real struggle in Japanese industry was over the moral implications of the employer-employee relationship. As they became clearer, time discipline to all appearances steadily tightened without crisis over the process.

Tokugawa peasants seem so far removed from the attitudes attributed to preindustrial English working people by Thompson that I cannot help wondering if he has not exaggerated the strength and prevalence of task-orientation in eighteenth-century England. The most convincing instances of task-orientation cited come from ethnographic accounts of premarket societies. Contemporary criticisms of the work habits of English common people, although bearing heavily on time, do not on the whole point specifically to task-orientation. They do indeed suggest a strong resistance to work on terms satisfactory to employers and moralists but do not necessarily reveal the reasons for the resistance. Thompson quotes the complaint of a writer in an agricultural magazine in 1800 that "when a labourer becomes possessed of more land than he and his family can cultivate in the evenings . . . the farmer can no longer depend on him for constant work."[97] This sounds like a wish for independence on the worker's part rather than necessarily a casual attitude toward time. He also quotes Francis Place who, speaking from experience, wrote in 1829 that working men ran from twelve- to eighteen-hour working days when they could no longer stand them and that "in proportion as a man's case is hopeless will such fits more frequently occur and be of longer duration."[98] This may show a lack of time discipline from an employer's viewpoint, but it is difficult to see what it necessarily has to do with task-orientation.

Thompson himself seems to be of two minds about the prevalence and strength of task-orientation. On the one hand, it was so deeply

97. Ibid., 77.
98. Ibid., 76.

seated that the first generation of factory workers had to be taught the value of time by their masters. On the other:

> The entire economy of the small farmer may be task-oriented; but within it there may be a division of labour, and allocation of roles, and the discipline of an employer-employed relationship between the farmer and his children. Even here time is beginning to become money, the employer's money. As soon as actual hands are employed the shift from task-orientation to timed labour is marked. It is true that the timing of work can be done independently of any time-piece—and indeed precedes the diffusion of the clock.[99]

This is a telling passage not only because it seems to place the beginning of timed labor rather far back in English history but also for the individualism it sees *within* the family of the small farmer in England.

Perhaps the conflict over time between employers and workers in eighteenth-century England was not over the value of time but over who owned it and on what terms. In the first half of the nineteenth century in the United States, work was regarded as ennobling only when it was independent, self-directed, and self-profiting or when it was undertaken in preparation for independence. The man who as a more or less permanent arrangement sold his time did so, according to Abraham Lincoln, "because of either a dependent nature . . . or improvidence, folly, or singular misfortune." Also, according to a nineteenth-century treatise on wages in the United States, the man who worked for hire "not only will not, but cannot, being a man, labor as he would for himself."[100] Boston's carpenters, masons, and stonecutters proclaimed in 1835 that "the God of the Universe has given us time, health and strength. We utterly deny the right of any man to dictate to us how much of it we shall sell."[101]

Many English working people in the late eighteenth century would have understood and sympathized with this statement. No Japanese in 1835 could possibly have understood the statement[102] or taken a favor-

99. Ibid., 86, 61.
100. Daniel I. Rodgers, *The Work Ethic in Industrial America, 1850–1920* (Chicago, 1979), 34–35.
101. John R. Commons, ed., *A Documentary History of American Industrial Society* (New York, 1958), 6:98. Quoted in David Brody, "Time and Work During Early American Industrialism," paper for the German-American Symposium, April 1984.
102. The word *kenri*, which came to be the equivalent of the English word *right*, was used in Chinese texts studied in the Tokugawa period to combine the words *power*

able view of it if he did. The consequence of this difference for the pre-industrial meaning of time in the two cultures may account in part for the greater struggle over time in English factories, and possibly also the slacker time discipline in English and American industry today. If so, the source of the divergence seems to have less to do with time sense (as Thompson uses the term) than with different conceptions of the individual in society.

(*kenryoku*) and *interest* (*rieki*). It was first used in Japan in the modern sense of legal or human rights in the mid-nineteenth century in translations of Western works on political theory and law. *Kenri* was an extraordinarily bad choice for the purpose, since the Chinese characters carried a strong suggestion of selfishness and a misuse of position.

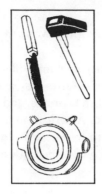

10

THE RIGHT TO BENEVOLENCE: DIGNITY AND JAPANESE WORKERS, 1890–1920

From its beginning, Japanese industry was marked by a scattering of large and heavily capitalized enterprises; as their size and number increased between 1890 and 1920, they became the scene of labor unrest. According to historical accounts of the period, management began efforts to bring workers under greater psychological control because of its fear of unions and government intervention and the need to reduce the amount of labor turnover.[1] The workers themselves appear

Reprinted from *Comparative Studies in Society and History* 26, no. 4 (Oct. 1984).

1. Hyōdō Tsutomu, *Nihon ni okeru rōshi kankei no tenkai* (Tokyo, 1971), is a classic and impressively scholarly statement of this view. For a different view, putting emphasis on paternalistic ideology, see Hazama Hiroshi, *Nihon rōmu kanrishi kenkyū* (Tokyo, 1964), 3–123; and Sidney Crawcour, "The Japanese Employment System," *Journal of Japanese Studies* 4, no. 2 (Summer 1978): 225–47. Ronald Dore, *British*

strangely abstract in these accounts. When they come into focus, mainly at moments of crisis, they are seen to be increasing their consciousness both of rights and of the need for organization and class solidarity.[2] Their consciousness issued at last in a sudden growth of unions between 1918 and the mid-1920s. Management intensified its efforts in response, and the measures it adopted—welfare services, greater security of employment, semiannual bonuses, separation pay, regular raises, factory committees—aided by a stagnant economy and unemployment throughout the 1920s, were successful in undermining worker autonomy. By the early 1930s unions were in retreat everywhere from large enterprises. The development of worker consciousness was stymied until 1945 when, in the aftermath of national defeat, the struggle was renewed.[3]

This, in drastically simplified form, is the conventional picture of Japanese labor relations before 1930. Two features of it in particular are troubling. First, it is difficult to understand the resistance to management that took place between the late 1890s and 1918 as being closely related to the growth of a consciousness of rights and of unionist ideals among workers. The first great strike, which brought the Japan Railway Company to its knees in 1899, was perhaps the best planned and organized strike of any before the 1920s. It took place at a time when the union movement was just beginning and occurred independently of it. This and other strikes independent of the early union movement, which had collapsed and all but disappeared by 1902,

---

Factory—Japanese Factory: The Origins of National Diversity in Industrial Relations (Berkeley and Los Angeles, 1973), 375–404, also stresses management's role in creating the employment system but emphasizes special conditions of late development as well as ideological influences on its decisions. Dore acknowledges the possibility that worker aspirations may also have influenced management decisions but does not follow up the suggestion. None of these studies, therefore, gives workers a significant role in shaping the content of management's reforms. An exception is Andrew Gordon, The Evolution of Labor Relations in Japan: Heavy Industry, 1853–1955 (Cambridge, Mass., 1985). Gordon sees management reforms as the outcome of a continuous interaction between the concrete demands of workers and management's own strategies. My own view is similar to Gordon's but differs in stressing the non-Western ideological background of workers' demands.

2. An influential example is Ikeda Makoto, Nihon kikaikō kumiai seiritsu shiron (Tokyo, 1970).

3. Gordon, Evolution, chaps. 9, 10.

were startlingly well disciplined. Workers formed workshop struggle groups, held meetings, debated issues, empowered delegates, conducted negotiations with management, voted financial support for dismissed workers, and ratified agreements. These collective abilities, whatever their origins, must have sprung from indigenous sources, possibly from the rich tradition of agrarian protest of the Tokugawa period. At any rate, there are striking parallels between early worker protests and Tokugawa peasant uprisings: the same submission of petitions for the redress of grievances, the use of a similar moral language, the same taking of loyalty oaths and use of shrines and temple grounds as meeting places, and the similarity of the roles of foremen and village headmen and of workshops and villages.

Second, workers used the language of rights sparingly before 1918. They were of course acquainted with the concept of rights from the Freedom and People's Rights movement of the late 1870s and 1880s and from the chapter of the national constitution dealing with the "rights and duties of the subject." Also, Japanese intellectuals who advocated labor unions based their advocacy on natural rights theory.[4] But workers themselves rarely used the term *rights*. Rather, expressing themselves in manifestos during labor disputes, in petitions to employers, in the charters of labor clubs and societies, in letters to newspapers, and in factory newspapers (some of which by 1920 were written by and for workers), workers appealed for status (*chii*) justice. Indeed, when they spoke of rights, as they sometimes did, for example, in demanding "an improvement in workers' rights and status," they often gave the word a meaning indistinguishable from that of *status*.[5]

4. From the beginning, advocates of labor unions associated unions with protecting and "expanding" the rights of workers but said little about the basis of such rights. Katayama Sen (1860–1933) made the most considered early effort to justify workers' rights in editorials published in *Rōdō sekai*. His argument was that the most basic human right was the right to life and hence the right to work; under present conditions of freedom of contract, workers had a "just right" (*seitō no kenri*) to strike in order to increase their bargaining power and employers had the right to discharge or lock workers out. This "just right" Katayama called a "natural power" (*shizen no ikioi*). *Rōdō sekai*, no. 8 (10 March 1898): 73–74; no. 11 (1 May 1898): 104.

5. Intellectuals also often found it difficult to keep the distinction between status and rights clearly in mind. Katayama Sen's journal, *Rōdō sekai*, no. 2 (1 December 1897), carried an essay questioning the existing class structure and asked by what "right" (*kenri*) the Japanese upper class enjoyed its position. Its answer was, not by superior virtue or understanding but solely on the basis of wealth. The clear implication

The idea of rights did not call forth the expressions of moral feeling that status did. The employment relation was seen as one between status unequals, similar to the relations between lord and vassal, master and servant, parent and child, calling for benevolence on one side and loyalty and obedience on the other. For ignoring the ethical code governing such relations, employers were denounced as unrighteous, cruel, barbarous, selfish, inhumane, and ignorant of the way of heaven and man.[6] Such injustice was to be overcome by employer reformation, bringing workers "improved treatment" (*taigū no kairyō*) and "higher status" (*chii no kōjō*), the two overarching demands of workers from the 1890s into the 1920s.

It would be a mistake to see in these demands either false consciousness or a mere prelude to rights consciousness. Status was the core of a changing and dynamic criticism of the factory, incorporating elements of thought from sources as various as Christianity and Marxism and giving benevolence and loyalty a new institutional—as opposed to purely personal—meaning. That meaning was defined in concrete terms as time went on: in the demands for the impersonalization of pay, benefits, and promotions, and for the downward extension to workers of benefits until then enjoyed exclusively by groups having higher status. There was no repudiation of status itself, but rather an effort to narrow the distance between one status and another, to free status of the incubus of caste. The demand was met in significant degree by management's reforms in the 1910s and 1920s. The demand was also adopted by the unions, which, proliferating after 1917, rephrased it (although incompletely) in the language of rights and class struggle. In what follows I attempt to trace one part of these complex developments: the transformation of status from a personal to an organizational concept. I begin with the concern of workers for status in society generally.

Factory workers were widely treated as near outcasts in Meiji and Taishō society, and many regarded the very name by which they were

was that the position of the upper class would have been justified if based on superior virtue and understanding—the traditional and still potent justification of high status.

6. *Tōyō taimusu*, no. 39 (25 June 1921): 2.

commonly called—*shokkō*—as a term of disparagement. Workers were thought of as forming a society (*shakai*), as if they were a group apart from society generally, and they were routinely described as being low class (*karyū*), inferior (*geretsu*), base (*katō*), little people (*saimin*), the defeated (*reppaisha*), and stragglers (*rakugosha*). Fuku-zawa Yukichi (1835–1901) pronounced factory workers not "good subjects." Mothers threatening naughty children used factory workers as the bogeymen, and they exhorted sons to study hard in school so as not to become workers. Schoolboys reprimanded the behavior of their fellows by exhorting them not to act like *shafu batei* (ricksha pullers and grooms), with whom public signs often linked *shokkō*.[7] A 1914 letter to a newspaper, admittedly written in indignation, recounts an incident its author witnessed outside the gate of the naval shipyard at Kure, where a quarrel took place between a factory worker and a coolie. A crowd formed to watch, and one "citizen," or nonworker, tried to stop the quarrel, while another made fun of his attempt. How strange, the second man said, for a human being to intervene in a quarrel between a factory worker and a coolie, and for "coolie" he used the word *inu*, meaning "coolie" in Kure dialect, "dog" in stan-dard Japanese.[8]

How workers came to a position of such ignominy is not the sub-ject here, but something must be said briefly of developments after the Tokugawa period. Although the four main status groups of Tokugawa society—samurai, peasants, artisans, and merchants—represented significant differences of status, they were all essential to society and all, therefore, honorable. Good order and the governance of society were held to depend, to an extraordinary degree, on each group per-forming its proper role without encroaching on the others. But with the Meiji Restoration, the legal bases of this order were swept away. Restrictions on residence, name, dress, and occupation were lifted, and a rapidly expanding school system was open to all males on the same terms. Social confusion and fierce competition reigned for the

---

7. Personal communication from a Japanese friend born about 1912; also see Ma-tsuzawa Hiroaki, *Nihon shakaishugi no shisō* (Tokyo, 1973), 126.

8. *Yūai shinpō*, no. 20 (15 January 1914): 5. For an account of the pioneer labor organization that published this newspaper, see Stephen Large, *The Rise of Labor in Japan: The Yūaikai, 1912–19* (Tokyo, 1972).

next several generations as people scrambled to better themselves or merely to hold their own. No contemporary caught the confusion better than the French illustrator Georges Fernard Bigot in his Japanese cafe and railway scenes, which are full of male figures in tall hats, pith helmets, Scottish capes, tams, Russian blouses, fur caps, hunting jackets—all mingled randomly with articles of Japanese dress.

Status after the Restoration continued to have much the same psychological and emotional importance as before, but judgment of it was now more sensitive, the outward signs less reliable. Status came to be seen not as inherited place and occupation in society, and thus contributing to social stability, but as the outcome of success or failure in competition. The redemptive association of status with occupation, vital for people at the lower end of the scale, simply slipped away. This change brought much anxiety but no other loss to people of a certain rank who managed to hold their own; for many others it was a misfortune. When judgment of them was no longer mitigated by knowledge of the work they did, with its place in the order of things and the honorable traditions surrounding it, little was left to value.[9] No one suffered more in this circumstance than factory workers, who, in addition to practicing new and little known skills in places full of dirt, smell, and noise, were often new to the communities in which they lived, crowded together in slums (called "caves" and "islands") with scavengers, pickpockets, street entertainers, ricksha men, carters, ditch cleaners, navvies, and the traditional outcaste group, the *eta*.[10]

As their letters to newspapers show, workers resented public scorn and might have fought back by championing their own and belittling middle-class virtues. That reaction has been known elsewhere in similar circumstances, and there are some signs that it emerged in Japan,

9. The names of major status groups in the Tokugawa period were also occupational names: warrior, peasant, artisan, and merchant, in that order. This nominal linkage of status and function disappeared with the elimination of legal status in early Meiji. The effect of the change on status judgments might be compared to a hypothetical situation in which, in speaking of baseball players, the position played was omitted and the players were identified only by their batting average. Thus a man who had been proud to be called a shortstop might find himself identified only as a .220 hitter.

10. Kagawa Toyohiko, who knew the slum people intimately from social work, believed that most slums had developed from *eta* (outcaste) communities and that few if any slums existed in which *eta* were not resident. Sumiya Mikio, *Nihon chinrōdōshiron* (Tokyo, 1958), 105.

too. Street songs and joke books ridicule middle-class hypocrisy, lechery, dandyism, and Western affectation.[11] A worker newspaper rages against intellectuals, asking, "How does it happen that people who know nothing of the world control everything?"[12] And a miner's song bespeaks a certain pride: "Don't despise a miner, a miner/coal is not grown in a grain field." Newspapers tell of workers behaving in purposely offensive ways in public, shaven-headed fellows who roared with laughter and sent people flying as they made their way down the street.[13]

But the overwhelming reaction of workers was to try, by cultivating respectable behavior, to overcome the stigma put on them. Workers filled the correspondence columns of labor newspapers with scolding letters, exhorting their fellows to practice frugality, sobriety, regularity, and night study. "Society's contempt for us is not because we are workers but because of our behavior" is a common theme of such letters.[14] To escape identification on the street, factory workers almost universally wore respectable street clothes to and from work, changing into and out of oily and sweat-stained clothes at the factory. A worker explained this practice in a letter to a newspaper, protesting at the same time the unjust view the public took of workers: "Because our countrymen despise us, we try to avoid their contempt by dressing outside the plant gate as merchants or students. If all of us were to walk down the street at the same time in work clothes, people would be astonished not only by our numbers but also by our good behavior."[15]

---

11. Kai Rōnin, ed., *Kokkei taika ronshū*, 2d ed. (Tokyo, 1888), 11–13, 39–48; *Marumaru chinbun* (a satirical magazine; in the collection of the East Asiatic Library, University of California, Berkeley).

12. *Tōyō taimusu*, no. 69 (5 April 1922): 5.

13. The announcement of the founding of an early labor organization, Shokkō Gundan (Knights of labor) in 1892 states that "workers get drunk, sing in the streets, push into crowds, and pick quarrels." Nihon Rōdō Undō Shiryō Iinkai, ed., *Nihon rōdō undō shiryō* (Tokyo, 1960), 1:175 (hereafter cited as *NRUS*). *NRUS* is a basic collection of materials on the labor movement to 1945, planned for eleven volumes.

14. *Yūai shinpō*, no. 30 (15 June 1914): 5.

15. Ibid., no. 3 (3 January 1913): 4. A short story in this same issue (p. 5) describes two young metal workers leaving the factory and commiserating with each other on their lives, which offered no chance for advancement, only the prospect of endless factory work. One says to the other, "The world is a strange place. When I am dirty with sweat and oil I feel that even my heart is soiled and wonder if we workers are not different animals from human beings."

The novelist Hirabayashi Taiko (1905–72), who worked in the central telephone exchange in Tokyo in the late 1910s, tells how the girls were obliged to wear uniforms to and from work, a requirement they hated because the uniform was well known and telephone girls were looked down on. Her roommate worked out an elaborate disguise of the uniform, which she put on and took off in the privacy of an alley just outside the exchange. Hirabayashi believes that one of the girls at the exchange committed suicide over the public shame she felt of her job.[16] Matsumoto Seichō (1909–), the prolific novelist and detective story writer, was born of poor parents, left school at the end of six years, and went to work in a small factory in northern Kyūshū. He tells of the extraordinary pains he took on the street thereafter to avoid meeting former classmates who were continuing in school, and how ten years later, aged twenty-five and employed as an apprentice lithographer, he was still dodging them. "From time to time I would run into my old elementary schoolmates walking along the street in Western dress. It was excruciating. Of course, I went back and forth to work in kimono and wooden clogs, but I changed into dirty clothes at work."[17]

Companies that offered special technical programs to give bright young workers training to enable them to become model workers and foremen found that, instead, these workers often used the training to become teachers or low-level government officials or to go into business for themselves.[18] Much concern for the education of children is expressed in worker newspapers, usually with an implied hope that, by education, sons might not follow in the occupational footsteps of the fathers. The Sasebo Naval Shipyard paper, analyzing worker budgets, complains that even a worker at the very highest pay level—represented by a foreman in his forties—would find it impossible to provide "higher education" (kōtō kyōiku) for his children. Consequently, the report laments, "children of the greatest ability . . . inevitably end up

16. *Sabaku no hana* (Tokyo, 1957), pt. 1, pp. 13–15.
17. Matsumoto Seichō, *Hansei no ki* (Tokyo, 1970), 35, 49.
18. The head of the Tokyo Industrial School explains that "the vast majority of factory workers today are completely different in both character (hinkō) and deportment (sokō) from school graduates, who therefore cannot bear to be classified along with workers." *Tōkyō keizai zasshi*, 23 January 1908, p. 15.

buried in factory soot."[19] A worker magazine demands a government program to defray school expenses for the poor in order to provide true "equality of educational opportunity," because "without the benefits of culture, just as the pollywog becomes a frog, our children grow up to become workers."[20]

Although education might rescue the sons, it was unlikely to do much for the fathers, whose best hope of overcoming the stigma of the factory lay in the improvement of worker status within it.[21] Organizational details differed from one factory to another, but all large enterprises divided personnel into three primary status groups corresponding broadly to blue-collar, clerical-technical, and managerial employees. New employees were assigned to one of these status groups according to their years of formal schooling: elementary school graduates or less became workers, middle and technical school graduates became clerk-technicians, and high school and college graduates became managers. Each status was accorded a qualitatively different treatment, or *taigū*, as prescribed in separate sets of regulations. Each group had a different mode of payment, different holidays, different benefits, different rewards and punishments, and a different toilet, dining hall, and gate for entering and leaving the plant. The material value of the prescribed treatment increased dramatically going up the ladder. So closely identified with treatment was status that the two words were used synonymously;[22] indeed, it was common to speak of clerical-technical "treatment" rather than clerical-technical "status."

19. *Kangyō Rōdō Sashō Rōaikai kikanshi*, no. 10 (1 September 1926): 1.
20. *Rōdō no Kyūshū*, no. 5 (12 May 1926).
21. An article in the Yawata Steel Mill's union paper expresses the connection between factory work, social stigma, and low self-esteem with remarkable clarity. Workers are despised (*keibetsu*) by society, the paper says, because factory employment is insecure and workers accordingly feel shame at being called *shokkō* (factory workers). "Thus they have no wish to remain *shokkō* and suffer the spiritual pain (*seishinteki kutsū*) of wounded self-esteem (*jifushin*)." *Tōyō taimusu*, no. 31 (5 April 1921): 2.
22. The dictionary *Kōjien* (Tokyo, 1977) gives the second meaning of *taigū* as "salary, status, and other such treatment (*toriatsukai*) in the workplace." Different degrees of *taigū* were often distinguished as high, middle, and low, warm and cold, and thick and thin. The Mitsubishi Shipyard (Nagasaki) personnel handbook of 1914, *Rōdōsha toriatsukaikata ni kansuru chōsa hōkokusho*, states, "Among employees at the Mitsubishi shipyard all those who are not *yakuin* [clerk-technicians] and do not receive *yakuin* treatment [*taigū*] are workers [*rōdōsha*]."

Each of the primary status groups was subdivided into additional statuses, in part by titles and written regulations and in part by less formal means. Workers were divided into unskilled, skilled, and supervisory classes, and each of these in turn contained many pay grades linked to discrete benefit levels and in some companies also marked by formal ranks.[23] Advancement within each primary group was possible, and even likely in time, since seniority always counted for something in promotions. But movement among primary groups, without additional formal education, was rare.

The near-impassable barriers separating the primary status groups had a rationale that did not require explicit statement. Status was not a classification of employees for limited technical or organizational purposes; it reflected supposed differences of individual moral worth.[24] Status was based on education, of which the overriding aim was moral instruction—duty, loyalty, filial piety, the obligations of man to man— and this had been the aim of education for three centuries. Individual exceptions apart, it was taken for granted that moral sensibility would vary with education, and consequently workers were routinely described as uneducated, unknowing, mindless, *and* immoral.[25] They were tirelessly reminded by middle-class sympathizers that, until they curbed a notorious propensity for drinking, gambling, whoring, and domestic quarreling, they would never achieve higher regard, and many workers agreed.[26] Charters of workers' clubs and proto-unions almost invariably listed among their objectives the improvement of workers' character (*hinkō, hinsei*) as well as the achievement of higher status.[27] When the striking engineers of the Japan Railway Company

23. Hazama, *Nihon rōmu kanrishi kenkyū*, 415–26, 162–67.

24. Workers' perception of this imputation is clearly seen in a worker's letter saying that, at his factory, foremen had in the past entered by the same gate as workers, but since the foremen thought this a reflection on their characters (*jinkaku*), they had recently persuaded management to let them use a separate gate. *Shibaura rōdō*, June–July 1923, p. 9. Shōda Heigorō, a Mitsubishi executive, thought that the public widely regarded the treatment (*taigū*) accorded workers as a denial of the morality of their characters (*jinkaku*). *Tōyō keizai shinpō*, 25 April 1907, p. 21.

25. *Rōdō oyobi sangyō*, no. 39 (1 November 1914); *Tokyo keizai zasshi*, 7 September 1890; "Shokkō gundan sōritsu shuisho" (September 1892); all the above in *NRUS*, 1:173–75; 3:174.

26. *Yūai shinpō*, no. 9 (3 July 1913): 1, 3.

27. See Naimushō, *Rōdō sōgi gaikyō* (Tokyo, 1917), 26–32, for examples.

won important improvements in treatment in 1899, a labor newspaper, without the slightest hint of irony, rejoiced that an improvement in the character (*hinsei*) and even in the speech of the engineers
was soon to be expected.[28]

The implications of status in the factory, where the statuses were
novel and the people in them often new to one another, were the cause
of much personal offense and resentment. Railway engineers, whose
positions required years of special training, complained that smooth-
cheeked boys had the temerity to address senior engineers as "Hey,
Tanaka," without the polite suffix *san,* merely because as middle
school graduates they were classified as clerical-technical personnel,
outranking engineers.[29] A worker's letter says that when he complained to a foreman that an unannounced change in working hours
would prevent his attending his night school class, he was told, "Who
do you think you are? You are only a worker"; he wanted to bash in
the man's face but thought better of it.[30] A Yawata worker testifies to
his rage when, walking home tired and sweaty after a ten-hour day at a
blast furnace, he was covered with dirt by a speeding company car
carrying a manager who was in all probability, he thought, on a private errand.[31] A worker tells about getting onto a streetcar, whose personnel had recently been put in uniforms, and being addressed rudely
by one of the newly outfitted conductors. "Putting a peasant in Western clothes," he concludes, "is more dangerous than turning a maniac
loose with a knife."[32]

In demanding higher status and improved treatment, the workers
were, of course, seeking more than higher pay and better working conditions: they were also seeking recognition of their human worth from
those with the power and the reputation to confer it. This was widely
acknowledged by writers on labor problems, many of whom held that
Japanese strikes were essentially "emotional" (*kanjōteki*) affairs rather
than economic struggles.[33] As a writer for the *Ōsaka asahi* explained

28. *Rōdō sekai*, no. 12 (15 May 1898): 8.
29. *NRUS* 2:9.
30. *Yūai shinpō*, no. 29 (1 June 1914): 5.
31. *Tōyō taimusu*, no. 51 (25 October 1921): 2.
32. *Yūai shinpō*, no. 18 (15 December 1913): 5.
33. Ibid., no. 7 (3 May 1913): 3.

in reporting on the Kure Naval Shipyard strike in 1912, "economic oppression" in Japan was always accompanied by "moral oppression," which he defines as the fact of being placed on an inferior moral level. The imputation of moral inferiority was, he says, more difficult for Japanese workers to bear than economic oppression. This made Japanese strikes emotional, likely to be set off by seemingly trivial incidents, whereas strikes in the West, he holds, were strictly conflicts over economic interests.[34] An earlier strike at Kure illustrates the point. It began when a new shipyard head, trained in Europe, ordered workers to travel to and from work in their work clothes. The new head saw the requirement as a way of making workers keep their work clothes clean; the workers apparently saw it as an unfeeling measure that forced on them the humiliation of walking through the streets in work clothes.[35]

The theory of moral oppression is borne out by the language of the workers themselves. Adamant in insisting that low wages and poor working conditions were expressions of employer contempt, they often compared their treatment to that of slaves, animals, or mere things and machines. They appealed to employers and the public to right this wrong by stressing, both in action and in words, their dependence upon the employer. Before 1917 requests for improved treatment were invariably in the form of a petition (*tangan*); striking workers collaborated with management in avoiding any appearance of a negotiation between equals; strikes were terminated—even when the workers won substantial concessions—by a return to work without a formal agreement in order that the employer, after the return, could announce the settlement terms as a unilateral decision on his part.

The following is part of a petition for higher wages at the Tokyo Arsenal in 1902. It appeals not to rights but to sympathy and a long record of loyal service. The language is cannily honorific and full of implications of dependence and humility difficult to translate without parody. The workers acknowledge that the setting of wages is a matter

---

34. *Ōsaka asahi,* in *NRUS* 4, 5 April 1912, 3:505–7.
35. There were work-rule issues in the strike as well, but the worker manifesto justifying the strike spoke to the clothing issue first. *NRUS* 2:61.

for management alone, yet they continue: "If out of extreme generosity and humanity you were graciously to adjust wage rates so as to restore our incomes [which had been reduced by inflation], that act of special favor [*tokuten*] would be a great good fortune to us. It would allay our worries and raise our spirit a hundredfold. We would work harder and yet harder, so that two results would be achieved at a stroke. We pray for your consideration of this petition."[36]

In such early petitions, workers sought to overcome moral oppression by claiming the existence of a patron-client relationship with the employer. They seem to have longed for the kind of acceptance enjoyed by Hugh Leonard's father, who was a gardener on the Dublin estate of a wealthy Quaker family named Jacob.

> Each Christmas Eve, he would be summoned to the pantry to receive a handshake from Mr. Jacob, at whose elbow stood Miss Grubb, ready to present him with a pound note, a tin of biscuits and a tumbler of Irish whiskey. He was unused to any drink stronger than a bottle of stout at weddings or funerals, and the whiskey made him garrulous and restless. He would come home, thrust the money at my mother with the grandeur of a nabob, sit, jump from the chair and announce with a sob in his throat that Old Charlie Jacob—who was his senior by five years—was the decentest man that ever trod shoe leather. He would say: "Show us the pound note again, Mag," and look as if it were the last ever to be printed. To him ten hour's toil each day was as natural as shafts to a drayhorse. The Jacobs were not only quality, they were his family.[37]

But the days for the personal touch, for the employer "to take the worker by the hand and call him by name," as the *Osaka mainichi* urged employers to do in 1917,[38] were long past in large enterprises, and workers increasingly knew it. One must not, therefore, interpret their petitions too literally; after all, a petition was often prelude to a strike. The submissiveness was at least partly intended to manipulate: to remind employers and the public of worker dependence and of the principle that power carries the responsibility of use with a decent concern for those subject to it, that otherwise it is nothing more than force

36. *NRUS* 2:64.
37. Hugh Leonard, *Home Before Night* (Middlesex, Engl., 1981), 32.
38. *NRUS* 3:565.

and fraud.[39] Despite the generally low opinion of workers, or perhaps because of it, the public was sympathetic to this message. A Home Ministry study of labor disputes in 1917 concluded that the public tended to side with the workers out of the conviction that, in all unequal relationships, the superior party has responsibility for setting the proper moral tone.[40] The workers both played on this sentiment and shared it.

It will be supposed that by emphasizing status, with its implication of dependence, rather than asserting the equality implied by rights, workers encouraged the very disparagement or moral oppression of which they complained.[41] They may well have about the turn of the century, but even then they were beginning to redefine status in a way that aimed at a radical change in the nature of authority and the place of workers in the factory.

This reworking of ideas, always around concrete issues, is too scattered and manifold to follow in detail, but three prominent themes may be noted and illustrated briefly. One was the inferential denial of the legitimacy of certain kinds of distinctions, in effect positing a finely graded status order without decided breaks, a hierarchy without class or caste. The second theme was the transformation of benefits from

39. From an early date, workers were sensible of the need to appeal to the public in the course of labor disputes. Dismissed workers at the Ōmiya factory of the Japan Railway (Nihon Tetsudō) issued a statement appealing for support by "brave and upright men of the age" (*yo no jinjin resshi*). *NRUS* 1:510.

40. According to the study, the public tended to blame labor disputes on employer despotism (*sen'ō*)—a word with strong Confucian overtones. Naimushō, *Rōdō sōgi gaikyō*, 20–21. *Osaka asahi* makes much the same point in analyzing strikes in 1907 when it compares employers and workers to rulers and ruled, adding that since "rulers should guide and instruct," it is the employer's responsibility to give such succor (*kyūsai*) to workers as would eliminate strikes. *NRUS* 2:87–90.

41. Most Japanese historians do not regard preindustrial experience and culture as contributing positively to the development of worker consciousness. Ikeda Makoto, for example, speaks of an early "unmediated producer consciousness" (*mubaikai na seisansha ishiki*) among workers, which arose from the confrontation with factory conditions. It was unmediated in the sense that it came from direct experience, presumably without the aid of ideology. This producer consciousness was then developed by intellectuals and union activists among workers into rights consciousness—that is, consciousness of "the right to live, the right to work, the right to collective contract and the right to strike based on justice." Ikeda, *Nihon kikaikō kumiai*, 130–80 (quotation, pp. 134–35).

expressions of the employer's personal benevolence into entitlements of service in a work community. The third was a demand for the promotion of qualified workers up the would-be classless status ladder on the basis of experience, irrespective of educational credentials and theoretically without any ceiling on possible advancement. It should be said immediately that this essay is concerned with the concept rather than the practice of status, although there were also changes in the latter.

Primary status groups were offensive to workers because the sharpness of distinction in the treatment accorded members of each suggested not merely differences in skill and seniority but in basic human worth. Managers were paid by the year, clerks by the month, workers by the day. Each group had a different title, and in the early years most companies had no comprehensive term embracing all groups, as though each represented a different order of being. Managers and clerks wore Western suits, workers uniforms or makeshift clothes. Only workers were subject to body searches on leaving work. There was a long and growing list of benefits—company housing, twice-yearly profit-sharing bonuses, separation pay, clubs, pensions, health care, and payments during illness and disability—that in most companies initially belonged mainly or wholly to managers.

After the turn of the century workers increasingly sought assimilation and the kinds of treatment accorded to higher status groups. They demanded, although at lower levels of payment or provision, the same bonuses, separation pay, housing and recreation facilities, and so on, as managers received. By the 1920s these issues seem to have become as important as wages, hours, and working conditions.[42] In response, benefits during the 1910s and 1920s were extended downward, although in a piecemeal and grudging manner, at first to clerical employees and then to workers.[43] In a gesture of assimilation, most com-

---

42. This general impression is strongly confirmed by a systematic check of issues in strikes that were reported during the year 1926 in the union organ, *Rōdō*, 112–15, 144–46, 173–76, 198–201, 230–31.

43. Company financial reports published in the *Tokyo keizai zasshi* from 1890 show bonuses (*shōyo*) first for directors and then increasingly for clerical-technical personnel; the earliest notice I have found in the magazine of a bonus for workers was in 1912, in the report for Fuji Gasu Bōseki (vol. 66, p. 1176). Notices of workers' bonuses became more and more frequent after 1912 and were fairly common by the 1920s.

panies invented or borrowed a general term for employees to be used in company documents in place of the serial listing of status groups, and companies also coined a respectful or at least neutral term for *worker*, in place of the old, disparaging *shokkō*.[44] After a long agitation by workers, the Yawata Steel Mill in 1922 abolished body searches as well as worker uniforms and cap insignia, and some other companies followed in time.[45]

In all of these reforms, the workers were intent on obliterating distinctions among primary status groups. Their fundamental claim was that distinctions of treatment *in kind* (although not in amount) were "discriminatory" (*sabetsuteki*),[46] a word used to protest against ascribed, as opposed to achieved, status. In using the word to criticize distinctions of treatment in kind, workers were unquestionably denying the legitimacy of primary status groups; at the same time, however, they were avoiding complaint against the existence of quantitative distinctions. Although they often questioned the size of the differentials— the number of holidays and the amount of bonuses to workers in comparison to those given clerical-technical employees, for example—they

44. The adoption of a term equivalent to "employee" that would include blue-collar workers might be regarded as symbolic inclusion of workers in the company. An unsystematic sampling of company semiannual reports suggests that the use of employee-equivalent terms came into common use in the 1910s. No such term appears in the reports for Nihon Kōkan in 1915, 1917, and 1918, for example, but one—*jūgyōin*—is used in the 1920 report. For Tokyo Shibaura, there is none in reports between 1904 and 1909, but *shiyō jin'in* appears in 1911. For Tokyo Gasu, none in 1903 and 1910, but *shiyōnin* in 1916. Most companies also show changes in the specific terms for white- and blue-collar workers. At Tokyo Shibaura, for example, *shokkō* for blue-collar in 1904 becomes *rōekisha* during 1909–25 and then *kōjin* during 1925–27. The company reports referred to here are in the collection of *Kaisha eigyō hōkokusho*, Hoover Institution and Library, Stanford University.

45. *Tōyō taimusu*, no. 70 (5 May 1922): 7; no. 87 (5 November 1922): 7. It is evident from the phrasing in the company newspaper's announcement of the change in dress regulations that workers were ashamed of wearing their uniforms and insignia in the town of Yawata. *Kurogane*, 15 July 1922.

46. The Yawata paper calls such distinctions "class discrimination" (*kuikyū sabetsu*), leaving no doubt of the pejorative meaning of the term. *Tōyō taimusu*, no. 28 (5 March 1921): 7. This was a new usage and evidently not one accepted generally: the dictionary *Dai Nihon kokugo jiten* (Tokyo, 1920) defines *sabetsu* as the equivalent of *kubetsu*, meaning simply "distinction" with no pejorative sense. *Daijiten* (Tokyo, 1935) also defines *sabetsu* as simply "difference" or "distinction" (*chigai, kejime*). I do not know the date of the first dictionary inclusion of "discrimination" as a meaning of *sabetsu*. *Nihon kokugo jiten* (Tokyo, 1976) gives the following as the second meaning of the word: "to treat a person as lower than another without just cause."

did not challenge the principle of quantitative differentials. Factory newspapers were full of letters of complaint about favoritism in promotions, but no letter advocated ignoring differences of skill and seniority in favor of the principle of equal pay for the same job. The hierarchical pay and benefit system, even among workers doing the same jobs in the same workplace, was taken for granted. When the Yawata management distributed a wartime bonus to workers in 1922, the Yawata workers' paper expressed resentment that the size of individual bonuses failed to correspond to status in all cases, so that some workers of lower rank received more than those of higher. The paper attacked such discrepancies as humiliating, lacking in human feeling, and threatening to the very order (*chitsujo*) of the factory.[47] After a factory committee was organized at Yawata, worker representatives made many suggestions for establishing new status distinctions among themselves but, at least for the committee's first ten years, none for eliminating or consolidating existing statuses.[48]

Second, since superior status carried a presumption of moral superiority, it was often associated with abuse of authority, especially perhaps on the shop floor. Foremen and workshop supervisors were notoriously harsh and contemptuous in dealing with workers. According to Yokoyama Gennosuke (1870–1915), a journalist with unrivaled knowledge of factory conditions at the turn of the century, these men were self-important martinets who thought workers never so well managed as when being upbraided, and they went at them "like samu-

---

47. *Tōyō taimusu*, no. 73 (5 June 1922).
48. The newspaper *Kurogane*, published by the Yawata Steel Mill for its workers, contains detailed summaries of meetings of the mill's factory committee, the Kondankai. Examples of workers' suggestions for increased distinctions among themselves, advanced at these meetings, include the following: in calculating separation pay, give greater weight to seniority of more than ten years; create retirement ceremonies for those retiring upon reaching the age limit (but not for those retiring otherwise); give full retirement pay to workers with ten years' seniority and half to workers with less than ten years' seniority; change "nonabsentee" awards to "good behavior" awards and create a separate "nonabsentee" award; provide allowances for workers who serve as city or village council members; determine admission to company housing according to seniority; provide a bonus for continuous service (*kinzoku teate*); establish a seniority bonus (*nenkō kahō shōyo*) like that in the army. There are also egalitarian suggestions, but they seem always to be aimed at eliminating distinctions between workers and higher status employees; there is, for example, a request that identification badges of all employees be identical. *Kurogane*, June 1920–February 1930.

rai berating peasants."[49] An engineer who returned to Japan in 1907 from several years in factories in America and England was shocked to see again workers on their knees before staff personnel.[50] Supervisors and foremen had a strong voice in hiring, setting beginning pay, recommending promotions and raises, and making work assignments, all of which they were apt to use to extend their personal sway over workers and, frequently, to extract gifts, bribes, wage kickbacks, and services.[51] At the Yawata Steel Mill in 1922 a middle-level manager was discovered using the firm's workers on company time on his nearby tea plantation and processing factory; he had been doing so for years but resentful workers had been afraid to protest.[52] An autobiography written by a worker in 1913 described conditions the author had found at a government arsenal some years earlier: "Bribery [wairo] was absolutely open. When the worker first entered the arsenal, he paid a fee to obtain employment. For every promotion thereafter he paid a fee ranging from grade one to grade ten. To become a foreman or assistant foreman a top fee was required. Character and ability hardly counted in promotions and raises. At All Souls' and New Year's the gifts to supervisors were enormous. Dozens of bottles of beer, hundreds of yen worth of clothing, and fish. Some men gave cash. Gifts that supervisors could not use at home they sold to merchants at discount."[53]

Because such conditions were common, any individual raise or promotion was suspect and the subject of intense speculation as to its warrant. A worker tells of rooming next door to four young metalworkers who were known to him only from their voices, to which he

49. *Naichi zakkyogo no Nihon* (Tokyo, 1959), 42–43, and *Nihon no kasō shakai*, in *Yokoyama zenshū*, ed. Sumiya Mikio (Tokyo, 1972), 1:158–59.

50. Hazama Hiroshi, "Japanese Labor-Management and Uno Riemon," *Journal of Japanese Studies* 5, no. 1 (Winter 1979): 79.

51. A report of the Agriculture and Commerce Ministry (Nōshōmushō) in 1900 states: "Hiring and firing and the payment of wages is left to *oyabun* [work bosses who were often also subcontractors]. In factories with large numbers of workers . . . the employer has almost nothing to do with these matters, permitting the bosses to collect fees from the workers under them and to advance and demote workers without regard for factory regulations." "Kōjō oyobi shokkō ni kansuru tsūhei ippan," in *Shokkō oyobi kōfu chōsa*, ed. Sumiya Mikio (Tokyo, 1970), 56. The power of *oyabun* and, later, foremen over hiring, firing, and wages, although gradually reduced, was still great as late as the 1920s in most large factories. See n. 59 below.

52. *Tōyō taimusu*, no. 73 (5 June 1922): 6.

53. *Yūai shinpō*, no. 29 (1 June 1914): 4.

was obliged to listen through the thin partition. Night after night, drunk or sober, they talked of scarcely anything but whether the difference in wages between themselves and this or that man in their workshop was justified by a difference in skill.[54] Pride was much at stake in such differences because the worker's main claim to pride was his skill, of which the wage was the ostensible measure. But not only pride was at stake; a large cumulative gap in wages for the same work could open between the man who rarely won a raise and the man who regularly did. Wages for persons doing the same work often differed by as much as 50 to 100 percent[55] and occasionally more, and in addition benefits increased with base pay.[56]

Clearly some workers must have benefited by the payment of bribes and kickbacks on wages, but literally no one defended these practices openly. Workers' letters to newspapers uniformly condemned them as corrupt, insisting that raises and promotions be based exclusively on factors such as skill, attendance records, and seniority, thereby divorcing advancement from the evaluation of attitude and diligence, which was regarded as inviting bribery, favoritism, and personal exploitation. Workers sometimes found ways of dealing with egregious cases of favoritism, by hounding and threatening the offending worker until he quit,[57] but they had no effective way of making favoritism an issue with management. The fact of improper influence in a raise or promotion could not be proved, and charges of corruption against higher-ups could bring discharge or other reprisal.[58] This situation changed, however, in the late 1910s and early 1920s because of two circumstances.

54. *Tōyō taimusu*, no. 15 (25 October 1920): 5.
55. Hyōdō Tsutomu, *Nihon ni okeru rōshi kankei no tenkai*, 2d printing (Tokyo, 1980), 192–202.
56. The Mitsubishi Shipyard at Nagasaki, for example, based payments for disablement or death on the worker's daily wage bracket (less than 35 sen, 35 to 60 sen, and more than 60 sen). Payments for the first bracket ranged from 150 to 500 yen; for the second, 375 to 700 yen; and for the third, 500 to 1,500 yen. *Rōdōsha toriatsukai-kata ni kansuru chōsa hōkokusho*, 72–73.
57. For an autobiographical account of such an incident, see *Yūai shinpō*, no. 26 (15 April 1914): 4.
58. In a widely publicized incident, the Japan Railway dismissed eight workers in 1899 for protesting the "despotism" and corruption of an overseer; the company forced the eight to move out of company housing within twenty-four hours and confiscated bonuses held for them as savings. *NRUS* 1:509–10.

First, unprecedented company profits during and after World War I, coinciding with rising consumer prices and a critical shortage of skilled labor, resulted in the winning of general wage increases by workers in large enterprises. The question inevitably arose of how the increase should be distributed. Almost invariably management wanted to distribute it differentially among workers, thus preserving the freedom to reward and punish individuals. Precisely to avoid this situation and the powerful extension of the personal authority of foremen and supervisors that would result, workers insisted on either uniform raises or a sliding scale of increases based strictly on measurable factors such as seniority and attendance records. Two of the largest strikes in 1917 were over this issue In one case, the company succeeded in retaining the freedom to vary raises to individual workers with a range of 5–30 percent of base pay, according to the company's judgment of the individual worker's deserts. But even in this case the permissible variation was at least limited, and workers had united on the principle of the impersonal determination of the level of wages.[59] In the other strike, the company, acting under pressure from public authorities, finally agreed to a formula by which two-thirds of the raise would be governed by determinant factors and one-third left to the company's discretion, a considerable victory for the workers.[60]

The second factor raising the issue of company discretion was the trend, in the late 1910s and 1920s, of extending to workers certain benefits previously enjoyed exclusively by higher status groups. In the case of benefits entailing monetary payments, such as twice-yearly bonuses and separation pay, companies everywhere retained a broad authority to determine both worker eligibility and the size of the payment on an individual basis. Workers sought to narrow or eliminate

59. This was the strike at the steel mill in Muroran in March 1917. Workers rejected the company's plan for a variable increase because, according to a local newspaper, they feared on the basis of past experience that individual raises would be based on the recommendation of foremen and that partiality and corruption would result. NRUS 3 : 567–72.

60. This strike, at the Nagasaki Shipyard, resulted in the revision of the formula used for distribution of a wage increase of 30 percent granted by the company some months earlier. The earlier formula had been 10 percent across the board and 20 percent on individual merit as judged by the company; the new formula was 10 percent across the board, 10 percent on attendance record, and 10 percent on merit as judged by the company. NRUS 3 : 573.

such authority and substitute a hard-and-fast formula. Separation payments had been made to retiring workers from an early date at the Yawata Steel Mill, for example, but the company issued no public regulation specifying the terms of eligibility or the amount of payments. It regularly withheld payments from workers who, as the company put it, "left for their own convenience," and workers were consequently left in considerable doubt as to whether they would receive payment upon separation and, if so, how much. Over many years the Yawata workers' paper argued that eligibility should be independent of the reason for quitting and that all regulations concerning separation pay should be detailed and public so that workers would have "the right to demand" (yōkyū no kenri) what was coming to them.[61]

The phrasing is significant. Benefits, once seen as expressions of employer benevolence and still sometimes referred to by that term in the Yawata paper, had now become entitlements based on service to the company. That was precisely the paper's point in insisting that separation pay was a reward for "past service" unrelated to the reason for quitting. This shift in the concept of benefits had been under way for some time and was by no means confined to workers. A personnel handbook in use at the Nagasaki Shipyard in 1914 called certain benefits extended to workers "benevolence," and the workers entitled to it were said to be "bathed in benevolence." But the handbook also spoke of these workers as having a "right" (kenri) to the benefits and at one point termed this a "right to benevolence."[62]

Third, workers sought to reduce the ascriptive element in the determination of status by attacking the value of formal schooling. Just as company benefits ideally ought to be of the same kind for all employees, thereby linking everyone ultimately in a common overriding status, so all employees should be able to move across internal statuses without prejudicial tests. For workers, education was such a test. It

61. Rōdō no Kyūshū, 15 May 1926, p. 2.
62. After stating that welfare payments covered by worker regulations were granted "benevolently" (onkeiteki) by the company, the handbook went on to distinguish three categories of workers with differential claims to such payments. Of the third category it was said that "workers in this category . . . have no right to the benevolence [onkei ni yokusuru kenri naki mono nari] established by these regulations." Rōdōsha toriatsukaikata ni kansuru chōsa hōkokusho, 1–2, 76–77.

was a test of the parents' ability to support the child in school, not of the child's educability or of what the child-become-man could do. Workers' letters and factory newspapers repeatedly complained of unequal economic access to education and of the unfairness of judging a man forever according to whether he had completed four, six, or ten years of school.[63]

The railway engineers' strike, which shut down the Japan Railway Company's Tōhoku line from Tokyo to Aomori in 1899, implicitly raised this issue. The strike was called in support of the demand on the company by the engineers for treatment equal to that of clerks (*shoki*). Calling themselves the Alliance for Improved Treatment, the engineers argued that, as engineers were charged with the operation of great and expensive locomotives, the true products of civilization (*bunmei no riki*), they ought to be accorded a degree of honor (*meiyo*) equal to their heavy responsibilities. It took eight years of training to become an engineer, and "these dangerous machines" could not be operated without exceptional judgment, perseverance, industry, and bravery. Thus, they continued, "our occupation is not base (*rettō*) but noble (*kōshō*); it should be accorded respect (*sonkei*), not contempt (*hisen*)." Nevertheless, engineers were given "cold" and "low" treatment in comparison to clerks and stationmasters, even though the duties of a stationmaster in a small station were trivial. He had only a few passengers a day to deal with "between naps," and his whole business could as well be taken care of by a station roustabout. Distinctions of treatment such as those between stationmasters and engineers, which were based on education and ignored actual responsibilities, were survivals from the feudal age. They sprang from the same attitudes that allowed youngsters just out of middle school to address senior engineers without the polite *san* and prompted the company to refer to clerks (*jimuin*) as "officials" (*yakuin*)—as if the engineers and other workers under them were subjects.[64]

After 1899 the arguments against formal education as the basis

63. For example, *Tōyō taimusu,* no. 31 (5 April 1921): 2; *Rōdō no Kyūshū,* 19 April 1924, 15 May 1926, 13 October 1926.

64. "Taigū Kisei Daidōmeikai Ichinoseki Shibu kiji," an account, published in 1899, by one of the strike leaders, Ishida Rokujirō. *NRUS* 2:16–35.

of an individual's status and authority within companies took many forms. One was to ridicule what the clerks actually did, as the Tōhoku engineers had done. Thus the Yawata workers' paper routinely referred to clerical personnel as "high class loafers" (kōtō yūmin) and to themselves as "producers."[65] Another was to deprecate the skills of school-trained foremen, supervisors, and engineers, who were said to be clever at theory and blueprints but unable to handle tools or machines or stand up physically to hard work.[66] Yet another was to impugn the characters of those with school training (foremen and supervisors), holding that technical education had a narrowing effect on the personality, resulting in what Nishio Suehiro (1891–), himself a fireman but not school trained, calls "fragmentary" (kireppashi) human beings—men without broad sympathies, common sense (jōshiki), or character (jinkaku) who treated other men like machines.[67]

The popular movement among workers in the late 1910s and early 1920s to elect their own factory foremen was partly aimed at ridding themselves of such superiors and partly at opening the way for the advancement of talented workers. Nor was the rank of foreman thought to represent a necessary ceiling on such advancement. Nishio makes it clear that the positions in which exceptional workers might replace fragmentary human beings included engineers and workshop heads (kōjōchō); the Yawata paper announced that workers who produced significant inventions ought to be awarded the doctorate of engineering, suggesting that they would then qualify for the highest management positions.[68] Although these claims on behalf of practical experience apparently resulted nowhere in concrete measures that made it easier to rise above worker rank without special technical training, they clearly affected management's confidence in the persuasiveness of the old equation, education = character = status = treatment. In responding in 1922 to workers' discontent with the size of differentials

65. Tōyō taimusu, no. 40 (5 July 1921): 1.
66. Tōyō taimusu, no. 40 (5 July 1921): 1; no. 70 (5 May 1922): 2; Rōdō no Kyūshū, 19 April 1924, pp. 12–13. School training was often derided as "half-baked learning" (namahanka gakushiki).
67. Kōjō seikatsu 2, no. 1 (July 1917): 16–17; also Tōyō taimusu, no. 28 (5 March 1921): 1.
68. Tōyō taimusu, no. 69 (25 April 1922): 2.

in pay and benefits between workers and clerical-technical personnel, the Yawata management used the astonishing argument that such differentials were justified by the heavier expenditures the parents of clerical-technical personnel had made on education.[69] The Yawata managers to a man probably did believe that education on the whole made a person more valuable technically and gave him a finer moral grain. But they apparently hesitated to voice that argument—unquestioned a couple of decades earlier—fearing that it would not convince workers. Instead, they made an argument that reduced status to a return on investment! Yawata workers may have won no immediate practical gain from this exchange, but they clearly won the argument, in a big way.

As with other changes they sought in the status system, workers linked their drive for access to advancement to the furthering of broad community interests. The engineers in 1899 spoke of their struggle for improved treatment as a "just war" (*meibun tadashiki gisen*) being fought with "sincerity" (*seii*) to reform the industrial world (*jitsugyō-kai*) and benefit the nation.[70] Nishio and his fellow workers who formed the Osaka Dōshikai (Brotherhood) in 1916, in part to open the way for the promotion of workers to higher positions, announced that their ultimate objective was to contribute to a rich nation and strong army (*fukoku kyōhei*).[71] The Yawata paper repeatedly argued that only if industry tapped the talents and energies of workers could Japan withstand foreign competition: "In present worldwide industrial competition, it is completely to misunderstand the times to give confidence only to people with academic credentials and to withhold it from those with seasoned practical skills. Industry cannot develop with such attitudes. Rather it must be made to stand on the principle of equality [of opportunity] regardless of educational degrees. . . . We must thus open the way for the promotion of men in accordance with their skill [*ginō*]."[72]

69. Ibid., no. 40 (5 July 1921): 1.
70. "Taigū Kisei Daidōmeikai Ichinoseki Shibu kiji," in *NRUS* 2:16.
71. *Kōjō seikatsu* 1, no. 1 (September 1916).
72. *Tōyō taimusu*, no. 69 (25 April 1922): 2.

No doubt workers did not see clearly where they were going, especially in the early years, but Abe Isoo (1865–1949), a Unitarian, socialist, and academic, defined the goal with surprising clarity. In a 1913 essay he attributed worker dissatisfaction to the nature of authority relations, which replicated lord-vassal relations and were based on the survival of "feudal" attitudes in Japanese society. In companies and factories the superior treated subordinates with arrogance and contempt, those subordinates in turn tyrannized their subordinates, and the man without subordinates took out his frustration and anger on his wife and children. Since everyone bowed before superiors and abused inferiors shamelessly, low morale and productivity were general. The remedy, Abe argued, was to transform what he called the present "person-based" (*taijin kankei*) into "enterprise-based" (*taijigyō kankei*) authority. Then no one would any longer be subordinate to a superior *as a person,* but only through that person to the enterprise, to which both superior and subordinate would be subject. In that sense, all employees would be equal and would work not to serve a superior but to advance the company and, through the company, to serve the nation and the emperor. Even the employer would have no purely personal authority; his authority, if any, would derive solely from his executive position in the enterprise. Thus, if the worker did his work for the company "loyally," he would owe no debt of gratitude to the employer and would have no reason to bow down before him.

Abe illustrated with an anecdote his distinction between person-based and enterprise-based relations. A young man he knew had taken a position with the Morimura Trading Company and was put in charge of its New York store. After some months he received a handsome bonus, and his seniors in the company advised him to thank Mr. Morimura and his wife. The young man flatly refused, saying that he would resign first; he worked for the company, not for Mr. Morimura, and certainly not for Mr. Morimura's wife. If thanks were necessary, however, let all employees of the company assemble in a great hall and thank one another for the effort that made the bonus possible. When word of this reached Mr. Morimura, he thought the young man's position entirely correct and arranged for the mutual-thanks ceremony to be carried out. If this attitude was adopted generally, Abe predicted, the world would see what the presently dispirited Japanese worker could really do.[73]

The essence of Abe's enterprise-based authority was the idea of a basic human equality independent of all status relations, a community or enterprise loyalty unmediated by personal ties. As will be seen, workers affirmed this equality and, indirectly, its relation to loyalty in the 1910s by insisting on recognition by the employer of their *jinkaku*—a Christian concept that entered the language about the turn of the century. *Jinkaku* signified the potential of all biologically normal human beings for autonomous moral development based on the reflection of divine intelligence in consciousness and memory, qualities that distinguished mankind from all other things in nature. Although all human beings were held to possess this potential, not all realized it fully or in the same degree. Its development, which came through self-consciousness (*jikaku*)[74] and was, significantly, called self-realization (*jiko jitsugen*), could be impaired, distorted, or reversed by dissipation, the denial of education, or dehumanizing conditions of life and work. Since man could realize himself only in society, and since he could contribute to society only by self-realization, to hamper the development of another person's *jinkaku* was both antisocial and an act of individual cruelty.[75]

As indicated by their widespread adoption of the term in the 1910s, despite an almost total lack of interest in Christianity, workers were quick to understand the egalitarian implications of *jinkaku*. The words *hinkō* and *hinsei,* which until then had been accepted as expres-

73. *Yūai shinpō* no. 14 (15 October 1913): 3; no. 15 (1 November 1913): 4.

74. I have the impression that until about 1920 "self-consciousness" among workers meant consciousness of personal dignity, respectability, and character, that is, consciousness of *jinkaku,* and that after 1920 it came increasingly to mean consciousness of working-class identity. Both meanings suggest pride, but the first pride is despite the fact of being a worker, the second is because of it.

75 The earliest use of the term *jinkaku* found in the collection of dictionaries in the East Asiatic Library at the University of California, Berkeley, is in the *Dokuwa jiten taizen* of 1905 under "Person, Persönlichkeit." The earliest reference in a Japanese-Japanese dictionary is in 1908 in *Jirin.* The first use of the word in the Christian magazine *Rikugō zasshi* appears to be in an article by Morita Kumato, published in 1897 in issue no. 177. (I am indebted to Andrew Barshay for these notes.) The dictionary *Gensen* of 1912 defines *jinkakusei* (*jinkaku*-ness) as a quality formed by "self-consciousness [*jikaku*], reason [*risei*], and autonomy [*jiko kettei*]."

sing the supposed moral correlate of status, emphasized overt behavior and might be translated roughly as "refinement" or "breeding."[76] These were qualities in which workers were painfully lacking, as they themselves recognized, and most early worker organizations, as noted earlier, were dedicated to improving the behavior of workers in order to raise their status—clearly a long-term ambition. Now, however, *jinkaku* defined morality as an inner quality, something close to conscience and independent of social position. For the first time it became plausible for workers to claim moral equality with their status betters and to suggest that if the performance of some workers fell short of the desired standard, it was not their fault but the fault of those who refused to recognize their humanity. Whether because of the influence of the idea of *jinkaku* or not, workers began to write letters, like this one appearing in 1914, that made far-reaching spiritual claims: "I am only a poor worker looked down on by society as rubbish. Yet I am a man who does not regard his life as his own. I am ready to give my life for my lord and country: like a train on a track, I will forever follow the way of righteousness [*seigi no michi*]."[77] A stanza of the Yawata union song struck a similar chord: "In this world of selfishness / Only the worker stands on righteousness."[78]

Since workers were morally equal or, as the song suggests, superior to their status betters, benefits enjoyed exclusively by the latter were morally unjustified. They were in fact brutal public denials of worker *jinkaku*. Under a regime of this kind, which denied their essential humanity, workers could not be expected to work with a will, a sentiment they asserted in letters such as this one: "Japanese industry cannot possibly develop if worker *jinkaku* is not respected. . . . Engineers, factory managers, and capitalists treat us as things and machines. Who

76. *Dai Nihon kokugo jiten* (1920) defines *hinsei* as *hitogara* (personal character or appearance), *hinkaku* (grace, dignity), *hin* (elegance, refinement). *Hinkō* is defined as *okonai* (behavior) or *hitogara* (as above). A contributor to the *Yūai shinpō*, no. 10 (13 August 1913): 10, praises the workers' recreation room, recently opened under the paper's auspices, as a means of improving the use of leisure time by workers and hence raising their *hinsei*. It is significant that, when workers at Yawata established a recreation center at their own expense with facilities for "moral cultivation" (*shūyō*) and for "group activities and sports," they announced that the new facility would raise worker *hinsei*—not *jinkaku*. *Tōyō taimusu*, no. 49 (5 October 1921): 2.

77. *Yūai shinpō*, no. 33 (1 August 1914): 5.

78. *Tōyō taimusu*, no. 57 (25 December 1921): 7.

with spirit will remain a factory worker under these conditions? I hear the criticism that Japanese workers are technically inferior and do not work hard, but that is because the treatment given them is such as to retain only inferior workers."[79]

The Yawata workers' paper, comparing what existed with what might be, expressed the same judgment: "It hampers the development of industry to treat clerk-technicians as lords and actual producers [*gengyōin*] as vassals. If Japan is to win the world industrial war, workers must make capitalists and managers realize this. If we succeed, then an era of cooperation will come about that will increase the benefits of industry and strengthen the peace and prosperity of the country."[80]

It is significant that workers sought equality by an appeal to the new idea of *jinkaku* rather than the older concept of *kenri*, or rights, advocated by unionists. Perhaps it was because *jinkaku* bespoke moral equality, which workers longed for but were denied, whereas rights implied an equality independent of moral differences. Also, workers seemed to strive for a community in the workplace that would transcend status. *Jinkaku* offered the basis for such community by affirming the worthiness of workers for association with persons of the highest company rank, whereas, according to union advocates, rights (*kenri*) were effective when workers organized and asserted them separately and in opposition to such persons.[81]

Workers' aspirations for equality and community are expressed in a cartoon that appeared on the front page of the Yawata workers' paper in 1920.[82] The cartoon, shown in Figure 10.1, portrays a hand-

79. *Yūai shinpō*, no. 29 (1 June 1914): 5.
80. *Tōyō taimusu*, no. 70 (5 May 1922): 2.
81. Early unionists, who were almost as one in advocating workers' rights, hoped that unions would serve as a basis for cooperation with management; but they foresaw that relations with management would also be marked at times by confrontation and strikes and so stressed the need for worker solidarity. Suzuki Bunji (1885–1946) associated unions with the struggle for survival, which was a "law of evolution" that operated at both the individual and group levels. *Rōdō oyobi sangyō*, no. 56 (1 April 1916), in *NRUS* 3:331–32.
82. *Tōyō taimusu*, no. 28 (15 June 1920): 1. The *Tōyō taimusu* was the organ of Dōshikai, a Yawata union that survived the strike of 1920 while participating in it, although two other unions, Rōyūkai and Yūaikai, which played more active roles in the strike, did not. The latter two were expelled from the mill, along with workers promi-

Fig. 10.1   Sense of Receiving Benevolence
SOURCE: *Tōyō taimusu,* no. 28 (15 June 1920): 1.

some young man in black hat and coat and striped vest joining, as partner in a three-legged race, another handsome young man, in cap, neckerchief, and work clothes. The first figure is labeled "capitalist" and the second, "worker." The two are arm in arm, striding ahead confidently; their common (third) leg, moving in perfect coordination with the others, is labeled "sense of [receiving] benevolence" (*kan' on*). At first glance, the cartoon appears an appeal to patron-client eth-

---

nently affiliated with them. In taking the Dōshikai paper to represent worker opinion subsequent to its strike, as I believe it did broadly, one must keep the events surrounding the strike in mind, since they must have dampened the expression of opinion in some degree. From a careful reading of workers' letters to the paper, however, I do not have the impression of a subterranean current of opinion very different from the views of the paper. Perhaps such a current could not be detected in any case. Yet the workers' letters are not cautiously phrased; they are vehemently expressed and cover a great range of subjects, from complaints of the most personal kind about working condition, overseers, and promotions, to highly abstruse criticisms of management.

ics between workers and management. But the actual message was considerably more complex. Patron-client relations were an anachronism for Yawata with its twenty thousand employees; moreover, the Yawata paper regularly attacked management for personalism in awarding promotions and raises, insisted on worker *jinkaku,* and demanded that separation payments be a matter of "right." Closer inspection of the figures in the picture reveals that "sense of receiving benevolence" is in fact lettered on the capitalist's, not the worker's, leg; although lettering on the worker's leg would have been difficult because it is partially obscured by the capitalist's leg, that problem could have been resolved simply by reversing the positions of the two figures. So the particular location of the label was unnecessary and perhaps deliberate, suggesting that both capitalist and worker were expected to receive benevolence. That intention is also suggested by the fact that the two figures are almost exact replicas of each other: the same height, age, and face, the same expression of confidence and resolution. They are identical in everything except dress, reflecting their different functions, which are clearly what bind them together. The two work in a common endeavor, which neither can accomplish alone, and both share in its benefits. The cartoon seems a pictorial version of Abe's enterprise-based community, in which one can imagine workers, managers, and clerks all assembling in a great hall to thank one another for their efforts.

The actual state of affairs at Yawata, by contrast, is represented in another cartoon in the same year, entitled "Inside the Yawata Steel Mill." That drawing, shown in Figure 10.2, shows a white-collar employee labeled clerk-technician (*shokuin*) and a worker labeled "producer"; they are side by side, opening their year-end bonus envelopes. The clerk's is for the equivalent of five months' pay, and the worker's is for three days' pay. The clerk, Western-featured and wearing Western clothes and smoking a cigar, prances in delight and self-importance in front of the chagrined worker, a cross-eyed, button-nosed figure half the size of the clerk, wearing wooden clogs and smoking an old-fashioned pipe. Everything about him is pathetic by comparison with the splendid form displayed by the clerk, who says condescendingly, "Ah, yes, for this too we have the producer to thank." The producer replies, "And for that reason productivity will not rise." Here we have

Fig. 10.2 Inside the Yawata Steel Mill

SOURCE: *Tōyō taimusu*, no. 23 (15 January 1920): 1.

something like the converse of the enterprise-based ideal: selfishness on the part of management, gross unfairness to the workers, the imputation of fundamentally different categories of human beings, and the worker's bitter prediction that so long as these conditions prevail he will withhold loyalty and effort from the enterprise.

Perhaps no worker in the prewar period encountered enterprise-based relations in industry, but many experienced something like them in the army. In his autobiography, Matsumoto Seichō describes his feeling of liberation on being drafted into the army from a provincial branch of the Osaka newspaper, *Asahi;* he explains that this exhilaration came in effect from moving from an organization based on ascribed to one based on achieved status. We noted earlier that he was ashamed at having to drop out of school because of family poverty and that for years he dodged former classmates on the street. As a worker at *Asahi,* he was excluded from company gatherings to celebrate the anniversary of the firm, the emperor's birthday, and the founding of the Japanese empire. He had little interest in the ostensible meaning of these ceremonies, but he felt the segregation keenly. When finally promoted to the advertising section and allowed to participate in such gatherings, however, he encountered a new and more personal form of discrimination. As a lithographer, he found himself a mere technician among salesmen, writers, clerks, and managers who daily made him feel the unbridgeable gulf between them and him. The branch head would stop by the section to chat with the advertising salesmen, exchange jokes, and hear the business news from the street, but he never had more than a perfunctory "good day" for Matsumoto, sitting nearby. At staff parties, where it was customary for the head and his assistant to make the rounds of the guests, exchanging drinks and pleasantries with each in turn, they would barely pause in front of him and hastily pass on. It was not that they disliked him, Matsumoto says; he was simply a person of no importance to them. For years this kind of thing went on, day in and out, making his life an unrelieved misery; and then came the war in the Pacific, and he was drafted into the army:

> Army life was a revelation to me. It turned out just as they told me when I arrived there: "Here social position, wealth, and age count for nothing. Everyone is on absolutely the same level." The equality I found among the new recruits gave me a curious sense that life was worthwhile. At *Asahi* I

was not just a cog in a wheel but a cog of no value. But in the army if one worked hard and studied and kept on good terms with the squad leader and older men, recognition was possible. At the newspaper my very existence was not recognized. Here I counted. Discovery of a human condition not present in the factory enlivened me in a strange way. People say that army life negates the human being: I had just the opposite experience. During my three months in training and then two years of regular duty, no one could possibly have been a poorer soldier than I; so it was not that I was full of martial spirit. My feeling was a reaction to life in the factory up to that time.[83]

Matsumoto's reaction to the factory status system testifies to the tension it caused among workers, although readers may wonder that he could find escape from this particular source of misery in, of all places, the army. Yet obviously he did. What bothered him at *Asahi* was not the inequality and absence of rights, as one might suppose, but the nature of that inequality: it was ascriptive[84] and segregated employees into superior and inferior humankind. The army seemed to him free of this kind of segregation. Everyone entered on the same level; prior differences of wealth, education, and family were obliterated; subsequent differences of rank were earned—hence Matsumoto's novel sense that he counted. At *Asahi*, by contrast, not only was he just a cog in a wheel, but a cog of no value.

Matsumoto's sense of liberation in going from factory to army, I suspect, was not unusual. His complaints about *Asahi* echo decades of worker criticism, and by 1920 the criticism was already calling for the reform of status along lines somewhat similar to those Matsumoto later found in the army. Status, in this reformist view, should carry no imputation of basic human inequality and should be earned; it should be free of any hint of personal subordination of one man to another; and it should be a mode of integration in a community rather than segregation from it. If these views were as widespread among workers as I believe, they suggest two possible revisions of commonly held inter-

83. Matsumoto, *Hansei no ki*, 49, 76–77, 81–82.
84. Status in the factory was based, automatically and rigidly, on education—an achieved status. But education became the basis of ascription in a work situation in which, although status derived from it, education was not an accurate predictor of performance. Although workers were widely aware and resentful of the ascriptive function of education in the factory, so far as I know they had no word to signify a meaning equivalent to "ascription," which might from their viewpoint be called false status.

pretations of the history of Japanese labor that I am not in a position to argue at length and hope merely to call attention to here.

First, the dramatic growth of the labor movement from 1917 to the mid-1920s was not, as is widely held, based on the growth of a consciousness of rights among workers. It is true of course that national union leaders and local union activists used rights language freely. But the ease with which the Yawata union paper could invoke employer's benevolence and workers' rights on the same issue should make for caution in translating rights language too literally into general worker consciousness. One even wonders about the people in the union vanguard, who continued at times (as they had since the late 1890s) to use the word *rights* in contexts that suggest a broad overlap of meaning with such concepts as status, power, and interest; consciously or not, union leaders appropriated status issues in the name of rights. They demanded an end to favoritism within the hierarchical pay system but not to the system itself. They emphasized company social benefits (bonuses, separation pay, housing, and so on)—issues tending to separate workers at one factory from those at others—at the expense of wage issues tending to unite them. They rarely mentioned, and never to my knowledge tried to give effect to, the notion of equal pay for equal work. I suggest that up to the mid-1920s the labor movement was based primarily on worker status ideology. The concept of rights was relatively new to workers. Their notions of status had been shaped by thirty years of local efforts to improve conditions in the workplace and were deeply rooted in the history of the struggles of villages and towns for hierarchical justice from regional lords during the Tokugawa period.

Second, management is given rather more credit than it deserves for the creation of the reformed system of Japanese labor management, insofar as that system may be said to have emerged before World War II. Management is usually seen to be moved to create the system by traditional paternalistic ideals, by a shrewd appreciation of the need to counter the threat posed by the labor movement, and by market-rational decisions under conditions of late development. No doubt there was something of all these factors in increasing the attention of large companies to worker welfare in the 1910s and 1920s. What is not explained by any of these analyses is how management, culturally far removed from workers and starting with nothing more substantial than vague declarations of moral concern for them (made under public pressure in the 1890s) could have hit upon the concrete measures it did, and why previously alienated workers responded so favorably that by 1930 the union movement was fading fast in large enterprises. I suggest that management's measures were largely the ones that workers had for years been demanding as improvements of status and "treatment." They were adopted by management piecemeal, reluctantly, with a considerable time lag. It is true that credit is due the unions for putting new pressure behind these demands, but the content of the demands was not significantly changed, despite much new rhetoric. Nor should we forget the accomplishments of the period before 1917, when unions scarcely existed. From the late 1890s there were periodic waves of strikes and labor disputes; by 1907 at the latest, management was aware of the seriousness of the labor problem, and during the next decade the large companies made a start at meeting the status demands of workers.

In the hierarchy of factors that shaped the reform of Japanese labor management, worker status ideology occupies an important place well into the 1920s.

INDEX

Designer: Mark Ong
Compositor: G & S Typesetters, Inc.
Text: 10/13 Sabon
Display: Sabon
Printer: Maple-Vail Book Mfg. Group
Binder: Maple-Vail Book Mfg. Group